CONSUMING POLITICS

CONSUMING POLITICS

Jon Stewart, Branding,
and the Youth Vote in America

Dan Cassino
and
Yasemin Besen-Cassino

Madison • Teaneck
Fairleigh Dickinson University Press

Associated University Presses
2010 Eastpark Boulevard
Cranbury, NJ 08512

The paper used in this publication meets the requirements of the American National Standard for Permanence of Paper for Printed Library Materials Z39.48-1984.

Library of Congress Cataloging-in-Publication Data

Cassino, Dan, 1980–
    Consuming politics : Jon Stewart, branding, and the youth vote in America / Dan Cassino and Yasemin Besen-Cassino.
       p.   cm.
    Includes bibliographical references and index.
    ISBN 978-0-8386-4145-3 (alk. paper)
    1. Youth—United States—Political activity. 2. Politics and culture—United States. 3. Mass media and world politics—United States. 4. Mass media and young adults—United States. I. Besen-Cassino, Yasemin. II. Title.
    HQ799.2.P6C38   2009
    306.20835′0973—dc22
                                                              2008055089

Contents

Acknowledgments

Dr. Besen-Cassino:

I would like to thank my colleagues in the Sociology Department at Montclair State University. All my colleagues and my chair, Dr. Jay Livingston has been very helpful in their discussions of this project. I also would like to acknowledge The Faculty Scholarship Program (FSP) program—it provided the release time to allow the completion of this project.

This book is for my parents, Zeynep and Edip Besen, who have been amazing parents. I would like to thank them not just for their endless support and encouragement but also for their stimulating intellectual discussion of young politics.

Dr. Cassino:

I would like to thank my colleagues in the Department of Social Sciences and History at Fairleigh Dickinson University, as well as acknowledge the support, in the form of granted release time, of Becton College. I would also like to thank the many colleagues and reviewers who have offered their time and comments on this project throughout its various stages.

Both authors would also like to thank the staff of Panera #3640 in East Orange, New Jersey, where this book was largely written.

Introduction

IN 1968, PEOPLE UNDER THE AGE OF TWENTY-FIVE WERE MORE INTER-
ested in politics than their parents, knew more about it than
older people, and were so politically engaged that the Gallup poll
had to add another category, "radical," to their list of political
views to try and measure the strength of the youth movement.
In 2004, people under the age of twenty-five were half as likely
as older voters to say that they were very interested in politics,
and only about one in six strongly supported one of the major
political parties. Radical, as a category, was dropped a long time
ago. The youth have gone from angry to apathetic, and the goal
of this book is to find out why.

THE MAKING OF APATHY
AND CONSUMING POLITICS

This apathy toward partisan politics can't just be taken for
granted. "Apathy," as sociologist Nina Eliasoph argues, "takes
work to produce" (Eliasoph 1998). While political observers may
take it for granted that political disinterest and disengagement
are the default state, apathy has causes, ones that arise from
everyday events. In this book, we'll be making use of in-depth
interviews and broad-based survey data and analyses to put forward a new model of why young people have become disengaged
from politics, and what can be done to bring them back into the
fray. Before doing this, however, we should review some of the
other explanations for young people's apathy.

The classic sociological argument is probably one that draws
on C. Wright Mills (1959): that young people lack what he calls
"sociological imagination," or the ability to connect their everyday experiences to larger political events. According to Mills,

humans try to connect their everyday, individual lives to the greater social and political structure in an effort to create meaning for themselves. This interplay between our daily activities and the greater structure is only accomplished through this sociological imagination, "a quality of mind" that helps connect the micro, personal, everyday details to the overall, macro, larger structure to create meaningful narratives and help people feel less powerless within a society. Without this sort of imagination, individuals fail to create ties between themselves and the larger social and political structure, and alienation results. This could offer an explanation as to why many young Americans find politics irrelevant. Due to their lack of sociological imagination, they fail to connect their personal lives and experiences to American politics. Sociological imagination, according to Mills, develops only as a result of extensive interaction with the outside world, through reading, talking, and exchanging ideas. Engagement with political matters, then, requires some degree of initial interest to make the search for and discussion of political information palatable: in essence, people lift themselves up by their bootstraps into caring. Without that initial interest, though, there aren't any bootstraps to begin with, and sociological imagination cannot develop.

Second, political apathy can be due to real or perceived structural problems. To the extent that young people see the political world as being impervious to any change, it may be rational for them to opt out of it entirely. If nothing you do will make any difference, why bother doing anything? We see claims such as this, for instance, in Ralph Nader's insistence that neither of the parties in our two-party system represent the people and that there's no real difference between them. To the extent that young people agree with such stances, and see no difference between the choices, their apathy is understandable.

Finally, another classic explanation of political apathy can be found in work on the perception of powerlessness. Hannah Arendt (1958) defines powerlessness as being caught in the "web of human relationships." Individuals in positions of power are able to set the definitions of the terms at stake, robbing those outside of those positions of the ability to develop their own interpretations of political issues (Eliasoph 1998). The policies that are put into place by leaders are seen as being resistant to all attacks, and may be impervious even to attempts to understand them. To the extent that they are, individuals may rightly perceive themselves to be powerless. This perception can be remedied only through active and meaningful political participation. Through learning, debate, and mass activity, individuals can create a personal understanding of politics and feel powerful as a result. As with the prior explanation, this requires a certain degree of existing political knowledge, and without it, powerlessness is inevitable. However, this ongoing pursuit of knowledge requires time, money, and a Habermasian public sphere: all things that young people in our society are generally lacking. Powerlessness, and the attendant feelings of apathy, could thus be seen as inevitable.

RESEARCH QUESTION

In this book, our focus is on the political attitudes of youth between the ages eighteen and twenty-four in the United States. Past studies of the topic have generally been content to document the overwhelming evidence of young people's political apathy (as outlined in chapter 1), and argue for targeted programs designed to increase their engagement, such as ad campaigns, celebrity appeals, interviews in popular media sources, and so forth. The apathy, in this approach, can be understood through behavioral markers: they don't vote, don't watch debates, don't register, so they must be apathetic. With few exceptions (such as Zukin et al. 2007), scholars generally haven't bothered to ask the young people themselves about their perceptions of the political world. Our goal is to try to gain an understanding of how the way in which young people perceive the political world leads to this apathy, so it can be attacked at the roots. Moreover, we allow for the fact that these roots may very well differ within the monolithic category of "young people," and so divide our analysis by the partisan group in which the individual respondents place themselves.

A bourgeoning literature points to the importance of consumerism and branding for the lives of many young people, and politics should be no exception. Many new studies argue that young people today put a high premium on consumption in all of the forms offered by a postindustrial capitalist economy. They consume everything from clothing to electronics to music to cars: all of these things, which might once have been items of necessity (as clothing is today in many parts of Africa), now serve a dual purpose as status and identity symbols. Today, young people are central to corporations. In fact, many companies target young people exclusively (Kline 1993). This is because young people have more disposable income than ever before, due to both parental allowances and their own earnings. They also have distinctive wants and needs. These factors result in the identification of young people as a "primary market" (McNeal 1992; Valkenburg and Cantor 2001) for many brands. Young people are also valuable to marketers because early choices, brand identifications, and purchasing habits often determine future consumption habits (McNeal 1992; Valkenburg and Cantor 2001). Furthermore, young people are important to marketers not only because of their own consumption habits, but also because they are what marketers refer to as "market influencers." In other words, they influence others' consumption decisions. They often have a say, for example, in the family activities, both necessary (like grocery shopping) and recreational (like vacations), giving them an influence over consumption greater than would be suggested by the funds at their command (Gunter and Furnham 1998; McNeal 1992). Many young people, for instance, start showing preferences for certain brands at rather early ages, before they buy products themselves by telling their parents and expressing their preferences (Reynolds and Wells 1977): something that should come to as no surprise to anyone who's seen a toddler in the cereal aisle. The creation of young people as a separate consumer market was a result of economic and sociological and cultural changes in our society. As parents' incomes and education increased, many parents started to have fewer children later in life. This, in turn, left many parents with the desire to ensure that their children had far more than the necessities of life (McNeal 1992; Valkenburg and Cantor 2001). With increasing income and education, more and more parents had the opportunity to realize this ideal or at least aspire to it. Those parents lacking the money to provide the right brands for their children came under intense pressure to do so, competing for status with their neighbors in this regard just as their children competed with playmates in the schoolyard. At the same time, the relationships between parents and their children began to liberalize. While old child-rearing techniques valued obedience, respect, and authority (Torrance 1998), new child-rearing techniques emphasize equality, compromise, and communication (Valkenburg and Cantor 2001). This too led to an increase in the spending influence of young people, whose opinions on brands and products are more likely to be respected.

Interest in young people as consumers emerged with the baby boom generation after the Second World War (McNeal 1992). The idea that young people have a distinctively different culture and taste that emerged at this time was later coupled with youth-targeted marketing. Especially in the 1950s, many corporations began to target young people (Davis 1990), especially through the emerging medium of television. This idea of youth as a separate group of consumers was enabled by the rapid growth in real wages after the war, particularly young people's wages. Newly emerging service and retail corporations marketed a wide range of goods and services ranging from clothing to food and drinks to entertainment to music (Stewart 1992). Young people were targeted by these companies as the potential consumers. While some corporations catered exclusively to young people as a distinctive group, others saw this as an opportunity to create brand loyalty by creating ties with young people at early ages. Especially since the 1980s, our society has witnessed the increasing importance of young people in our economy as consumers. Despite their declining numbers relative to the 1950s, young people today remain a powerful source in making economic decisions (Tootelean and Gaedecke 1992).

Young people's consumption has been paralleled by their incorporation into the adult labor market at early ages. Throughout the world, young people work while still in school, or are forced to leave school to work. Only in the United States do large numbers of relatively affluent young people work while still in school, seemingly to fulfill social rather than economic needs (Besen 2005)—a finding we'll discuss in more detail in the next chapter. While the labor force participation of young people declined in the 1980s and 1990s, it has stabilized today. Currently, many teenagers work part-time while still in school (Greenberger and Steinberg 1986; Manning 1990; Entwisle et al. 2000), and this part-time work and the earnings it brings are closely related to sustaining their consumption habits.

Given young people's buying power—enhanced by the factors we've discussed—their interest in consumption, and their presence in the adult labor market, much ink has been spilled documenting their consumption habits. Typical studies of consumption base their understanding of consumer behavior on consumer socialization (Ward 1974). Scholars working from this base argue that consumption requires a set of knowledge, skills, and attitudes. These necessary tools of consumption are socially learned through interaction with media, others, and the products themselves. Young people are particularly thought to be socialized into consumption patterns through social interaction. Mowen and Minor (1998), for instance, define consumer behavior as a four component process. First, young people feel a desire to buy, so the process starts with wanting and preference. Second, the feeling of wanting is followed by a search to fulfill these wants and wishes. Third, the search results in a particular choice and a purchase. Finally, the process is completed by the evaluation of the product and other alternatives. This is an ongoing process, heavily affected by the society it is embedded in.

So, in our society, people are socialized into their roles as consumers from a very early age (Gunter and Furnham 1998). Their choices in these roles are believed to be influenced by a number of factors, including their parents' buying habits (Furnham 1993), school environments (Nappi 1973), and, perhaps most importantly, their peers and mass media (Carlson and Grossbart 1988; Perachhio 1992). The children can be influenced as early as they can understand conversations or television, and they make their preferences known as soon as they are able when accompanying their parents in shopping trips (McNeal 1992).

While these preferences are most visible, and at adult levels of sophistication (John 1984) when children begin making independent shopping trips in their "tween" years (McNeal 1992), their preferences are measurable much earlier. Young people between the ages four and twelve show very sophisticated brand consciousness (McNeal 1992). In fact, brand consciousness and recognition among young people often exceeds the cognitive perception and developmental levels expected of people at their ages (Ward et al. 1977). With appropriate training and education, many young people before the age of eight develop consumer knowledge and skills well ahead of their age (Moschis et al. 1980).

In the earliest years of young people's socialization, the most important source of this consumer and brand education is mass media, particularly television (Adler et al. 1980). It has been argued that newspapers, books, and magazines also have some role in brand education (Wartella et al. 1979), though literacy is obviously a factor in their influence on very young children. Peer influence becomes more important in later years, particularly in their mid-childhood to teenage years and continues to shape young people's consumption choices (McNeal 1969). In addition to these effects, parental choices keep influencing young people's consumption choices in later years (Ward et al. 1977).

Adolescence is a crucial time for consumption patterns and habits to develop. While consumption patterns and brands are learned much earlier, they take full shape during adolescent years. This also coincides with the time when young people's disposable incomes increase, partly through increased parental allowances and partly due to their own part-time work (Moore and Moschis 1978). Many of the brand affiliations and buying habits created during these years last well into adulthood. During this period, young people start to have a greater say in household purchases (Gunter and Furnham 1998), and the range of media to which they are exposed dramatically increases, as exposure to magazines, music, and lately, the Internet, increases substantially (Avery 1979; Lyle and Hoffman 1971; Moschis and Moore 1981; Moschis and Churchill 1978). While the influence of media on young people remains quite strong during adolescent years, there are other factors influencing their consumption decisions. Parents become less influential (Gilkison 1973), while peers become more so (Coleman 1961; Moschis and Moore 1979).

In addition, nearly all of the money that young people get ahold of is spent. While there is some evidence of saving, for the most part, saving money is just a way for these young people to defer their consumption on a major purchase (Mintel 1990). Young people, beginning in their teenage years, consume leisure activities that will take them outside the home (Dunlop and Eckstein 1995; Gunter and Furnham 1998). They consume brands that have a social meaning and are associated with social acceptance and popularity. Consumption of certain items and particular brands of certain items is a way of seeking social acceptance and showing that you belong in a social group. Aspiring athletes might well define themselves on the basis of the shoes that they wear or the jersey number that they pick out. You know who you are, and who you belong with, based on the consumption choices that you make.

It is no surprise, then, that consumption is closely tied to identity for many young people. By and large, they individuate themselves through the products and services they consume. Many scholars argue today that consumption for young people is an important symbolic activity closely related to their self-expression and self-identity (Kamptner 1991). Buying products, for instance, is a way of self-expression (Gunter and Furnham 1998): the clothes at Old Navy, The Gap, and Banana Republic may all be manufactured in the same factory, but the meaning of shopping at those stores couldn't be more different. As such, it is essential for young people to have very sophisticated brand awareness, preferring particular brands to unbranded products of the same type (Stewart 1992): a failure to understand the differences between these brands would be nothing less than social suicide. These brands are not simple differences in choice, but are social signifiers and ways of distinction, by which young people distinguish themselves from others. They are sources of identity and create a sense of belonging to groups. Often, having certain brands and being associated with certain company's products create a sense belonging and a sense of identity.

ROLE OF BRAND

Branding is a particularly important topic in understanding consumption because so much of consumption is consuming particular brands of products. Not surprisingly, given the amounts of money at stake, there is extensive research on how people use products and particular brands to create and communicate their identities and images (Belk 1988; Chaplin and John 2005; Escalas and Bettman 2003; Kleine, Kleine and Allen 1995; Sirgy 1982; Solomon 1983; Wallendorf and Arnould 1988). Brands are excellent tools for expressing individual identity because they represent a wide range of personalities (Chaplin and John 2005; Fournier 1998; Gardner and Levy 1985; Muniz and O'Guinn 2001; Schouten and McAlexander 1995). Typically, individuals will try to choose products with images that are congruent to their actual or desired self-images (Birdwell 1961; Dolich 1969; Gardner and Levy 1955; Sirgy 1982). This makes these brands especially important for young people (Chaplin and John 2005): the more in flux your view of yourself is, and the more driven you are to define yourself to others, the more important the brands you consume—and become associated with—are.

Consumption of Other Things

Young people's consumption is not limited only to products and services. New studies show that young people consume not just goods and services, but other things that are not typically commodities. For example, recent studies of youth employment in suburban United States show that many teenagers "consume" part-time work. For many affluent, white teenagers in the suburbs, working is a fun activity that they enjoy during their free times (Besen 2004; 2005; 2006). The consumption patterns we've been talking about, then, are not limited to traditional commodities like clothes and music and electronics, and neither is the role of branding. Many teenagers view part-time work as a social activity that they participate in during their free time from school. Work provides them with the social space they lack in the suburbs to meet new people and to see their existing friends. As far as these young people are concerned, part-time—and sometimes even full-time—work is a social activity, not too different from going to the movies or hanging out at a coffee shop. It lets them become a part of the "in group" along with the other young people who are working in a certain place. The jobs, just like the other commodities they consume, are branded, holding meaning well beyond the tasks that they're expected to do and the pay that they receive. Just as a T-shirt from one store is preferable to a functionally equivalent T-shirt bought from a less desirable store, a job in a store with a desirable brand is better than a job with the same duties in a less desirable location. By working for that company, many young people feel like they "consume" the cool, desirable brand.

It is here that *The Daily Show with Jon Stewart* enters the narrative. When it comes to television programs, "consumption" generally means the simple act of watching the show, and, if the network has its way, the ads that go along with it. This means that, traditionally, maximizing the consumption of a show, and the profits that go along with it, means appealing to as many people as possible: in other words, broadcasting. People don't have to like the show that much, just enough to not turn it off when it comes on. Someone obsessed with the show and someone who just happens to have it on that night are functionally equivalent as far as the producers are concerned.

However, that's no longer the case. The transition away from this model was evident early on in HBO shows like *Sex and the*

City and *The Sopranos:* they earned their keep not on the basis of the breadth of their audiences, but on the depth of the devotion of these audiences. They didn't just watch the shows, but were willing to subscribe to HBO even when the shows were on hiatus, and were willing to spend substantial amounts of money on DVD sets. They also became an important part of the brand of the network, which tried, with some success, to have their success rub off on other programs. The value of programs was no longer tied to how many people watched it, but also how much they liked it and wanted to be associated with it beyond the half-hour or hour a week it was on. The show, in other words, becomes more than a show: it becomes a brand in and of itself.

One of the most successful television brands in recent years is *The Daily Show*, not because of it viewership—though that's a necessary component—but because it has resonance disproportionate to its viewership. Our surveys reveal that it is the most highly regarded information source for young people and that people associated with it are viewed much more positively than those associated with Fox News or NPR, for instance. Somehow, it has turned political information into something desirable, something that young people want to be associated with. Moreover, it does this while providing just as much objective information as its rivals. In doing all this, it gives us a blueprint for making politics, in general, more desirable, and reversing the disengagement that we see throughout our interviews.

CONSUMPTION AND POLITICS

In *The Selling of the President 1968*, Joe McGinniss sounded the alarm about how that year's presidential election, pitting Republican Richard Nixon against Democrat Hubert Humphrey, had been carried out. Instead of being a frank exchange of ideas, McGinniss made the case that the content of the campaign was being dictated by ad men: that candidates were being sold as if they were soap. In the first televised campaign, that of Dwight D. Eisenhower against former ambassador to the United Nations Adlai Stevenson, the ads were generally issue based. Stevenson's ads featured him, or a supporter, talking about his issue positions and qualifications. Eisenhower's ads were spiced up a bit by a cartoon band animated by the Walt Disney Studios, but that was still just window-dressing for the message: here's the candidate, here's what he says he will do, and here are his qualifications.

Nixon's ads—and his entire campaign—in contrast, seem modern by comparison. In 1960, Nixon had used the old methods of campaigning, presenting himself forthrightly to the voters, and lost. The traditional narrative about the 1960 presidential debates is that people who watched the debates on television thought that Kennedy won, and those that listened to it on the radio thought that Nixon had won: a triumph of image over substance. As Malcolm Gladwell points out in *Blink* (2005), the problem wasn't that television viewers had been deceived by Nixon's image, but that they had seen the real him. Unlike those that listened to the debates on the radio, they came away from the debates thinking that Nixon was untrustworthy, and, as it turned out, he was. The modern style of campaigning that Nixon's staff and advisors created, to a large extent, during the 1968 race was a response to these problems. For instance, Nixon and his advisors knew that they had been criticized for looking shifty during the 1960 campaign—so when they filmed commercials, they made sure that no one was in the studio unless they were directly in his line of sight, so that he didn't look from side to side. They were self-consciously trying to brand Nixon, with top speech writer Raymond Price writing in a memo that they had to decide what "vision of the nation's future" that the candidate "wants to be identified with." For the first time, surveys were carried out to measure what people thought of twenty-six aspects of Nixon's personality—firmness, sense of humor, stinginess—as well as those of Humphrey, and the ideal candidate. Closing this "personality gap" through the use of television became a high priority for the campaign.

Every aspect of the campaign was carefully scripted. Nixon held televised meetings with rooms full of handpicked enthusiastic voters who screamed their support and gave him easy segues into the dozen or so talking points that he had prepared for the occasion. The fact that these programs were only broadcast locally meant that he could shift the talking points slightly depending on whether he was in the north or south, speaking to urban voters or rural voters. These programs were artfully produced by Roger Ailes, who had been a prop manager on *The Mike Douglas Show* when he met Nixon, and went on to become the president of the Fox News Channel.

The commercials made a point of framing "law and order" as the major issue in the campaign, going so far as to refer to safe streets as the "first civil right." Nixon's stump speech, in which he pledged to take the offensive against criminals, was intercut with images of antiwar protestors, deserted streets, and black criminals being hauled off the police. When coupled with these images, Nixon's words were put in a whole new light: this was the power of television, to add inflection and meaning without saying anything offensive. Twenty years later, a similar strategy of indirect references to race under the cover of law and order politics was a key component of George H. W. Bush's election campaign (Mendelberg 2001).

This campaign wasn't the first one to utilize these techniques. Nixon's chief media advisor, Harry Treleaven, had previously put many of them to good use in the 1966 Texas race that gave George H. W. Bush his first term in Congress. It was, however, the first time that they had been used in a national campaign, and a successful one at that. It was also—as the connection to the 1988 campaign makes clear—far from the last time that they would be used. In recent years, though, these sorts of tactics took a leap forward, largely through advances in marketing technology that were brought to bear on political campaigns by Karl Rove (as described in Halperin and Harris 2006). In the middle part of the 1990s, supermarkets began offering shoppers discount cards for their wallets or key chains that in many instances hich took the place of coupons. But when shoppers used these cards at check-out, marketers could track exactly what they were buying, how often, and cross-reference that information with the demographics of the shopper, and, most critically, their ZIP code. Those same marketers could combine that information with everything else known about consumers in that ZIP + 4 to create a highly detailed profile of them. For instance, people living in a certain ZIP code might subscribe to *Time* and eat Captain Crunch, while the folks in the next ZIP code over read *Mother Jones* and shop at Whole Foods (Weiss 2000). Advances like this meant that marketers could target consumers very narrowly with direct mail and telemarketing. Rove was the first to make wide use of the notion that that the factors that make someone buy one product over another would also lead them to prefer one set of issue stances, and one candidate, over another. The ads became ever more slick and targeted, and the organizations behind the candidates became tighter, faster to react to criticism, and occasionally vicious in doing so.

The loser, in all of these advances, was content. Instead of standing for something, as candidates might have done in the past, as Stevenson did in 1952 and 1956, or Goldwater did in 1964, these techniques meant that candidates could be all things to all people. Frank debates on radio or television—to the extent that they had ever occurred—gave way to exchanges of sound bites, the eight- to twelve-second statements favored by news producers. The relentless packaging of the candidates begun in the 1968 campaign meant that all most voters would ever see of the candidates was the packaging, the image: something no more substantial than an ad campaign in the cola wars. Candidates, as far as we can tell, saw this is a necessary evil—Nixon deplored what he saw as stunts—but it was what they felt that they had to do in order to get elected. Once in office, the stunts would be over and the serious business of governing would commence. As the years passed, though, the stunts, the image building, the branding took up more and more time even when the candidate was in office, and the campaign, in essence, became nonstop.

It's possible, of course, for those voters with a deep knowledge of politics, and the ideological content behind the images and the branding, to find content in the talking points, but not everyone has that knowledge or the drive to seek it. For those voters who have come of age in the era of the nonstop campaign, what Halperin and Harris (2006) call the political "freak show," it may not seem like there's any content there at all. The ad campaigns, the packaging, the branding, have worked—but too well. Today's young voters see politics as being nothing but the brand, missing whatever ideological content is left. There's also no reason for them, as far as they're concerned, to try to learn more about the parties or the candidates. As with any other ad, if the brand appeals to you, if you want to be associated with it in the eyes of others, buy it; if not, forget about it. Moreover, partisan political activity isn't a necessity like food or transportation: if you don't like any of the brands that are offered to you, you can opt out completely. This, we argue, is the state of young people's politics in the United States today, and while it isn't hopeless, we have to understand it if we want to change it.

Now, the link between politics and the sort of economic consumption that we've been talking is not unprecedented in the literature, even if we're talking about a different aspect of it than most researchers. Many studies show that economic consumption and spending habits of young people is strongly associated with how young people vote (Gunter and Furnham 1998). Results from the *Economic Values Inventory* (O'Brien and Ingels 1985) show that the economic values are strongly predicted by political values. In fact, economic values are more closely related to political values than they are to religion, gender, and personal economic experience (Furnham 1987). Studies also show that young people who said they would not vote were more economically alienated than those who said that they would. Feeling economically alienated leads to political alienation as well (Furnham 1987; Gunter and Furnham 1998). While such studies argue that political and economic alienation go hand in hand, the relationship has been explored mostly to explain economic values and consumption habits. For instance, political beliefs explain young people's economic beliefs and consumption patterns (Furnham 1987): young people are socialized into certain economic values and consumption patterns, through political discussion at home. However, the relationship between political and economic relationship might not be that straightforward. While it is true that political beliefs influence consumption patterns and economic values, politics itself could be consumed as a product of consumption. It is important to explore this intertwined relationship in-depth instead of portraying it as a simple linear relationship.

For young people, voting may be perceived as similar to work, as an object of consumption, as a fun activity to be consumed during leisure times. More importantly, it is a branded activity, one that can provide identity and distinction to young people. Recent research suggests that many political issues have been employed by corporations to be marketed along with their products to enhance their brand loyalty and rebrand their brand images. Pringle and Thompson (1999) show that more and more corporations employ social issues in their marketing strategies. Political and social issues like hunger, breast cancer awareness, human rights, and global inequality (Pringle and Thompson 1999) have been used as a way. This wide range of political issues become objects of consumption and are marketed to consumers as a part of their product images.

METHODS

In exploring young people's political attitudes, we have opted for a multi-method design. We have combined qualitative, quantitative, and experimental methods. It is important to combine these different methods for the most comprehensive understanding of young people's political views. These three methods have different strengths that complement one another. Qualitative interviews provide in-depth information and accurately describe the political views of young people. They allow us to see the process of political involvement and show how young people become involved (or not involved) in politics. They also let us see, from the perspective of actors, how young people see politics and what the image of politics and political parties are. Quantitative methods help us establish causal relations between the economy and the political views. Quantitative data analysis on secondary datasets also expands our sample beyond the in-depth interviews. This large, representative sample also allows us to see the over-time changes in young people's political involvement. Finally, experimental methods isolate effects in a controlled environment, eliminating potential confounding effects. Such methods allow us to capture the effects of television shows such as *The Daily Show with Jon Stewart* and *The Colbert Report* on political processing and understanding.

First, we have conducted originally designed surveys and structured interviews, which are presented in the appendixes. These surveys and interviews are specifically designed to compare young people's political values and their consumption habits. They include detailed questions about how young people view politics and other consumption related activities. These surveys consist of four sections. In the first section, we explore the images and stereotypes that young people associate with different political groups as well as other brands. In the second section, we test the way young people see politics and how they relate to it as well as where they get their political information and how they see the relative strength and weaknesses of different sources of information. The third section explores the issues that young people relate to and value. In the final section, we identify the demographic, background information of the respondents. These surveys also include open-ended questions in which the students are encouraged to elaborate on social and political issues and offer an in-depth understanding of political issues from their perspectives. The transcriptions of these surveys resulted in about three single-spaced pages, resulting in a total of about 170 pages of text.

While we do not claim that these fifty surveys and interviews, carried out at two universities in New Jersey (one public, one private), represent a cross-section of all young people in the United States, the characteristics of the sample correspond fairly well to those of national samples. Males are slightly overrepresented in our surveys, comprising about 60 percent of the sample, and whites are slightly underrepresented, comprising about 70 percent of the respondents, with the remainder split between Hispanics (about 20 percent) and African Americans. In the 2004 American National Election Study, which we'll use as a baseline throughout, approximately 23 percent of the respondents between eighteen and twenty-four were Democrats, about 21 percent Republican, and the remainder (56 percent) were independents (including those who indicate they lean toward one party or the other, a factor that can be somewhat problematic, as we discuss in the next chapter). This corresponds very closely with our sample, of which about 20 percent were Republican, 20 percent Democratic, and 60 percent independent.

Pilot studies were run three months prior to the beginning of the study. Based on the results of the pilot study, the questions on the survey were revised to add questions in areas that had generated the most content and remove those areas that our respondents simply didn't understand or relate to. In order to ensure complete confidentiality and anonymity, we have devised an anonymous Web submission system for paper surveys, which resulted in double blind process. The anonymity of the process is especially important because it removes many of the biases that often plague research done with convenience samples. Oftentimes, participants' responses are biased by the fact that they're going to be turning in the results to an experimenter shortly after they finish, and they want to give that experimenter whatever it is that they think the experimenter wants and avoid expressing socially undesirable opinions. For most of the surveys, we control for these problems through the Web submission system. Rather than turning their responses over to an experimenter, participants use an experimenter-provided password to log on to a Web-based email service. From there, they paste their answers into the body of an email, which is sent to the experimenter. Because all of the participants have been given the same password for the email service—and they know that they've all been given the same password—the participants know that their responses cannot be tracked back to them, a certainty augmented by the normal expectation of Internet anonymity.

As for the questions on the survey, they've been designed to try and minimize the problem of respondents giving what they believe to be the correct answer: as in much of survey research, the correct answer is the enemy of the truthful one. We don't, for instance, ask what the Republican Party believes in, or about the leaders of the Democratic Party, because any factual questions will point respondents toward trying to give that correct answer. While an Internet-based response modality has many advantages in terms on anonymity, it makes it easy for respondents to look up the correct answers to factual questions. Instead, we try and get at the brands that are associated with political groups by asking respondents to describe a typical member of that group. The images that respondents report tell us a great deal about the sort of people that they think associate with that brand, and, therefore, how attractive that brand is to them. A respondent who sees members of one of the parties as fat, or poor, or ill-kempt—as many of the respondents did—obviously wouldn't want to be associated with that brand, or that party.

Two of these questions seemed to throw off our respondent's expectations. In addition to asking about the types of people that they associate with political parties and with media organizations such as NPR and Fox News, we ask respondents to describe typical employees at Starbucks and McDonald's. These questions serve two purposes. First, they allow us to compare the images associated with these brands with that of the media organizations, including, critically, *The Daily Show*. Second, they allow us to see how that respondent describes something typically seen as undesirable and low class (McDonald's), and how it differs from a solidly upper-middle-class brand like Starbucks. The extent to which the description of a McDonald's employee resembles that of a Democrat, a Republican, or a *Daily Show* viewer tells us a great deal about the premium the respondents put on these brands.

The second part of the survey tries to get at respondent's more general views about political leaders, issues, and structures.

These questions ask the respondents to agree or disagree with a number of statements and are designed to allow respondents to express their engagement with the political system as well as bring in examples to support their viewpoints. Questions about the quality of modern political leaders, for instance, can elicit general responses about leaders being out of touch with the people or specific responses about George W. Bush or Hillary Clinton. Again, a premium is put on avoiding questions that may have, or may be perceived to have, correct answers.

In the third section of the survey, we ask a series of questions that mirror those asked on standard statewide surveys, about President Bush, the war in Iraq, and issues such as a reinstatement of the draft that are expected to be relevant to young people. Having these questions on the survey allows us to roughly compare their responses to recent statewide surveys to see if there are any wide discrepancies. While we can't compare the results of fifty surveys, especially fifty surveys taken from a nonrandom sample, to six hundred random responses in a statewide survey, we can identify trends. If, for instance, our respondents overwhelmingly say that the war in Iraq was a good idea when a random statewide sample is overwhelmingly opposed, we can draw some conclusions about the sample.

In the last part of the survey, the respondents are asked a series of demographic questions, some of them standard, some of them not. As in most political surveys, we ask respondents about their partisan affiliation, their age and sex. Other questions make sense only in the university setting in which the surveys were distributed. For instance, it doesn't make sense to try to gauge the socioeconomic status of college students by asking about their income: it simply doesn't apply. Asking about their parent's incomes would generate more refusals even than asking about their own. Instead, we try and measure the socioeconomic status of their families by asking about how many houses they lived in growing up. Barring exceptions like a military background (which several respondents noted in this answer) families in lower socioeconomic strata tend to move about a great deal more than families from a higher strata. Similarly, we don't use standard questions used to measure political engagement and interest, such as asking about campaign contributions or vote turnout. College-age respondents may well not have been old enough to vote in the last election or not have established residency; financial campaign contributions among these groups are almost unheard of. As such, we ask the respondents about the political science classes that they have taken or are currently taking. Even students who aren't political science majors report taking such classes as electives when they're interested in politics. Students who take political science as their major field of study can be expected to have a relatively high degree of interest, given their choice of majors, and knowledge, at least from their classroom experiences. This section also asks about how long their family has been in the United States (by asking how many of their grandparents were born in this country), religious affiliation and church attendance, and whether or not they hold a job.

While this methodology of in-depth interviewing is common in sociological research, it has largely fallen out of favor in political science. We want to stress, though, how important it remains for the sort of research we are doing here. Quantitative research is one of the best ways to find correlations between attitudes and behaviors: when people think or do this, they also tend to think or do *that*. In certain cases, guided by theory, past research, and the use of careful statistical controls, it's even possible for quantitative work to assign causes: people tend to do that *because* they do this. What it cannot do well, however, is tell us *how* people do something, and that's really what we are most concerned with. It's easy to use numbers to show that young people are less engaged in politics than older cohorts, and that they are less engaged than young people were thirty or forty years ago. If we want to change that, though, we need to uncover what sociologists call the "lived experience" of young people's political disengagement. Only by starting from their actual experience and re-creating their perspective can we create what Glaser and Strauss refer to as a "grounded theory" of young people's politics (Glaser and Strauss 1967; see also Glaser 1992 and Strauss 1987). How do young people see politics from *their* perspective? While their political views have been reduced to apathy because many do not vote, that is simply a result. We want to see the process: how do they distance themselves from the political world. Through that, we can see the ways in which politics is consumed as a product. We also explore the ways in which certain brands such as *The Daily Show with Jon Stewart* and *The Colbert Report* are able to mobilize young people.

We should also discuss the nature of our sample. We have made no effort to contact and interview a cross-section of American young people, and so can make no claim that the interviews are representative of that population. For that, we have turned to survey analysis and quantitative research. Rather, our interviews are designed to provide a great depth of information from a limited sample to allow us to understand exactly how these particular young people relate to the political world. The restriction of the sample to relatively affluent young people pursuing a college education makes their responses less representative, but it gives us a tighter focus on the young people that we should be most focused on mobilizing. These are the young people that, in past years, would have been most politically engaged, and so the ones whose disengagement now requires the greatest explanation.

The trends that we find through a close reading of their responses tell us how they have become alienated from politics and provide a model for how others have been alienated. On the individual level, this may not tell us much—a particular young person could have become alienated for all sorts of idiosyncratic reasons—but the trends we find cutting across the interviews can tell us a great deal about young people. Combined with theory, and parallel with quantitative work, we're confident that these interviews can tell us a great deal about how the political system can bring young people back into the fold.

We have coupled these surveys provide and detailed, in-depth information with quantitative analysis of large-scale datasets. We have employed reliable and representative datasets that have been used nationally and globally by many social scientists. In the first chapter, we have used the General Social Survey and a new dataset complied from CBS, Gallup, and *New York Times* surveys. Chapters 2 through 4 include data from the American National Election Study. Finally, chapter 6 that makes predictions about the future use polls conducted by the Fairleigh Dickinson University's Public Mind polls conducted between July 2006 and April of 2007. Since the phenomena we explore, namely the political and consumption habits of young people, are rapidly changing phenomena, it is important to use very recent data. These recent and reliable datasets and the statistical methods employed are discussed in detail in the later chapters.

Finally, we have employed experimental methods. We have randomly assigned college students into two groups. We measured the initial political involvement and analysis of political news of fifty subjects. After an initial measurement, we have assigned young people to two random groups. The first group is asked to watch *The Daily Show with Jon Stewart* or *The Colbert Report* every night for four consecutive nights. The second group is asked to watch another news show for four consecutive nights. At the end of the four days, both groups were given a post-test, during which they were asked to describe current events and also to explain a different political event. Here, we test for political knowledge as well as ability to process political information.

In all cases, we have tried to make the analyses as approachable as possible. When we use statistical coefficients, we present the results as being changes in the probability of something happening, rather than changes in the expected value of a dependent variable. Details that aren't expected to be of interest to the casual reader have been placed, as much as is possible, in the endnotes, for the use of those who want to dive deeper into the subject at hand. For these same reasons, we have made extensive use of excerpts from the surveys and in-depth interviews, which do the work of showing what's going on, rather than just telling about it.

Chapter by Chapter Breakdown

Chapter 1 explores the reasons why young people are apathetic toward politics through quantitative methods. In this chapter, we explore the role of consumerism and branding in the ways in which young people relate to politics. The following three chapters look at the inner differences among youth as Republican, Democratic, and independent youth do not relate to politics the same way based on in-depth, ethnographic interviews conducted with youth between the ages eighteen to twenty-four. Chapter 2 focuses on young people who identify themselves as Republicans. This chapter shows that Republican youth relate to politics through strong leaders. They report feeling powerless vis-à-vis the government as well as unable to relate to current leaders. Fear and distrust of the government and an inability to relate to the contemporary political leaders are the major reasons why Republican youth become less politically involved. Chapter 3 focuses on Democratic young people and shows the importance of issues in how they relate to the political world. This chapter argues that Democratic youth disengage from politics because they feel like issues they find relevant are not addressed in the political arena. Chapter 4 focuses on young people who identify themselves as politically independent. They are typically seen as the "remainder" or "other" category, but this chapter shows that they have a distinctive identity. The reason why independent youth are alienated from partisan politics is because of their dislike for partisan politics. They feel that there are structural problems in our current political system, which makes them lose interest in the current political system.

Chapter 5 uses an experiment to see how shows like *The Daily Show* and *The Colbert Report* impact young people's ability to learn about politics, and apply the knowledge that they gain to new political issues. This chapter compares and contrasts the effects of these shows with more traditional news outlets like CNN and broadcast networks and points to the importance of these brands in teaching young people about politics and related issues. Finally, Chapter 6 examines the effect of the war in Iraq and the potential long-term impact of current issues as today's young people come to dominate the political sphere. We also examine the cognitive processes underlying all of the effects that we've discussed throughout the book.

CONSUMING POLITICS

1
Work, Politics, and the Making of Apathy

ONE OF THE MAJOR GOALS OF THIS BOOK IS TO PUT THE ROLE OF politics in young people's lives into context, to understand how it fits in with all of the other aspects of their lives, and how this leads them to participate in partisan politics, or ignore it completely. To do this, we will first examine the role of work in young people's lives, for two reasons. First, among today's young people, politics is just one of many concerns, like work, that are competing for time and attention: seeing how young people in the United States deal with work tells us not only what politics is going up against, but how they approach what they see as alternative activities in general. Work is a central activity in today's teenagers' lives in the United States, competing not just for young people's limited free time, but for many young people it is an important source of identity. Therefore, it is important to see how work and politics interact in providing an identity among young people. Second, work is important in relation to another important activity in young people's lives: consumption. Many young people today work to maintain their consumption habits. In fact, a bourgeoning literature shows that young people not only use work for as a means of sustaining their conspicuous consumption habits, but they also consume the work activity itself. Many scholars point to young people today relating to unrelated activities such as work and education through consumption. In this chapter we aim to show that young people consume politics just like they consume other activities. By showing how, exactly, young people consume an activity like work, we can identify the signs that will tell us that they are consuming politics, as well.

Also in this chapter, we take a look at the empirical evidence showing that young people are actually disengaged from the political system. Certainly, the young people we interviewed are, but we want to make sure that this isn't just a fluke of the small sample size necessarily attendant with qualitative work. When-ever, possible, we back up our hypotheses about the consump-tion of politics—and work, in this case—with quantitative analy-ses. In this chapter, we'll make use of national survey data from two sources, testing the consumption of politics hypothesis first directly, on the individual level, and then indirectly, by looking at the relationship between partisanship and the economy. In both cases, we'll show that young people—and more educated young people, at that—treat partisanship in the same way that people treat any brand that helps to define them to others, and even in the way that they treat a consumer product like a refrig-erator. The consumption of politics is a big shift in how the cur-rent generation sees the political system, and the purpose of this chapter is to provide a framework for this understanding.

We also have to demonstrate that one of the main characteris-tics of young people's political views—a failure to identify with either of the major parties—is actually a bad thing. As we'll show, political independents, as opposed to those individuals who iden-tify with one of the major parties, are at a severe disadvantage when trying to understand and engage in the political system, making the trend against partisanship a cause for concern.

PARTISANSHIP: HOW POLITICAL PARTY IDENTIFICATION IS FORMED

For both of the analyses in this chapter, and throughout the rest of the book, we're using a standard party identification measure as a way of telling how political someone is. Basically, party iden-tification is whether someone is a Republican or a Democrat, but to political scientists it's a great deal more complicated than that. Party identification (often abbreviated to "party ID") is the most important tool in the political scientist's predictive arsenal. It does a good job of predicting almost every political behavior that we're interested in, from the vote choice, to campaign volun-teering, to which issues are important. It's also a fairly recent construction, dating back only the 1950s.

Before then, and the groundbreaking work of Angus Campbell and his coauthors (Campbell et al. 1960), political scientists and pollsters categorized people politically based on which presiden-tial candidate they had supported in the previous election: a Truman voter was a Democrat, a Dewey voter a Republican. This sort of behavioral measure fits in very nicely with the behavioral theories en vogue in psychology at the time, but Campbell and his colleagues saw it as an oversimplification. Rather than defining political party based on which party a person had voted for— or even which party a person was a registered member of—they defined it as a psychological attachment to one party or another that was generally manifested through vote choice and political behaviors, but also through political attitudes and statements. Researchers in the field quickly settled on measurement of this psychological attachment through a two-question sequence, yielding a seven-point scale. First they ask the survey respondent, "Regardless of who you voted for in the past election, do you consider yourself a Republican, a Democrat, an independent, or what?" Respondents who say that they are a member of one party or the other are asked if they consider themselves to be a not-so-strong member of that party or a strong member of that party. Those who call themselves independents are asked if they lean toward one party or the other.[1] All told, this yields a seven-point scale (though five point variations, which don't differentiate between strong and not-so-strong partisans, are also in evidence), ranging from strong partisans of one party; to not-so-strong partisans; to those who lean toward that party; to full independents, who don't lean toward either party; to the leaners and partisans of the other side.[2]

According to traditional models, people begin to identify themselves with one party or the other sometime between the ages of eighteen and twenty-four, and stay with it for the rest of their lives.[3] While some events may be able to change it—America saw a marked decrease in the number of Republicans after the Watergate scandal—it's generally stable. Even when an issue makes it so that individuals are at odds with their party, they stay with it. Take the effect of the 1964 Civil Rights Act on the Democratic Party. While it is difficult to imagine a bill that would alienate the white southern base of the Democratic Party more than one that outlawed discrimination in restaurants, schools, and theaters, and provided federal remedy to any violation. Even President Johnson, having shepherded it through the House and Senate, reportedly said that it meant that the Democrats had lost the south for a generation. The interesting thing about this is that they didn't—at least not immediately. Southerners who had been

Democrats since before Andrew Jackson didn't suddenly become Republicans. Rather, they became what we knew as "boll weevil Democrats," Democrats who were generally in favor of tax cuts, deregulation and muscular national security policy, and always against civil rights, women's rights, and other rights outside of state's rights. Despite having almost nothing in common with the liberal Democrats who swept into the House and Senate in the 1960s and 1970s, the southern Democrats stayed true to their party, returning Democratic incumbents to the Congress while increasingly voting for Republican presidential candidates. It was their children who became Republicans—the group now referred to as "NASCAR dads." Once partisanship is set, it seems, there's not much that can be done to change it.

More recent models, like Michael Mackuen and colleagues' macropartisanship theory (Mackuen, Erikson and Stimson 1989; Erikson, MacKuen and Stimson 1998; Green, Palmquist and Schickler 1998; Abramson and Ostrom 1991, among many others), have held that partisanship does shift a bit in response to lesser political events, like unpopular policies or a bad economy, but the basic wisdom about partisanship has remained the same: get them early and you get them for life.

In effect, party identification is seen as an element of an individual's identity, in the same way that being middle class, or Hispanic, or male, or homosexual, might be a part of identity. It should be more or less relevant depending on the circumstances, but it's always there. Upon traveling to a foreign country, national identity might be most important: being an American, as opposed to a German. In a discussion of economic issues, class identity, or even occupation might be the most relevant consideration. At a gay pride parade, sexual identity would probably come to the fore. In the same way, a political context is expected to make party identification relevant.[4]

The gradations of party identification have been shown to predict every kind of meaningful political behavior and attitude. Strong partisans, for instance, are more likely to vote for their party's candidates in general elections, more likely to vote in primary elections, more likely to contribute time or money to a campaign, more likely to be in agreement with the party's candidate on any given issue. This party identification also impacts the way people learn about political issues: strong partisans have been shown to pay more attention to politics than those with weaker partisan attachments—and to be more biased in their choice of which information to consume and who to believe. This shouldn't be surprising. After all, partisans have a much stronger stake in the political system than independents, and so we'd expect them to care more, to pay more attention. Without such partisan attachments to make politics more important or guide them in what to think about the political world, it becomes difficult for independents to learn about politics or to be engaged in it if they do learn.

To understand why, let's look at the fight in the House and the Senate over President Bill Clinton's impeachment. To a hypothetical strong Republican, this is a simple issue. Bill Clinton is a bad man who took advantage of a naïve intern, then lied about it under oath, thereby committing perjury and demonstrating his contempt for the rule of law. Members of the House of Representatives saw this clearly and did their constitutional duty by voting to impeach him, while the Senate was too worried about Clinton's popularity to follow through and remove him from office. It's a simple issue to a hypothetical strong Democrat as well: Clinton didn't technically lie in his deposition, and, if he did obfuscate, it was about matters that weren't anyone's business but his and Hillary's. Republicans in the House, seeking revenge for their defeat in the 1996 budget showdown, tried to use this to remove him from office, but their more levelheaded counterparts in the Senate refused to go along with it.

Of course, both of these narratives ignore important details about the fight over impeachment, but they have a few advantages over a more complete account. First, they're simple, breaking everything down into cause and effect: he did this, so they did that. Second, they each have clearly delineated good guys and bad guys. One side is in the right, one side is in the wrong, and once you know who's who, figuring out which side to support is a no-brainer. It could be argued that this is one of the factors behind the success of ideologically biased information sources such as Rush Limbaugh and Fox News: by providing simple explanations, based around narratives of good and evil, they provide an easy way of entry into the often complex political world (see Lakoff 1996).

Independents, lacking this in-built sense of good guys and bad guys, have a much harder time constructing a narrative. Clinton did something inappropriate with an intern while on government property, but it was consensual, to the extent that relations between the president and an intern can be consensual. He lied about it, but may have not been technically guilty of perjury, but probably shouldn't have been asked questions about it in the first place if the Paula Jones lawsuit was a politically motivated and/or financed attempt to bring the president into disrepute through the legal system. While lying under oath is a crime, if he actually lied, rather than just danced around the truth, it isn't clear if that's exactly what the founders had in mind with "high crimes and misdemeanors" and we could go only like this ad infinitum. The point is that not knowing who the good guys and the bad guys are means that the decision of which side to support requires an enormous amount of knowledge and effort to even decide what the relevant issues are, much less what conclusion should be reached. While this sort of effort may be interesting and even enjoyable to political scientists, pollsters, pundits, and others who are both passionate about and expert in political minutiae, it isn't nearly as compelling for the average citizen. As independents don't have the same stake in the outcome that partisans do, they wind up with two strikes against them when it comes to engaging in political issues.

Even by the low standards of American politics, independents make a poor showing. Just prior to the 2004 election, 30 percent of individuals who identified themselves as full independents said that they were "not much interested in the election," compared to 9 percent of strong Democrats, and 8 percent of strong Republicans. The difference is even evident when comparing independents who don't lean toward one party or the other with those that do: just 15 percent of leaners say that they aren't interested in the election, half the proportion of independents that don't lean. On the other end of the spectrum of interest, just one in four non-leaning independents said that they're "very much interested" in the election, compared with 60 percent of strong partisans and 38 percent of those who lean toward a party.

In the same study—the 2004 National Election Study—nearly half (42 percent) of independents said that they didn't care very much whether Kerry or Bush won the election, compared to 11 percent of respondents in all other categories; 23 percent said that they have hardly any interest at all in the election, three times as many as in the aggregate of all other categories.

Independent voters also don't know very much about politics: 27 percent of independents think that the Democratic Party is more conservative than the Republican Party; 23 percent think that the Republicans are more liberal than the Democrats. Only 14 percent of respondents overall made such an error. In the past, errors such as these were used as evidence that respondents didn't actually have political attitudes at all, but were merely providing the answers that interviewers wanted to hear (Converse 1970, 1974; Pierce and Rose 1974; see also Schuman and Presser 1980 and Norpoth and Lodge 1985).

Finally, the problems of independents extend even to the voting booth: overall, 70 percent of respondents interviewed after the election claimed to have voted: while this is surely an exaggeration, only 46 percent of independents claimed to have voted. In reality, 55.3 percent of the voting-age population turned out to vote in 2004.[5] Assuming that independents were no more or less likely to lie about voting than respondents in other partisanship categories, only 36.4 percent of independents showed up at the polls in 2004, an election with the highest turnout for any election since 1968.

These figures are at odds with the generally accepted belief that people independent of partisanship make *better* citizens and voters than those individuals tied down by party affiliations. Dennis (1988) find the first scholarly reference to this belief in Merriam and Gosnell's (1949) book, *The American Party System*, which refers to "intelligent men" who "leave the party . . . where some principle was involved" (Gossnell 1949: 196). Earlier references to the undesirability of partisanship—if not the virtues of being an independent—can be found even in the *Federalist Papers*, which speak at length about the dangers of factions. In our interviews, even independent voters consider themselves to be more politically savvy than partisans, but, as we've shown, it just isn't the case. Moreover, the source of these beliefs, as we'll show in chapter 4 (which deals exclusively with independents) seems to be negative beliefs about the parties, and about anyone who would choose to associate with them. While the parties themselves may be bad, by any empirical measure, distance from them is worse.

OPTING OUT OF POLITICS: THE MAKING OF APATHY

The political apathy of today's youth can be seen largely as a result of this disengagement from the parties. Rather than being an essential part of civic and social life, partisan political action is an end, a way to fulfill other social needs, by helping to build an identity or ease social interactions. Furthermore, we're going to argue that different groups within the general category of young people are looking for different things within the political world, and won't become engaged in politics until they see those things.

Before we do any of this, though, we should sketch the evidence for young people's disinterest in party politics. We've already talked about the consequences of young people opting out of the partisan system, but we should establish that it is, in fact, happening.

On almost any scale of political knowledge and engagement, young people fare worse than their older counterparts. Traditionally, we measure political knowledge through a series of questions asking people to match the name of an officeholder with the office that he or she holds. In the 2004 American National Election Study, the names were Dennis Hastert (speaker of the House), Dick Cheney (vice president), Tony Blair (English prime minister), and William Rehnquist (chief justice of the Supreme Court). Even though the numbers of young people included in the study are relatively small—about 150 in this study, a problem we'll run into again, with other studies—the trends are clear enough: 47 percent of respondents over the age of twenty-five were able to identify Hastert, compared with 18 percent of those eighteen to twenty-five. And while nearly everyone (around 90 percent of both age groups) was able to identify Cheney as the vice president, the young people fall far behind in identifying Blair (72 percent, compared with 85 in the older category) and Rehnquist (35 percent versus 59 percent). They're also less likely than older groups to know which party had control of the House and the Senate than older respondents, with 24 percent thinking that the Democrats had control of the House at that time, and 22 percent thinking that they controlled the Senate, despite the Republicans having held majorities almost continuously in both chambers for nearly ten years at that point.

But maybe objective political knowledge isn't the best way to measure their interest in politics. After all, they simply haven't had as much time to absorb political information as older voters have. Maybe they make up for in passion what they lack in knowledge. When we look at the strength of their partisan attachments, though, they fall well short of older respondents. Only 17 percent of young people identify strongly with either the Republican or Democratic parties, compared to 35 percent of older cohorts. When asked if they're a Republican, a Democrat, an independent, or what, 56 percent of people eighteen to twenty-five claim to be unaffiliated with either party, a rate about 20 points higher than older respondents.

We could excuse this, too: attachments to a party take time to build up, and they haven't had it. Maybe, in this case, their actions speak louder than their words. After all, they're just as likely as older respondents to report watching television programs about the campaign, or hearing speeches, even if they're less likely to have read anything about it. They are far less likely than older voters to have contributed money to a political campaign or party (2 percent versus 11 on both) or another political organization (0 percent versus 7). But that could be because they don't have as much money. Maybe on free activities, like voting, they'll be the equal of the older voters: but they aren't. Even the lower rates of voter registration among young people (21 percent aren't registered to vote, compared with 8 percent reporting not being registered in the older group) doesn't explain the difference: even registered young people are less likely to vote than registered older voters. About 12 percent of registered older voters didn't show up at the polls, compared to 21 percent of those eighteen to twenty-five.

In fact, the only things that the young people do at higher rates than older respondents have to do with projecting an image: they're a bit more likely to display a campaign button, bumper sticker, or sign (24 percent versus 20 percent) and slightly more likely to try to influence the votes of others (52 percent, versus 48 percent among older voters). Other recent work on young people's political views has had similar findings. Zukin and his colleagues (2007) find that when the current generation of young people (whom they refer to as "DotNets") engage in traditionally political activities like boycotts, they don't see them as political. Instead, they see them in terms of consumerism, and in terms of the image that their participation in these activities gives off to others. In terms of knowledge, participation, and engagement with normal, partisan politics, young people are far worse than their older counterparts: they just don't seem to care. And it isn't even as though they're trying to hide it: when asked how interested they are in following political campaigns, they're half as likely as voters over twenty-five to say that they're very interested and twice as likely to say that they're not much interested.

As we'll discuss in more detail in chapter 3, this alienation from the political system isn't new. In the late 1960s, for instance, was a period of great dissatisfaction with the way the country was being run, especially among the young people being drafted to fight in an unpopular war. So many young people were dissatisfied with the choices offered by the political system that the Gallup poll had to add a new category, "radical," to describe their political views. And while, at that point, they didn't vote at the rates that they were expected to after the passage of the Twenty-sixth Amendment, the engagement with politics, the interest in it, and the knowledge was there. In 1968, for instance, young people eighteen to twenty-five were, on the whole, more interested in the outcome of the election than older cohorts (83 percent were "somewhat" or "very much" interested, compared with 78 percent among all others), and while they were slightly less likely to be registered, registered young people were just as likely to report casting a ballot as those in older cohorts (89 percent of those registered over the age of twenty-five, 90 percent of those under twenty-six). In addition, they were just as likely as older respondents to get information from any source about the election, more likely to read about in magazines (38 percent versus 30 percent), and were more likely to know objective facts about the election, like which party had the most seats in the House before and after (about four points ahead on both questions). The point being that all of it *was* there, and, today, it just isn't: *that's* what we're trying to explain.

THE TIME CRUNCH

We can begin with the simplest explanation for what happened to young people's political engagement: they're off doing something else. Learning enough about politics to want to get involved —to say nothing of that involvement itself—takes time and effort that young people may be putting into other activities. One of the major sources of this time crunch is employment.

The first indications of this relationship come from the interviews that we conducted with young people in New Jersey.

Almost universally, their responses to questions about politics and political activism touched on their experiences at work, or the demands placed on themselves or others by their work.

Theresa, an eighteen-year-old self-identified independent told us, "People are so busy [that] not a lot of people have time to pay full attention to the games the politicians play. There are so many more important things to be done and taken care of. You can't really do anything about the issues, so why pay attention?" She sees work and politics as two activities completing for her free time. The contrast is between politics, can be safely ignored —as you can't do anything about it—and activities like work, that require attention. Given her limited time, she chooses work over politics. Adrian, also an eighteen-year-old independent echoes the sentiments and puts more of the blame on how much people have to work. "In our society today," he says, "people are rushing around and so busy with their jobs that they really don't pay too much attention to these political issues." Politics, for the young people we spoke to, is just another activity competing for the little free time they have and is often a casualty in the time crunch.

Aside from being linked as competitors in the time crunch, politics and work are also linked in our analysis of young people's lives because they are both activities that have made the transition—at least among many young people—from a necessity to a choice. In the United States, work used to be something that young people did when they had to (as it is in most of the world today: Besen 2006[a]) today, especially for better-off young people, it's something that they choose to do.

Because of this, work and partisanship are competing for more than just scarce time in young people's lives: they're competing for a role as a source of identity. To understand why, we go back to the teenagers in Besen's research (Besen, 2004, 2005). Besen's study of suburban teenagers working at a national coffee chain shows that they work for social rather than economic reasons. The money isn't the driving force—many of them spend most of their check in the store where they work—and the hours and duties are equivalent to some of the worst jobs they could have. For them, working isn't about the job or the money—it's about establishing an identity in a way that isn't available to them elsewhere. They don't just work at Starbucks, or The Gap, or Abercrombie & Fitch, they incorporate it into their identity. Once they've done so, there's less reason to seek out other ways to differentiate themselves from their peers, or make new friends. The same logic can be applied to politics. Politics, like work, can be a source of identity, hence consumed by young people. You don't need to be the liberal guy, or the conservative girl, if you're already the Starbucks kid.

Education is also very important here. The effects we're talking about only really pertain to young people who have a college education or are on their way to getting it:[6] That's telling us something important about the different meaning of work to more- versus less-educated young people. For young people with less education, work is much more likely to be a way to earn a paycheck and less about defining who you are or who you want to be. Unlike jobs at Abercrombie, people don't typically take jobs at McDonald's to make friends and get an employee discount. As such, politics remains a viable way to establish a social identity and find like-minded people.

This idea of work as branding doesn't apply only to teenagers and college students, but to young adults as well. Four of Forbes' top 5 best companies to work for—Google, Wegman's (a specialty food store in the Northeast), the Container Store, and Whole Foods—could be considered lifestyle brands that people would want to be associated with. They all also beat out less cool brands on the list—like S.C. Johnson and W.L. Gore (makers of Glide Dental Floss: not exactly the sexiest product), also in the top 10—despite paying less and asking workers to put in longer hours. The Altria Group, despite largely promoting from within, offering generous pay packages and benefits, and resisting moving jobs overseas, has a relatively high turnover, and doesn't make Forbes' list: after all, who would want to work for a company formerly known as Philip Morris?[7]

So, young people are using work—traditionally something that you *have* to do, rather than something you *choose* to do—as a way of expressing their identity. Besen's research show that those young people that have a choice about whether or not to work flock to jobs that have positively perceived brands: Starbucks rather than McDonald's, Abercrombie and Fitch rather than Sears, regardless of the content of the job. This brand becomes integral to the way in which they present themselves in the world, and other potential sources of identity—musical taste or academic achievement, for example—fade in comparison.

WORK AND PARTISANSHIP

Our first analysis focuses on full-time work as a predictor of partisanship among young and old cohorts. If it is the case that partisan politics is competing against work and other potential sources of identity for young people's attention, those work full-time should be less partisan than those who do not. Furthermore, this effect should be greatest among more educated young people, for whom branding is a consideration in the work decision, as opposed to less educated young people, for whom work is more likely to be a means of survival.

Testing this hypothesis will require responses from a broad range of responses. When we're studying how people process information, it can be useful to use what we call a convenience sample, meaning undergraduates that we can easily get our hands on. When we're looking at broader social trends, though, we have to use some sort of broadly representative survey data that includes information on work history as well as political views, and has enough respondents that we can make inferences about different age groups.

Fortunately, we have just such a dataset in the General Social Survey (GSS), one of the primary data sources for sociology. Taken every other year since 1972 with a few exceptions, the GSS data, when pooled over a couple of years asks the questions we need from enough respondents to make the analysis work. In this case, we're using all of the respondents to the GSS between 1996 and 2004 (the most recent year for which data was available), giving us a total of just less than ten thousuand cases, of which about 12 percent are twenty-five years of age or younger.[8]

In this case, we're not really interested in measuring whether someone is a Democrat or a Republican, we simply want to know how engaged they are in the political system. Normative judgments aside, both Democrats and Republicans know a lot more about politics, and are more likely to participate in politics, than independents, so we'll leave the question of which party young people are joining alone for now. This means that we'll be predicting which of the four categories of partisanship people fall in to: strong partisans, not-so-strong partisans, leaners, or independents, based on the individual's self report.

We want to isolate the effects of working on young people's partisanship, so we have to control for all of the other factors that we know lead people to have strong political views one way or the other. These include the big three: race, gender, and class (represented here by education and income), as well as a few others, like religion. Since we think the relationship between working and partisanship changes as people get older, we also need to include age as a predictor and some interaction effects, which will tell us about exactly how the relationship changes.[9] An ordered logit model gives us the relative importance of each of these in predicting partisanship.[10]

First, we have to make sure that the overall model works in predicting what it's supposed to, and it does seem to. There are four categories, and the model predicts which category someone is going to be in correctly 38 percent of the time, about a 50 percent increase over chance. If we allow for a little leeway, the model predicts the outcome within one category about 75 percent of the time. Because the numbers in the model can be diffi-

Table 1.1: Ordered Logit Prediction of Strength of Party Identification

N = 9202		PCP = 37.9		
LR chi2(11) = 689.74		+ or - One Category = 74.0%		
Log likelihood = -12051.899		Modal Category = 35.9%		
Pseudo R2 = .0278				

Predictor	Coef	Std. Err.	z	P>z
Full Time Work?	-2.878	0.511	-5.63	0.000
Years of Education	0.060	0.010	5.74	0.000
HH Income	0.022	0.004	5.27	0.000
Fundamentalism	-0.196	0.025	-7.71	0.000
Race: Black?	0.611	0.059	10.31	0.000
Race: Other?	-0.240	0.081	-2.98	0.003
Female?	0.022	0.039	0.57	0.569
Age	0.021	0.001	14.45	0.000
Full Time x Age	0.052	0.011	4.68	0.000
Education x Full Time	0.214	0.036	5.92	0.000
Education x Full Time x Age	-0.004	0.001	-5.03	0.000
Cut 1: Lean Towards Party	0.187	0.180		
Cut 2: Not So-Strong Partisan	1.274	0.180		
Cut 3: Strong Partisan	2.886	0.182		

Figure 1.1: Predicted Strength of Partisanship by Work Status and Age

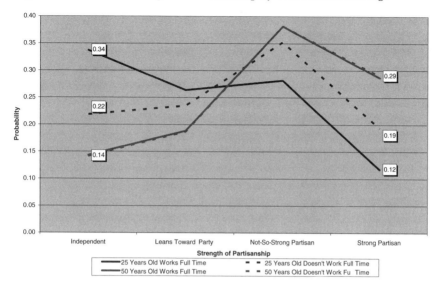

cult to interpret, the most important results are presented graph-ically in Figure 1.1.

We can see all of the estimated effects in Figure 1.1, which plots the strength of partisanship by age and work status for two different ages: twenty-five (representing young people), and fifty, for older cohorts.[11] In it, we can see that among the younger group, those who work full time are much more likely to be inde-pendent and much less likely to be strong partisans. Among the older group, the lines overlap almost completely: working doesn't make a bit of difference on older people's partisanship.

In Table 1.1, which contains the results of the regression, full-time work is a significant predictor of the strength of party iden-tification, but we're more interested in how it works among young people. Looking at the interaction effects, it seems that full-time work makes young people less partisan and older people slightly more partisan. This is exactly the prediction that the consumption of politics model would make about working, especially when we include the effects of education as well. A college-educated young man who works full time has a 34 per-cent chance of being an independent and a 12 percent chance of being a strong partisan. His high school-educated counterpart has a 22 percent chance of being an independent, and a 19 percent chance of being a strong partisan.

For some, the effect of education on partisanship among young people is going to sound very counterintuitive. After all, one of the things that political scientists know about American political behavior is that more educated and wealthier people are more likely to vote, give money, volunteer, or write a letter to their representative, and we can easily see why. Adults on the early shift may not be able to get off work to vote on a Tuesday morning or be able to arrange child care to get to the polling place. More educated people are also going to have more money to give to candidates and have more free time on their hands to learn about the issues, write letters, or go to rallies. Even if the less educated individuals have the same amount of time, it has been argued that it's going to require more effort for them to engage in politics: essentially because they're going to have to learn how to do so from the ground up, while more educated individuals presumably already have some of the skills they need.[12] The fact that the relationship is the opposite of this among young people —less educated individuals are more engaged in partisan politics—points to the strength of this finding about young people.

Our results also allow us to rule out some alternative explanations for the findings about young people and work. It could be the case that young people who work full time are less partisan simply because they have less time on their hands. But if that were the case, the effects of education would go the opposite direction. Even among those who work full time, more educated people are going to have more time on their hands to learn about and engage in politics than their less educated neighbors.

We also have to make sure that our model is actually measuring the strength of people's party identification and not just a propensity to be, say, a strong Democrat, and there's one result that's troubling in that respect. According to the model in Table 1.1, black respondents, relative to whites, are expected to be more partisan by a significant (though not very large) degree. However, while 37 percent of the blacks in our sample identify themselves as strong Democrats, less than 2 percent say that they are strong Republicans. We have to be sure that our model is not confounding increased strength of partisanship with increased propensity to be a member of one party or the other.

To test this, a second model, using the same variables, was run, with a different dependent variable: the various categories of partisanship. In this model, full-time work increases the likelihood of being an independent or leaning toward one of the parties, but has no impact on the likelihood of being a strong or not-so-strong member of either party. Additionally, none of the interactions between age, education, and full-time work have a significant effect on being a member of either party. As such, it does not seem that working makes individuals significantly more likely to join one party or the other, just more likely to be partisan in general.

Now all of this strongly suggests that young people are treating partisanship—and by extension, politics—as a way to identify themselves, when other methods, like work, are unavailable or unappealing. As we'll see in later chapters, in which we hear from the young people who choose to be partisans, they treat membership in a political party in much the same way that the workers at Starbucks treat their jobs.

We're going to need more evidence, though, if we want to say that they're consuming politics in the same way that they're consuming things like soap or refrigerators. For that, we'll turn to a second analysis that looks at a broader time period and incorporates information about the overall economy.

PARTISANSHIP AND UNEMPLOYMENT

So, at least among educated young people, work and politics are in competition—but that's not the same thing as saying that politics is being consumed. We know that work is being consumed among young people when we see a negative correlation between the need to work and the likelihood of working: taking a bad job to pay the rent isn't consuming work, but taking a bad job when you've got all the money you need is. For these young people, work is a primarily a source of identity, not money, so it becomes more prevalent when there's a surplus of other resources. We can apply the same logic to partisanship

If partisanship is being consumed in the same way that work is, it should be more prevalent when the economy is good and there are more resources at young people's disposal. This is basic economics: if something is a luxury good—something wanted, but not really needed—demand for that good will fall off when the economy goes sour, whether the consumer is directly affected by the economic downturn or not. We see examples of this all of the time. When housing prices go down, people spend less at the mall. When the unemployment rate increases, people tend to save more and spend less, in case they lose their jobs as well. A decline in the stock market can lead to a slump in demand even at stores like Wal-Mart, where relatively few customers have money in the market. We expect that for young people, partisan politics will work in the same way. If politics is really something consumed, when the economy slows down, young people—but not their older counterparts—should become less partisan.

There are a number of reasons why this is a very strong hypothesis. First, there isn't any direct relationship between money and partisanship. While it's easy to understand why people who are worried about their job might be less likely to spend money, it's harder to see why they would be less partisan. It only makes sense if partisanship isn't something that people need to do, but rather something they do for pleasure, something that only comes up when there's nothing more important to occupy them.

Second, this is a strong test of the consumption of politics model since it seems to be at odds with the first analysis. Previously, we established that when educated young people have jobs, they are less partisan. Now, we're arguing that when the economy is good and more young people have jobs, they should be more partisan. However, what we're really dealing with here is the perception of the economy, rather than any direct effect on those working. After all, in the last six years, the difference between extremely high levels of unemployment and extremely low levels is about 4 percent, making it unlikely that our respondents are being directly affected. Moreover, even if they are being directly affected by unemployment—that is, laid off—it should work *against* our expectations, so we can still trust any confirmation that our analysis gives us.

Finally, we'd expect that partisanship should decrease among young people when the economy turns bad because of changes in the political debate during periods of economic downturn. When the economy is doing well and tax revenues[13] are increasing, the political discourse is over how to spend the money the Congress finds itself with: a question that always seems to find a ready answer. When this isn't the case, when tax revenue is less than expected, politicians and parties have to debate from where the cuts—or at least less-than-expected increases—have to come from. In such a situation, the choices are all bad. Every program funded by the federal government is there because someone lobbied hard for it, and cutting any of them will therefore cause uproar. The brands represented by the parties, therefore, simply aren't as attractive as they are in good times, and we'd expect that young people would turn away from them. There is some support for such a stance in previous research. Burden and Sanberg's (2003) analysis of budget rhetoric in presidential campaigns finds that the relative balance of the budget has a strong impact on the tone of candidates' speeches. Positive tones are associated with a positive balance: not surprisingly, when the government has money, the politicians sound more hopeful. The links may not be direct, but they are clear: a good economy leads to a positive budget balance, and positive-sounding politicians make for a more attractive partisan brand.

Nor is the analysis of direct links between the economy and partisanship is unprecedented. Weisberg and Smith (1991), for instance, examine the impact of economic indicators on partisanship, and also find indirect effects of the economy on partisanship mediated by presidential approval.[14] Generally, such studies have looked at the effects of economic variables such as unemployment, inflation, and disposable income only on presidential approval, and with highly mixed results. Some have found that inflation has an impact, but not unemployment (Kernell 1978; Monroe 1978; Norpoth 1985), others have found that only unemployment has an impact (King 1989). Others have found that both are important, but only for certain periods of time (Ostrom and Simon 1989; Kiwiet and Rivers 1985; Norpoth and Yanek 1983). Lebo and Cassino (2007) offer an explanation for the variability of these findings: the relationship between the economy and presidential approval is mediated by partisanship, with members of the party not holding the presidency making much greater use of the economy in making their presidential approval decisions than members of the president's party. All of these studies, though, are missing a few elements that are critical to our hypotheses. First, they don't examine the relative impact of these factors by the age of respondents. There is ample reason to believe that young and old individuals deal with economic factors differently, but nearly all of these studies operate on the aggregate level (aggregate approval and aggregate partisanship to aggregate economic factors) and can't tell us about differential effects by age. Second, they assume that whatever the effects are, they are stable throughout the period studied, which may be why so many of them are limited to one presidency or even one term of a presidency. We want to examine the potential evolution of the link between partisanship and economic factors and allow the relationship to change over time.

As in our previous analysis, isolating the effect of one factor on partisanship means that we have to control for all of the other factors that may be involved. In this case, that means we control for education, age, marital status, and race, in addition to the factor that we're really interested in and interactions between that factor and the other predictors. Because we're dealing trying to predict people's political views, we also have to take account of a few other factors. For instance, it could be the case that young people are more likely to be Republicans when the president is Republican or when that Republican president is popular. As such, we'll control for the overall popularity of the current president and divide the analysis based on which party is in control of the White House at the time. It's also possible that young people are more likely to be a member of a party if they personally approve of a president of that party. By definition, young people have less experience with political parties and politicians than older individuals, and so they could be more prone to confuse liking an individual president—Clinton, Reagan—with liking that party. Alternately, they might decide not to be a Democrat during the Carter administration or a Republican during the George Bush administration.

In order to be sure of our results, we have to control for all of these factors. For most of them, this simply means including them in the analysis along with the variable of interest: the strength of the economy, as measured by the unemployment rate, and interactions with it. When it comes to figuring out how the relationship between the economy and young people's partisanship varies based on the party of the president, though, it's easier to split the analysis up into several sections, corresponding to the Carter administration, the Reagan and George H. W. Bush years, the Clinton years, and the first term of the George W. Bush administration. While it's possible to simply combine these periods by the party of the president—Carter and Clinton, Reagan and the Bushes—we want to be able to tell if things have changed over time. Also, the dataset is large enough that we can run the analysis separately for each of these periods without losing much accuracy.

For this analysis, we needed more than what is available in pre-existing datasets like the GSS, so a new dataset of individual-level data was compiled from the Roper Center of the University of Connecticut. Basically, we have at least one survey in every quarter of every year since the beginning of the Carter administration in 1977. All told, this is about 200,000 people, and at least 14,000 in each of the periods: plenty to carry out a detailed analysis. The one problem with such a dataset is that not all of the surveys include the detailed question about party identification that we used in the first analysis, and we're left without being able to differentiate between leaners and independents, and strong and

Table 1.2: Logit Regression results

Diagnostics	Administration(s)											
	Carter			Reagan/Bush			Clinton			G.W. Bush		
Number of Observations	12,085			78,969			45,884			24,585		
Percent Correctly Predicted	0.457			0.406			0.391			0.400		
Percent in Modal Category	0.448			0.375			0.363			0.360		
Percent Improvement Over Chance	0.372			0.219			0.174			0.201		
Percent Improvement Over Mode	0.020			0.082			0.078			0.110		
Predicting Republican	Coef.	Std. Err.	z	Coef.	Std. Err.	z	Coef.	Std. Err.	z	Coef.	Std. Err.	z
Age	0.030	0.018	1.63	-0.015	0.005	-3.03	-0.014	0.009	-1.50	-0.007	0.008	-0.81
Individual's Approval	-0.594	0.138	-4.29	0.030	0.050	0.59	0.610	0.066	9.29	-1.035	0.095	-10.92
Mean Approval	2.236	4.940	0.45	-3.423	0.739	-4.63	-5.665	2.691	-2.11	0.632	2.479	0.26
Squared Mean Approval	-0.032	5.815	-0.01	3.545	0.559	6.35	3.364	2.284	1.47	-0.204	1.725	-0.12
Unemployment Rate	0.076	0.107	0.71	-0.178	0.020	-8.86	0.040	0.044	0.93	0.107	0.070	1.52
Age by Individual's Approval	0.004	0.003	1.34	0.011	0.001	10.65	-0.023	0.001	-16.71	0.032	0.002	16.55
Age by Mean Approval	-0.056	0.023	-2.37	-0.018	0.005	-3.24	0.042	0.011	3.75	-0.018	0.009	-1.91
Age by Unemployment Rate	0.000	0.002	-0.17	0.002	0.000	4.59	-0.003	0.001	-3.45	-0.003	0.001	-2.33
Age by Unemployment Rate by Education	0.000	0.000	0.01	0.000	0.000	1.72	0.001	0.000	7.76	0.001	0.000	5.55
Individual's Gender	-0.023	0.047	-0.49	-0.029	0.018	-1.65	-0.034	0.023	-1.47	-0.016	0.031	-0.52
Individual's Education	0.166	0.063	2.65	0.026	0.022	1.20	-0.180	0.032	-5.60	-0.144	0.043	-3.35
Race: White	0.606	0.320	1.90	0.169	0.046	3.65	0.105	0.052	2.01	0.076	0.060	1.27
Race: Black	0.110	0.329	0.33	-0.184	0.053	-3.48	-0.173	0.060	-2.87	-0.240	0.073	-3.28
Constant	-3.046	1.398	-2.18	1.858	0.338	5.50	2.095	0.898	2.33	0.201	0.880	0.23
Predicting Independent	Coef.	Std. Err.	z	Coef.	Std. Err.	z	Coef.	Std. Err.	z	Coef.	Std. Err.	z
Age	-0.016	0.018	-0.92	0.005	0.005	0.97	-0.032	0.009	-3.44	0.010	0.008	1.25
Individual's Approval	-0.256	0.117	-2.18	-0.030	0.048	-0.61	0.432	0.065	6.65	-0.335	0.094	-3.57
Mean Approval	-7.552	4.478	-1.69	-1.800	0.742	-2.43	-6.318	2.706	-2.33	-4.152	2.530	-1.64
Squared Mean Approval	10.171	5.256	1.94	2.409	0.564	4.27	4.593	2.292	2.00	2.859	1.757	1.63
Unemployment Rate	-0.130	0.099	-1.32	0.032	0.019	1.67	-0.033	0.043	-0.77	0.251	0.070	3.59
Age by Individual's Approval	-0.001	0.003	-0.35	0.006	0.001	5.94	-0.013	0.001	-9.74	0.012	0.002	6.03
Age by Mean Approval	-0.013	0.022	-0.60	-0.023	0.006	-4.12	0.037	0.011	3.19	-0.016	0.009	-1.67
Age by Unemployment Rate	0.000	0.002	0.22	-0.002	0.000	-4.24	-0.001	0.001	-0.88	-0.005	0.002	-3.28
Age by Unemployment Rate by Education	0.000	0.000	0.34	0.000	0.000	3.07	0.001	0.000	7.80	0.001	0.000	4.58
Individual's Gender	-0.052	0.043	-1.22	-0.087	0.017	-4.98	-0.071	0.023	-3.13	-0.011	0.032	-0.36
Individual's Education	0.084	0.056	1.51	-0.005	0.022	-0.22	-0.165	0.031	-5.24	-0.140	0.043	-3.25
Race: White	0.197	0.241	0.82	0.087	0.044	1.98	0.073	0.050	1.45	-0.014	0.059	-0.23
Race: Black	-0.115	0.249	-0.46	-0.254	0.050	-5.04	-0.218	0.058	-3.74	-0.205	0.071	-2.87
Constant	2.447	1.258	1.95	0.541	0.337	1.61	2.821	0.904	3.12	1.006	0.899	1.12

Coefficients in bold face significant at $p > .05$, two-tailed.

not-so-strong partisans. This isn't that big a handicap, but it does mean that any results we get about the effect of unemployment on partisanship is especially strong, enough to make independents out of partisans, and vice-versa, rather than just independents into leaners.

As with the last model, we first need to make sure that the model worked, and the diagnostics look good. All four of the models do substantially better than chance, and somewhat better than the modal category, in predicting the partisanship of respondents. Also as with the previous model, we've presented the most relevant results in figures.

Several of the control variables have interesting effects on young people's partisanship. First, the popularity of the president has a significant effect on partisanship in most of the period studied. On average, an increase in the president's approval rating from 30 to 50 percent changes the likelihood of an eighteen-year-old belonging to either party by 4.2 percent; for fifty-year-olds, the change is 3.8 percent. The biggest effects are during the Clinton presidency: where a twenty-point increase in presidential approval is expected to make young people 3.8 percent less likely to be Republican and 8.4 percent more likely to be Democrats. In the same period, the change in likelihood among middle-aged respondents is far more typical: they become 2 percent less likely to be Republican and 3.7 percent more likely to be Democrats. The same increase in George W. Bush's approval ratings leads the young to be about 6 percent more Republican (compared to 4.4 percent for middle-aged respondents), though there is also evidence of a polarization effect in the most recent period. By itself, this suggests a sort of consumption at work: as Clinton and George W. Bush became more popular "brands," young people became more likely to identify with their respective parties.

These effects are independent of the effects of individual-level presidential approval on partisanship. Approving of the president's job performance generally led individuals to be more likely to identify with the president's party and less likely to identify with the other party. Unlike the effects of aggregate approval, though, these effects were larger for fifty-year-olds than for eighteen-year-olds. Averaging across the administrations, approving of the president had a mean impact of 5.0 (with a range of 1.5 to 8.4) percent on the likelihood of identifying with a party among eighteen-year-olds, and an effect of 8.9 (ranging from 5.7 to 10.2) percent among fifty-year-olds. This would indicate that while they are more likely to change their partisanship in response to the general popularity, they are also more likely to maintain their partisanship even if they disapprove of their party's president.

Taken alone, during the Bush years, education seems to make individuals more Democratic. However, the overall negative effect of education is muted by the interaction effect of age and unemployment rate by education. While the coefficient on the three-way interaction effect is less than one percent of the size of the main effect of education, this means that at average rates of unemployment (6 percent), the main effect of education is canceled out for individuals when they are about twenty-three years old. Among older individuals, higher levels of education lead them to be less likely to identify with the Democratic Party and more likely to be either independent or a Republican.

Once we control for the effects of all of these variables, we can isolate what we'll call the base level of partisanship. This base level tells us how many Republicans and Democrats we would have if a president's popularity, or a respondent's education, wasn't a factor. Since we've controlled for all of the factors that we expect should impact partisanship, we can look for the effect of the overall economy on young people's partisanship in what's left.

In the first two periods analyzed—encompassing the Carter, Reagan, and George H. Bush administrations—higher levels of unemployment made respondents less likely to identify with the president's party. Under Clinton, the effects were in the same direction but are not significant, and under George W. Bush, higher unemployment makes individuals more likely to identify themselves as independents. However, we are not concerned with the general relationship between unemployment rates and partisanship, but rather the conditionality of these effects by the age of the respondent. The variable representing this—the interaction between age and unemployment rates—is significant in all of the periods, except the Carter administration. Also, the further interaction between the age of the respondent, the education of the respondent, and the overall unemployment rate is also significant in the two most recent periods, including the Clinton and George W. Bush administrations. When put together, these results are telling us that the economy is having some effect on partisanship and affecting people differently by their age. Because

Figure 1.2: Predicted Likelihood of Belonging to Party, by President and Unemployment Rate, age 50

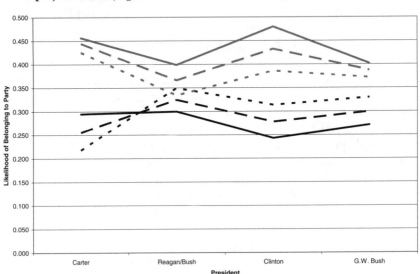

Likelihood of identifying with Republican Party in black; Democratic Party in gray. Lines become more solid as unemployment increases. Likelihoods estimated from regressions in Table 1.1.

of the complexity involved in sorting out all of these effects individually, we'll look at the outcome of all of them jointly.

Before we discuss how young people's partisanship responds to economic indicators, it useful to set up a baseline: how older individuals have responded. With the exception of the Carter administration, there's a clear pattern. Regardless of the party of the president, high levels of unemployment lead the older voters (age fifty) to be more Democratic and less Republican; low levels of unemployment lead them to be more Republican and less Democratic. During the Clinton administration, for instance, a 4 percent unemployment rate leads to a predicted partisan divide of about 31 percent Republican and 38 percent Democrat. At 8 percent unemployment, that gap widens to 24 percent Republican and 48 percent Democrat.

This fits in very nicely with conventional expectations about how Americans see the major parties (Hansen 1998; Modigliani and Modigliani 1987). Historically, they have tended to trust Republicans to handle the economy more than Democrats. As such, when the economy turns sour, people become more Republican. This holds up, apparently, even when it is a Republican administration that's apparently mishandling the economy. There are shifts in the size of the effect—biggest during the Clinton years,[15] smallest during the Reagan and George H. Bush administrations—but the pattern is remarkably stable since the 1980s.

This stability is in marked contrast to the shift that has taken place in the relationship between unemployment and partisanship among young people. In the Carter administration, increases in unemployment lead young people to be more likely to be Republicans and less likely to be Democrats. This, however, is where the similarities with older voters end.

Under the Reagan and Bush administrations, young people's partisanship is even more responsive to unemployment: the same

Figure 1.3: Predicted Likelihood of Belonging to Party, by President and Unemployment Rate, age 18

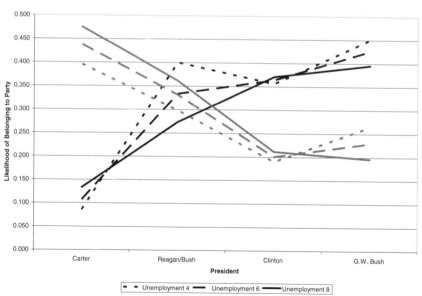

Likelihood of identifying with Republican Party in black; Democratic Party in gray. Lines become more solid as unemployment increases. Likelihoods estimated from regressions in Table 1.1.

four point increase in unemployment leads them to become about 6 percent more Democratic, and almost 13 percent less likely to be Republican. While older Americans' partisanship remained fairly steady after the Reagan and Bush administrations, young American's partisanship remains in flux. During the Clinton administration, in which older people demonstrated their greatest degree of economic responsiveness, young people's partisanship barely fluctuates in the face of changes in the unemployment rate. A 4 percent increase in unemployment leads to changes of less than 2 percent in the likelihood of identifying with either of the parties.

Finally, during the George W. Bush administration, the conditionality of partisanship on unemployment rates returns, but in a pattern rather different from that of older respondents and from any previous periods. Rather than becoming more Republican when unemployment is low and less when unemployment is high, young people are more likely to be members of either party when unemployment is low, and more likely to be independent when unemployment is high. A four point increase in unemployment leads eighteen-year-olds to be 6 percent less likely to be Republican, and 7 percent less likely to be Democrats.

In effect, young people are acting exactly as the consumption of politics model would hold. A bad economy leads young people, but not older cohorts, to become much less partisan. During the George W. Bush administration, a hypothetical increase in the unemployment rate from 4 to 8 percent[16] would increase the number of eighteen-year-olds expected to be independent by thirteen points, or 44 percent, from 29 percent to 42 percent.

It could be argued that this effect is due to the increased likelihood that young people will lose their jobs in a bad economy. After all, when it's time to let employees go, those with fewer skills and less seniority will be the first out the door, and young people are more likely to fit the bill. There are good reasons, though, to believe that this is not the case. If the results were simply a function of increased unemployment, or fear of unemployment, leading to young people paying less attention to politics, we wouldn't see the education interaction present in the model. When the unemployment level increases, more educated young people—who are less likely to be in fear of their jobs—are more likely to become independent, on the whole. If we were purely looking at a job security effect, we would expect the opposite to be true. Further evidence for this point can be found in the results for older individuals. Less educated older workers, too, should be more in fear of their jobs than more educated workers, regardless of their age, but the effect simply isn't there.

Because our data doesn't follow individual voters from month to month, or year to year, we can't be sure how long-lasting these effects are. Traditional theories like those we discussed earlier, would argue that they should persist for years. According to these models, partisanship rarely changes past a person's early twenties, so an individual who has learned to tune out will stay tuned out. Other models, like the macropartisanship model suggested by MacKuen (MacKuen, Erikson, and Stimson 1989) and his colleagues argue that partisanship, at least in the aggregate, shifts around in response to fleeting events, and so the increase in the number of independents may not be permanent.

Regardless of the length of the effects, the presence of the hypothesized relationship is clear. In the same way that others buy fewer durable goods, take fewer vacations, and put more money into savings when the economy goes sour, young people become less partisan. As we've seen, this means that they pay less attention to political news, are less likely to vote, and less likely to care about the outcome. In a bad economy, one explanation would hold, young people simply become disillusioned with both parties. For older voters, and even for young voters during previous administrations, this wasn't the case. Rather, a bad economy was a sign that a shift was needed, toward, perhaps, more competent economic leadership or less spending on social programs. This is arguably a rational response; that of today's young people seems decidedly less so.

CONSUMING WORK

All told, these results tell us a great deal about the relationship between partisanship and work, and, therefore the relationship between partisanship and consumption. As partisanship is one of —if not the—most important predictors of political knowledge and behavior, such results bear heavily on the political behavior of young people.

Our first study shows that when young people work, they're much more likely to identify themselves as independents, rather than as members of either political party. Among twenty-five-year-old white males, working full time led to a drop of about 7 points in the likelihood of being a strong partisan and an increase of about 12 points in the likelihood of being an independent. Moreover, the results for the control variables indicate that this effect isn't the result of a time crunch. From the previous work of one of the authors, we know that young people (especially the relatively affluent whites that the Monte Carlo model is based on) use work as an opportunity to brand themselves: hence the preference for being a barista at Starbucks over flipping burgers at McDonald's. What these results show is that when young people get their identities through their jobs, they don't need to identify with a political party. From these results, we'd also expect that any activity that gives young people an identity, a way to brand themselves, would lead them away from partisan politics as well: something that comes up frequently in our interviews. This is important because it means that politics doesn't occupy a privileged place in the lives of young people, that it isn't something that you do—or don't—regardless of your circumstances. Rather, being a "Democrat" or a "Republican" is about the same thing as being a "GAP employee," a "Yankees fan," or a "country music listener."

In the second study, we were able to show that economic factors have a direct effect on the partisanship of young people and in a much different pattern than they do for the older Americans. In recent years, this relationship has shifted such that a downturn in the economy leads to a decrease in membership in both parties. Why? One reason may have to do with increased demands on young people: when unemployment goes up, they have more to worry about. The other reason that presents itself has to do with the tenor of political debate in a bad economy. Put simply, politics isn't as much fun when the economy is bad: rather than worrying about how to spend money, the parties have to fight over where to cut funds. The brands represented by the parties just aren't as attractive, and young people, therefore, turn away from them.

These results lend substantial quantitative support to the premise that politics is just another thing to be consumed, and the consequences of that may be profound. Of course, we can't determine the mechanisms by which this happens solely through the quantitative results, and this will be one of the main topics that we'll explore in the upcoming chapters.

2
Republicans

A typical Republican (in our area) is someone who is usually wealthy. They wear polo shirts, plaid shorts, and drink martinis. They are usually racist and look down upon people who have less money than them. They may be of any age; if your parents are wealthy and Republican chances are you will be also. Republicans drive fancy European cars but they do not put gaudy decorations or accessories on them because that would make you a Democrat. Republicans like to drink Starbucks instead of Dunkin' Donuts and they play the stock market instead of the lottery.

—Billy, a twenty-four-year-old Republican

BILLY IS A TWENTY-FOUR-YEAR-OLD FULL-TIME COLLEGE STUDENT at a private liberal arts college. Born to affluent, suburban, Republican parents in the New York tristate area, Billy identifies himself as a Republican. When we ask him about his party affiliation, he does not even hesitate to answer "Republican." Though he is sure he is a Republican, he adds, "I could care less about politics." While he is a self-professed "political agnostic," for him political disinterest and political party affiliation are two different things. He describes politics as "totally irrelevant to what I want to do in my life." His apparently strong political views are almost entirely at odds with his general apathy, and this apathy is what we're trying to understand. To do so, we'll first examine the views of Billy—who exemplifies many of the statements made by the Republican respondents—as well as the other young Republicans we spoke to in depth to try to find the roots of their apathy. We'll then describe what political science and political psychology have to say about what Republicans *should* sound like, and see how similar Billy and his cohort are to older Republicans. Finally, we'll then piece together the clues from different areas that the respondents talk about in order to pinpoint the cause of this apathy and what could be done to reverse it.

IMAGE OF A REPUBLICAN

Billy's definition of Republicanism is devoid of issues and political ideology. However, he has a very clear idea about what a Republican is. When we ask him to describe an average Republican and Democrat, he says: "A typical Republican (in our area) is someone who is usually wealthy. They wear polo shirts, plaid shorts, and drink martinis. They are usually racist and look down upon people who have less money than them. They may be of any age; if your parents are wealthy and Republican chances are you will be also. Republicans drive fancy European cars but they do not put gaudy decorations or accessories on them because that would make you a Democrat. Republicans like to drink Starbucks instead of Dunkin' Donuts and they play the stock market instead of the lottery."

The difference between the two parties, according to Billy, is explained only through consumption habits and choice of brands. What differentiates Republicans from Democrats, according to Billy, are the consumption patterns of these two groups. Republicans consume more sophisticated, expensive, and often branded products. Starbucks rather than Dunkin' Donuts or the stock market rather than the lottery: *that's* Republicanism. Political apathy and partisanship aren't at odds because this notion of partisanship doesn't necessarily have anything to do with actual political views.

The parties, in this view, are brands to be consumed by young people, just like Starbucks and Dunkin' Donuts. Billy also doesn't see any real difference in the content of the two parties, just the ways in which they do things. They both gamble: one on the stock market and one on the lottery. You can change from one to the other easily and quickly, too: putting gaudy accessories and stickers on a European car makes you an immediate Democrat.

Other Republicans see the differences in the same way. Rachel tells us that a typical Republican is "probably an upper-middle-class or upper-class citizen," while a Democrat is "middle class or near (slightly under) the poverty line." The Republican youth seem to be making distinctions between the parties based on their relative incomes. Republicans and Democrats may be doing the same things, but Republicans are doing the expensive versions. Are they completely off-base? After all, while there may be wealthy businessmen skewing Republican, much of the party is made up of socially conservative southerners, who aren't thought to be especially wealthy. There are also plenty of rich liberal Democrats in the public eye, in Hollywood or on the Upper West Side. So, how accurate are these beliefs about the disparate wealth of Republicans and Democrats? It is easy to blame the statements of the young respondents on the brand of the parties as representing, respectively, the wealthy and the disenfranchised, but before doing so, we should see how valid these beliefs are. It is difficult to compare dollar amounts of income across time, but the American National Election Study solves the problem by putting the amounts given into percentiles. So, rather than knowing that someone made $3,000 per year in 1952 or $46,000 in 2004, we know that both are at about the median of income—half the population above and half below—for their time.

Most commonly, we try and find differences between groups based on the mean or median: in this case, though, there is no real difference between the mean incomes of Republicans and Democrats. Nor does there appear to be a substantial difference in the standard deviations attached to the means, which measure how far away from the means the income of either group is likely to get. There is, however, a vast difference in the skewness of the means. A negative skew, like that displayed by the Republican mean, indicates that much of the data is clustered in higher income groups, while the positive skew of the Democratic mean indicates the opposite. Moreover, while the mean of the two group's income is about the same, the median income of Republicans is higher than that of Democrats, indicating that there are a lot more wealthy Republicans than there are wealthy Democrats.

A closer analysis of the full range of the distributions fills in the blanks. In 1952, 26 percent of strong Republicans had incomes in the top 5 percent nationally, compared with about 10 percent of strong Democrats. By 2004, the numbers had shifted only a little: 14 percent of Democrats reported incomes in the top 5 percent nationally, while the percent of Republicans doing so stayed relatively stable at 28 percent. Meanwhile, the number of Republicans and Democrats reporting incomes in the bottom 15 percent dropped: for Republicans, it fell from 14 percent in 1952 to 9 percent in 2004, and among Democrats from 27 percent to 18 percent in the same period. As when dealing with the reported rates of voting in chapter 1, we don't necessarily believe that all of these numbers are reported truthfully—it's difficult to imagine how 10 percent of respondents in 2004 have incomes in the top 5 percent nationally—but they should hold up for the purposes of comparison.

These differences remain even when we look only at white respondents. In 2004, 16 percent of white strong Democrats had incomes in the lowest 15 percent, while 11 percent had incomes in the highest 5 percent. When racial minorities were not included in the tallies of Republicans, 12 percent identified themselves as being in the lowest household income category, and fully one-third in the highest 5 percent. While race certainly has an impact on these figures, it doesn't seem to be the deciding factor in the Republican income advantage.

All told, this means that while the Republicans and Democrats are, on average, about equally wealthy, Republicans are far more likely to be in the upper income brackets and rather less likely to be in the lower ones. The gains made by Democrats in the past fifty years have reduced this difference, but not nearly enough to eliminate them. As such, the differences in income identified by the respondents is not, in and of itself, evidence that they are basing their views of the parties on shallow stereotypes. However, the way in which these views of the parties are reported speaks volumes. It isn't just that Republicans and Democrats are associated with different income groups, but rather that they're associated with brands representative of those income groups. They are attributed consumption patterns that differentiate them, branded consumption patterns that separate the Republicans from the Democrats.

ISSUES

According to most accounts of partisanship, a party is defined by its issue platform. Downs (1997), for instance, argues that individuals should choose a party based on their expectations about what a party will do once in office and the impact that those actions will have on themselves. Parties, then, only function as useful labels when they are consistent over time, when past performance is some indication of future results, and issues are the main point of continuity. The definition of Republicanism advanced by many of our respondents, however, doesn't seem to include any issues.

In fact, Billy tells us that "I don't know how much they actually care of what the party's views are, instead they care that they can distinguish themselves from the other party." The difference between Republicans and Democrats in the United States is not issue driven, but rather based on illusions. He adds, "It doesn't matter what their views are anyways because they never do anything that they say they're going to do. They can definitely talk the talk, but I don't think that they can walk the walk, maybe they're just confrontational people who need to argue with others because they can't admit they're wrong." For Billy, even if the two parties want to appear different, in essence they are very similar. Barbara, his eighteen-year-old classmate, believes that "they [the two parties] want the same things to be achieved." She believes that there are no differences in their goals and aspirations. However, in the short term they focus on different topics. Steve, another nineteen year old, points out that now, "the Democrats' main issue is withdrawing the troops from Iraq, while the Republicans want to keep some troops for peacekeeping and to train the new police force. The Democrats also want to downsize our armed forces, while the Republicans want to keep our armed forces where they are or make them stronger." What differences there are don't come from the philosophy of government, but rather from approaches to specific issues: there's no mention of ideology, of overarching ideals or values that constrain the parties, but rather a few easily understood issues positions, like the war, or guns, or the environment. This could be seen as an improvement over some of the other Republicans—after all, there's at least some notion that the parties have political content—but this is undercut by the cynicism with which the Republicans we spoke to view these issues. They aren't real beliefs, but ways to win elections.

Even a few years ago, the inability to draw a clear ideological line between the two parties could have been seen as a reflection of the parties, rather than a sign of political inattention. Traditional theories of electoral politics, in fact, hold that it is in the best interests of both parties to blur the lines of distinction between them and move to match the preferences of the median voter in any given district.[1] In the famous 1960 presidential debates between Richard Nixon and John Kennedy, for instance, a key point was the question of American response to the potential Chinese invasion of two islands, Quemoy and Matsu, seen as potential staging sites for an invasion of Taiwan. Nixon said that any invasion would necessarily result in action, as it would be a sure sign of aggression against Taiwan. Kennedy argued that he would only act against an invasion of Quemoy and Matsu if it was a sign of aggression, which it probably would be. More recently, many observers complained that the 2000 presidential debates between Bush and Al Gore failed to draw many meaningful distinctions, as the debate was not over whether or not there should be tax cuts, but rather how large those tax cuts should be; not over whether to save money for future social security, but about whether such funds should be in a "lock box."

In recent years, the biggest differences between the parties come from social or cultural issues such as abortion, homosexuality, flag burning, and the role of religion in public life. These are generally considered to be "easy" issues (Carmines and Stimson 1989), because there are a clear set of alternatives and little confusion between what policies will lead to what choices. Tax reform, for instance, might be a hard issue, because no one is entirely certain what the impact of altering a certain tax break will be on overall tax revenues or the activity the tax break is designed to promote or discourage. Gay marriage, on the other hand, is an easy issue: if a law is passed allowing homosexuals to marry, then same-sex couples will get married. If a law is passed banning it, they won't. Often, debates on these issues are more symbolic than consequential, used to demonstrate differences between the parties in advance of an election, as was claimed of the attempts to pass constitutional amendments outlawing flag burning and gay marriage in the summer before the 2006 midterm elections.[2] Such attempts have ensured that these issues remain salient to voters, and the most recent American National Election Study shows that the vast majority hold views on these issues.

The inability to draw a distinction between the parties on these issues, then, represents more than a lack of attention to politics and political discourse, but rather an unwillingness to believe that the expressed differences actually represent any differences. Our interviews indicate that respondents know that the parties espouse different views—even if the respondents generally don't name the issues—but believe that those views are insincere. "Overall they [the parties] are fighting for the same issues just at different sides of the issues," Rachel says. "Like abortions . . . Democrats are pro-choice, Republicans are pro-life; yet, let either side say something and they both claim to be trying to protect the life of the mother and the baby."

It simply doesn't matter what politicians say, because nothing that they say can believed: all of it is political theater. In this, the respondents are attributing to the politicians the same type of political views that they hold themselves: the content of a political message only matters to the extent that it brands the message and the messenger. It isn't only that the respondents don't have a sense of personal ideology, but rather that they don't seem to believe that anyone has an ideology. Everyone is simply trying to appeal to one group or another; the words and concepts are, in effect, meaningless, and can be safely ignored.

SOCIAL CHANGE

One recurrent theme throughout the interviews we conducted was the relative powerlessness of young people. Oftentimes, Republican young people articulate how powerless they feel to change the system or create social change. In fact, many young people tell me, social change is not possible. Billy explains: "you can't change this system. If you are unhappy you have the freedom to move to a different country. I think that you could certainly try, but there would be a lot of people upset at you trying to change their evil ways. . . . For example, you can only win an election if you have money, and you can donate enough to the president's campaign that he will pardon you if you kill people."

Social change is not even a possibility he can entertain. For Billy, political or social change is simply not an option in the United States. If you're not happy with the system here, the only option is to leave and relocate.

Interestingly, almost none of young Republicans we spoke to linked their skepticism about social change to structural barriers. Rather, they told us that while change is theoretically possible, there is little people can do on the individual level to create it. "You really cannot change the political system by yourself. You would need people to follow you and have everyone come together," says Lauren. "I feel as though change is definitely possible but it is something that has to occur because of a want for it by the people. By want I mean something that people are not just going to let be ignored or overlooked because it doesn't seem important to others at the time." The mechanisms they identify for social change are also limited. "Voting, I guess," Steve says. Voting is as much as an individual can do to change the system, but even then he reminds us, you need large number of people agreeing with you.

Even if some short-term goals are achieved through individual participation, unless large groups of people collaborate, these changes fail to exist in the long run. As Barbara argues: "There has to be more than one person to believe in the same things for it [referring to social change] to work."

Based on their understanding, many of these young Republicans do not see themselves as potential actors in social change. Change in our system stems mostly from the acts of the president and people in authority: power comes from the top down, not from the bottom up.

For reasons we'll discuss later, the sentiment underlying these statements—that social change is undesirable, that we should simply accept society the way it is—is about what we would expect from Republicans. That said, the way in which these sentiments are phrased is jarring. Republicans might be expected to reject social change, but that rejection is supposed to be rooted in an acceptance of inequality and anxiety about the uncertainty that such change would bring. Like the statements made by other partisan groups, the Republicans we surveyed don't seem to be anxious about the possibility of social change because they don't see it as a possibility. It isn't that social change would be bad, it's that social change is an impossibility. There is, however, a great deal of acceptance of inequality.

The feeling of powerlessness in changing the social system is often accompanied by feelings of anonymity and alienation. In their relation to the government, these young Republicans feel at the mercy of the government and just a number on the database.

"If the government wants to take more tax money they will," Billy says. "If they want to send me to Iraq, they will. They can listen to my phone calls and track my footprints on the Internet. All I am is a number in a database to them."

Due to this powerlessness and the feeling that they cannot change things, they choose not be involved in politics. Billy tells us:

> A typical person who's really interested in politics is someone who cares way too much about something they cannot change. They take life too seriously and want to be heard, but ultimately they are just unhappy because they're powerless. I have a friend who loves politics but it's the only thing that he talks about, and he believes our current government is the most evil thing ever. He wants to make sure everyone knows how he feels about particular problems, but it doesn't matter because he can't change anything at all. I told him to move to a different country if he's so unhappy here, he said he's moving to Africa to get back to his roots.

The feeling of powerlessness and alienation from the system defines Billy's and the other Republicans' views of the political system. As Rachel tells us, "politics only affects me directly when any type of election comes around and then it feels as if everyone wants to get to know you and see what concerns you have in hopes of getting your votes." No one really cares about their views, and they, as individuals, certainly cant change anything, so why should they care about politics?

APATHY

This apathy is also partly due to the perception of governmental policies. While many young Republicans feel that government is too powerful, they do not believe that they are directly affected by governmental policies yet. Barbara tells us, "I am still young and I just recently turned eighteen. I still haven't figured out yet what [governmental policies] could affect me." Many young Republicans believe that government policies should be affecting them, so it is important to keep them in check; however, many young people say they cannot identify how the government policies affect them.

Barbara believes this is because adults do not tell them the truth regarding how the government polices affect them. Cynthia, a twenty-year-old transfer student who recently relocated from a Red state from a Blue state, on the other hand, believes this is because of age. She believes that government policies affect people, but they tend to affect her parents mostly. Cynthia argues "being that I claim nothing and I have no responsibility except for signing my tax papers, they do not affect me directly except in the larger sense."

The elements of government that Republicans do see impacting themselves directly are mainly drawn from a fear of state power. Steve tells us, "I have always researched my rights thoroughly, and been on top of laws that could directly affect me. I always like to make sure I am operating within acceptable bounds of government policy, so I don't get arrested or flagged in some FBI computer somewhere. . . .The government should keep tabs on its citizens, to keep an eye out for spies or terrorists. But they should not go so far as to jeopardize our rights as a citizen."

ROLE OF THE STATE

This distrust of state power is a recurrent theme in the statements made by the young Republicans. While they generally approving of certain actions, like the invasion of Iraq, government in general is thought to be a bad thing. Billy tells us that "most people in the government don't care about the job they're doing. They're in a position of power and they will abuse it until they get caught, but money can usually buy you out of getting caught also so it's all good. There are good people, but it's a dirty game. The people who get caught either ran out of money or were so stupid they exposed themselves or compromised the ability for others to do dirty tricks."

For Billy, the people in the government do not care about citizens, especially not young people like himself. Furthermore, there are no checks and balances to ensure effective job performance. He believes that money and connections lead to an abuse of power: if you give enough money to the president, he told us, you could get a pardon for anything. Partially, his cynicism stems from the fact that these positions, not individual people, lead to the abuse of power. While individual people might be effective and competent, the organization itself leads to abuse of power.

The mistrust of the government among young people is accompanied by a feeling of fear of the government. Billy, for instance, understands that "government policies need to be put in place," but "they shouldn't make me feel paranoid." He describes his relation with the government as one of fear and distrust. "I don't trust anything, and I will never trust the government," he says. Steve has a more positive view of governmental power, telling us that the government needs to "keep tabs" on terrorists, but consistently pairs such statements with references to constitutional rights, and the need to make sure that the government stays within certain proscribed limits.

The fear and distrust of the government among young people has often been associated with social protest and political activism. Historically, student protests of the 1960s and 1970s often coupled fear of the government with political action. However, young people today verbalize their fear and distrust of the government, yet their feelings do not translate into political activism. When we ask about it, Billy answers: "If they [the government] want to do something, they're going to do it, who's going to stop them? Do I take out my musket and form a militia or do I just conform to whatever the hell they say or do?" Even though he is not happy with the way things are, he does not even consider being politically active.

Despite the prevalent feelings of distrust and fear of the government, many conservative young people do acknowledge the role of the government. When asked about what the role of government should be, Billy tells us: "I believe the government does have to be involved in some of our affairs, but certainly not all of them. I'd be happier if I didn't have to worry about someone listening to my phone calls or getting searched every time I board a plane because my Hispanic features resemble those of a terrorist. This country has become such a superpower that it needs to have a government that dictates what we can and cannot do, but I don't think that it should be at the expense of our freedoms or our peace of mind."

This lack of trust in the government is especially consequential for Republicans. Following Hetherington's (2004) theory of political trust, Rudolph and Evans (2005) find that trust has larger effects on the policy preferences of conservatives than on those of liberals or moderates. Liberals and Democrats, we would expect, would support spending on social programs no matter their level of trust in the government. Conservatives and Republicans, on the other hand, aren't expected to think that such spending programs are inherently good and could easily turn against them if they don't trust the government administering them. In a way, Rudolph and Evans argue, supporting government programs means that conservatives are trading off their ideological preferences for potential personal or societal gain, and trust in the government can play a critical role in this calculation.[3]

What then, to expect from young Republicans who don't trust the government? Because they don't believe that money allocated for social services will be spent wisely, they should oppose any such spending—precisely the pattern we see here.

TIME

Time constraints are important factors to consider in understanding politics. Today, young people are overscheduled and overstressed and presumably have much less leisure time to devote to political activity; many scholars have pointed to the time constraints that young people have today. Especially given that many American youth work while still in school, political activity might suffer due to time constraints. After all, political involvement is a very time-consuming process that requires dedicated attention, from following up newspaper articles to writing to local representatives to voting to volunteering for campaigns.

Billy works part-time in an office in addition to being a full-time college student. However, he assures us that it is not the lack of time that leads to his political indifference. "If they really cared they would make the time," he says, referring to other young people. "They can feed you anything and you'd believe it. I think people are either too stupid, don't care, or a combination of both. I have the time to care about politics but I don't care because I'd rather spend my time listening to good music." Steve is even more explicit: "Most people do have time to worry about political issues, but they choose not to care. For example, a person may feel they cannot make a change in our government, because they are just one person out of millions, therefore they choose not to care about political issues."

Political involvement is, therefore, just another activity like listening to music or going to the movies or doing a sport that is fighting for his time. They may have the time, but they'd rather do something else with it.

MONEY AND INEQUALITY

Throughout our interviews on politics and political views, one theme that young people kept bringing up was money and class inequality. While we expected young people to emphasize ideologies and issues, many of the Republicans felt strongly about money—not surprising given their views of money being the only underlying difference between the parties. Billy characterizes a typical Democrat as "a person who has to work hard to make money, they may have a good job, but they weren't trust-fund babies. Some Democrats do not like to work at all." He remembers that when he was young, he was often told that "Republicans work hard and don't like to give their money to poor people, and Democrats are poor people that want Republicans' money." Inequality in society is not a structural issue, but a matter of preference: Republicans work hard, Democrats would rather just get their money from the hardworking Republicans, and enlist the government to do this on their behalf.

Billy, himself, like many young people we interviewed works long hours. While he characterizes most of the classes he takes in college as "irrelevant," work is very important and useful in his opinion. Therefore, he feels strongly about government assistance and welfare.

In this, the young Republicans we spoke with are in accord with the expected attitudes of Republicans in general. Attitudes toward inequality have often been regarded as one of the major distinguishing characteristics of conservatives. In general, conservatives are thought to see society as necessarily being hierarchical: some people will always be on the top, and some people will always be on the bottom (Giddens 1998). Attempts to change this, creating a more egalitarian society, are therefore folly at best, and against the natural order at worst. Even if the people at the top don't always deserve their money and privilege, the people at the bottom certainly don't deserve it.

INFORMATION SOURCES

One of the problems young people encounter is their distrust in the news sources. As a conservative young person, Billy identifies Fox News as his source of political information. However, despite his choice of channel, he does not feel happy with the news he receives from the channel. He characterizes it as "clueless rich people argue on a screen." One of the factors that bothers him is the unequal representation of more affluent people. He feels that nonaffluent people in this society are not equally represented, their concerns not addressed and their opinions not voiced in that channel.

Jenna, a twenty-one-year-old college student agrees that she cannot fully relate to the news media. She says she would like to get more information, but she does not like the news sources available to her. Even though she identifies herself as a politically active and engaged Republican, she says she does not like the more Republican news sources. She is one of the rare young people we met who is very interested in politics. Due to her interest in politics, she chose political science as her major and is currently thinking about a career in politics. Despite this, she complains about the lack of sources of information. She says: "I get mostly all my information from the media, my parents, group discussions, the Web, readings like the newspaper, and some of the scholarly journals like the ones in the library and things. Oftentimes, I try to stay more up to date by reading different types of newspapers in hopes of gaining a better perspective of the things that are going on the world and in America," but she is disappointed by the available options.

She sees the typical Fox News viewer as "old" or "middle aged." Therefore, because she associates the brand with being older and less fashionable, she does not like to be associated with it.

Democratic news mediums such as NPR are not attractive to her either. We had assumed Jenna's dislike for NPR was due to her political and ideological differences and differences in issues. However, the dislike for NPR is not due to the content of NPR: as far as she is concerned, radio, like Fox News, is for old people.

Therefore, even though she feels that getting her information while she is commuting to one of her two jobs or to school would fit her busy schedule well, she does not want to be associated with the radio. It sounds like an outdated brand for her, therefore she prefers newer, fresher, and younger brands.

Cynthia agrees: she has never listened to the NPR because she finds the pace slow and the speakers boring. Interestingly, she also describes NPR as a Republican channel that appeals to mostly conservative people. While she might not be aware of the content, she has distinctive images about the image and branding of NPR.

The time of the news shows is very important to Jenna, too. She says that earlier new shows are for older people because Jenna says older people prefer earlier shows. However, shows later in the day are cooler brands and are for younger people.

That is why she believes shows like *The Daily Show* are cooler. "Mostly younger people watch *The Daily Show* because the hour it comes on is a little later and mostly we are the people who are up at that time to watch. Also, older people just want the news flat out, and are not really into the whole satirical thing." She finds the brand cool and attractive. Barbara says that the show appeals to a younger audience like people younger than thirty.

It is not just a news show for these young people. Even though the content is more liberal, many young Republicans identify it as a way of escape from a political world they are alienated from. Steve, a nineteen-year-old Republican says: "A *Daily Show* viewer is tired about hearing about the grim news all of the other stations report. They like to hear the lighter side of the news reports, and hear the reporters make some jokes. *The Daily Show* reporters like to remind the viewers they are human, too, by the way they act, while other reporters just read the news and get off of the air. These viewers like to be reminded that the reporter on the other end is also human." Therefore, rather than simply reporting events, shows like these provide an opportunity to escape and vent.

Billy, on the other hand, is dissatisfied with other sources of political information. The two main sources he identifies as Democratic sources of information are *The Daily Show with Jon Stewart* and NPR. However, he characterizes a typical *Daily Show* viewer as one that "smoke(s) pot while watching the show, they think they know a lot about politics because they are watching the show." He is equally cynical about NPR. He believes that NPR listeners, too, believe that thy have a grasp on politics because they tune in. He adds "I don't care how fair or nonbiased it may be to someone, it's all make-believe."

Even for the young Republicans who seek out political information, then, none of the mainstream media outlets are appealing: they're simply too old. Of all of them, only *The Daily Show* is consistently viewed positively, or as appealing to young people, even if it isn't always taken seriously (it is, in their words, the haven of those who are smoking pot or just wanting a laugh). This speaks to the importance of *The Daily Show* in young people's political worlds, a topic we'll explore more in a later chapter: even those who would be expected to disagree with Jon Stewart's message see the appeal of the messenger.

Partisanship and Ideology

We're going to end the next three chapters by describing what we would expect statements made by the various types of partisans to sound like, so we can establish the ways in which the young respondents to our surveys are similar or different. In many cases, though, the research that gives us an insight into these partisan categories isn't based on partisan differences, but rather on ideological differences. As such, we should take the time here to discuss the distinctions between partisanship and ideology, and why expectations derived from one can be applied to the other.

The first reason that we can use ideology to shape our expectations about partisan groups is that the members of ideological categories are increasingly the same people who are members of the partisan categories that we're interested in. In philosophy, and disciplines that draw heavily from it, like sociology, ideology has a broad meaning, referring to an organized, consistent set of ideas: a way of looking at the world, really. In the American political science, however, it has a much stricter definition, generally referring only to the placement of an individual on a scale between liberal and conservative. The form of this scale is very similar to the scale used to measure party identification: as many as seven points, with "moderate" at the middle. Also, like the questions for party identification, the question has two stages and allows for moderates who lean toward one ideology or the other.

It has not always been the case that conservative and liberal ideologies have been aligned with political parties in the United States—as discussed in chapter 4—but they certainly are now. The current relationship between partisanship and ideology, as well as the relationship thirty years ago in 1974, can be seen in Figure 2.1.

Today, 44 percent of strong Democrats consider themselves to be liberal, and only 7 percent consider themselves to be conservatives. On the other end, 68 percent of strong Republicans call themselves conservatives—14 percent call themselves extremely conservative—and only 1 percent are liberal. The first year in which the seven-point ideology question was asked, 1974, was well after the parties began to align according to ideology, but the difference between then and now is still striking. In 1974, only 29 percent of strong Democrats considered themselves to be liberals, down 15 points from today, and 61 percent considered

Figure 2.1: Partisanship and Ideology, 1974 and 2004, from American National Election Study

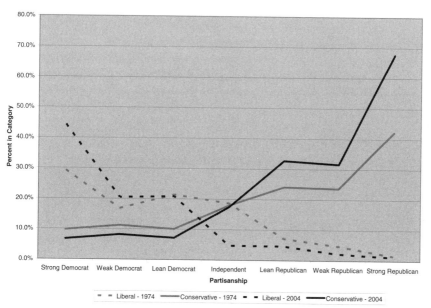

themselves moderates, up 12 points from 2004. To put it differently, 91 percent of liberals are today Democrats, and 67 percent of conservatives are Republicans.

Second, while not all members of a party are members of an ideological group, those ideological groups provide our best guess as to what members of partisan groups should be like. Perhaps because there are only two major parties in American politics, these parties are broad coalitions. The Republican Party, for instance, is comprised not only of laissez-faire libertarians who want to cut taxes and government, but also of religious groups that want to increase governmental regulation of private behaviors. The majority of the Democratic Party may be in favor of abortion rights, but it is also the home of conservative African-American voters who are strongly against them and may even be unaware of the discrepancy (Abramowitz 1995).

If we are thinking about the views that typical members of a party should hold, however, we are fairly safe in using ideology as a guide. Liberals, in general, favor a high degree of personal autonomy on sexual issues, and Democrats, by and large, do the same. Liberals tend to believe that government intervention is necessary to regulate markets for the greater good, and Democrats follow suit; the same arguments can be made for conservatives and Republicans. While parties and ideologies don't match up perfectly, the basic views, and the impulses that guide those views, are essentially the same.

Finally, it should be noted that the biggest deviations from the basic ideology associated with a party tend to come from groups that have historic, rather than recent, links to that party. African-American voters are rather more conservative on many issues than mainstream Democrats (and more liberal on others). Traditionally Republican westerners could be said to be increasingly out of touch with the rest of their party on many issues, not the least of which is immigration reform. The sample in our interviews, though, is comprised largely of white, affluent, suburban college students, who are unlikely to identify with these sorts of outlying groups within a party, and when they do, we'll be sure to identify them. Without historic ties to a party to cloud the reasons for partisan affiliations, we can expect that our respondents will be closer to their chosen party's ideology than a random member of that party might be.[4]

WHAT MAKES SOMEONE A REPUBLICAN?

Billy's image of Republicans—old white men driving their Cadillacs to the country club—fits in nicely with the traditional model of conservatism. In this understanding, individuals are thought to be conservative out of their own self-interest. After all, members of the upper classes have traditionally been more conservative than those who are less well-off (Sidanius and Ekehammer 1979). Just the word *conservatism* implies that the individual has something—perhaps political or social power—to conserve. This argument, however, applied mostly to economic issues, and ignores the social issues that are increasingly the source of political polarization (see chapter 6 for more on this). It also ignores the realities of modern American politics, in which southerners are not only the most reliable votes for the Republican Party, but also have the lowest mean income of any region.[5]

Rather, modern theories of conservatism argue that people hold conservative views in order to satisfy some deep psychological need. People hold these psychological predispositions regardless of their social class, though their political expression may be dependent on social position. For instance, Jost et al. (2003b) argue that the privileged may be conservative to satisfy a need for social dominance, and the lower classes may be conservative to reduce feelings of threat.

This problematization of conservatism is due to the links that have been made between conservatism and what has come to be called right-wing authoritarianism. This history of seeing conservatism as a social problem rather than a valid political choice has its roots in the aftermath of the Second World War. Faced with the atrocities committed by the Nazis, social scientists rushed to explain how a seemingly modern nation could succumb to such forces.[6] The most important of these responses put the blame at the feet of certain psychological predispositions, which were jointly called authoritarianism. (Adorno et al. 1950).[7] These predispositions included a propensity to follow orders, dogmatism, intolerance of ambiguity, and a desire for social dominance (as in Sidanius 1993). If the Republicanism of our young respondents is based on the same sort of motivated social cognition (Jost et al. 2003a) that is thought to lead older individuals to the Republican Party, we'd expect that the same underlying desires would be evident in the interviews. Alternately, it's possible that our respondents are embracing the Republican Party purely as a brand that the find attractive for entirely different reasons that are absent from individuals studied in the past.

We should note that George Lakoff (1996) has convincingly argued that there are substantial differences between economic and social conservatives in these underlying forces. Economic conservatives, for instance, may be more motivated by perceived self and class interests, while social conservatives are more motivated by threat. A shared political vocabulary, however, leads them to have a shared attachment to the label "conservative" and to the Republican Party. In other countries and contexts, it's entirely possible that these groups could comprise two different parties—the Conservative Party operating out of New York, for instance, seems to have little interest in social conservatism. In the United States, however, they tend to operate together, and the psychological underpinnings of their views are similar enough that they can be grouped here without too much difficulty.

To determine if the young Republicans interviewed in our study are really different from those of previous generations, we have to identify the general themes that we'll be looking for. If the Republicanism of the respondents is basically the same, there are three basic psychological motivations that we'd expect to see in the interviews. The first is a general acceptance of authority and a disinclination to question the source of that authority. Milgram's experiments on obedience to authority are the most dramatic examples of this predisposition. In these experiments, participants were told by an authority figure—in the initial experiments, a researcher in a lab coat—to subject another participant (actually an employee of the experimenter) to electric shocks in order to stimulate learning. Whenever the other participant made a mistake on a word recall test, the participant was instructed to give a shock and increase the level of the next shock. As the experiment wore on, the learner (who was not actually being subjected to any shocks) followed the script set up by the experimenter, making more and more mistakes, and receiving shocks approaching the level marked as "Danger" and, later "XXX" on the console. The learner screamed that he had a heart condition and wanted to leave, but the subject was instructed to continue the experiment and to continue shocking the learner even after he screamed in agony and stopped responding altogether. In the initial experiment, twenty-six out of forty-five of subjects continued shocking the learner to the point where they reasonably believed that the learner had been killed.[8] Further studies revealed that the degree of compliance increased with the proximity of the learner and the subject—few subjects were willing to go as far as the dangerous levels of shocks when they had to hold down the hand of the learner—and the authority of the experimenter: Yale scientists yielded greater compliance than private researchers, and instructions given in person more weight than instructions given by phone. Researchers such as Altemeyer (1996, 1998) have argued that conservatives are much more likely to uncritically accept authority in this manner, putting their faith in whatever leaders are seen as legitimate. Conservatives should be unwilling to criticize their leaders, and react harshly when others do. In the interviews, this should reveal itself through references to political leaders, whether in office, or in the media. These references may very well include negative remarks towards those who are critical of those leaders for any reason.

Second, Republicans are expected to be relatively intolerant of ambiguity. This line of research goes back to the work of Else Frenkel-Brunswik (1948, 1949, 1951)[9] who argued that certain individuals had a propensity to cling to stereotypes and to see any deviations from these stereotypes as a threat that should ideally be hidden or eliminated (Budner 1962). Men should act like men, women should act like women, and any behavior that goes against what they're supposed to be is a problem. In addition to being the hypothesized root of a great deal of sexism, such views can also result in homophobia, racism, and all sorts of other beliefs based on the application of group stereotypes to individuals. While this may sound simplistic, this model actually offers a great deal toward the understanding of prejudice. Rather than arising from ignorance, or lack of exposure, racist, sexist, or homophobic behaviors are the symptoms of a deep psychological predisposition.[10] This may explain why efforts to combat racism through education have generally resulted in better educated racists, rather than any real decrease in racism.[11] It is unlikely that any of our interviews will yield overtly racist, sexist, or homophobic sentiments, but any arguments against these groups on principled grounds could easily be seen as evidence that the young Republicans have motivations similar to their forebearers.

Finally, psychologists argue that conservatives are acutely sensitive to threats of any sort and that many of the behaviors associated with conservatism and authoritarianism can be seen as ways of reducing the perceived level of threat. Wilson (1973), for instance, found that political conservatism was strongly related to the fear of death, and many studies have found that indicators as disparate as purchases of attack dogs, police budgets, sales of superhero comic books[12] (Sales 1973), conversion to harsher religious sects (Sales 1972), and support for the death penalty (Doty, Peterson, and Winter 1991) all increased in times of political upheaval. The key link is drawn by Stanley Feldman and Karen Stenner (1997), who show that threat of any sort tends to make individuals with high levels of authoritarianism more intolerant and punishing than normal, even as individuals without authoritarian predispositions become less so. Fear of nuclear war, for instance, led authoritarian individuals to be less tolerant of gay rights and more likely to say that blacks would be successful if they simply tried harder.

In these studies, the nature of the threat potentially facing individuals changed from one study to the next, but in recent years the threat of terrorism has become dominant for obvious reasons. If it is the case that the Republicans in our study are responding in the same way as older Republicans, we would expect them to perceive more threat in the political and social environment than members of other parties and to make special reference to the fear of a terrorist attack. As Howard Lavine and his colleagues (1999) show, the threat of dire consequences resulting from an electoral outcome have a special significance to these voters, and we would expect this to be evident in their interviews.

SIMILARITIES AND DIFFERENCES

The apathy expressed by the Republican respondents toward politics in our survey seems to be based in some of the same characteristics traditionally associated with Republicanism. Like traditional Republicans, our respondents are untrusting of government in general and fearful that the power of government could be easily used against them. Several of them created vivid scenarios in which the government forced them to do something, and noted that there was nothing that they could do about it. There is little difference between the antigovernment views expressed in these interviews and the antigovernment views that have been held by Republicans for decades: if the government is given too much power, it will necessarily abuse it. To the greatest extent possible, it follows, government control should be minimized and its actions carefully watched.

Generally, though, we would expect this distrust of government to be balanced by a great deal of trust in individual leaders. Conservatives are expected to be generally uncritical of leaders that they view as legitimate, and so while the government itself may be entirely untrustworthy, *our* guy is defending us from it. That guy—be it Ronald Reagan or George W. Bush—is trusted, even when government itself isn't, and for the Republican respondents, that guy simply isn't there.

There are a number of indications that the young Republicans we studied are open to a leader whom they feel they can trust. Several of the responses make reference to past political figures like Reagan, as someone who was able to keep the government under control, but references to current leaders make it clear that they don't fit the bill. For the young Republicans we spoke to, then, turning apathy into action is simply a task of finding leaders that they trust, that they can get behind. Older Republicans had this in Goldwater or Reagan, and no such leader has yet come to excite these young Republicans in the same way. Give them a leader and Billy, and his friends, will follow.

In our interviews, many of the Republicans talk about "politicians" with disdain: "they" don't say anything important, "they're" just trying to get elected. It could be argued that in disparaging elected officials—or those hoping to be elected officials—in such a way, our Republican respondents are at odds with the expected profile of older Republicans. However, there are a couple of indications that this isn't the case. First, the young Republicans who make such statements never attribute them to any particular individual. At the time of the interviews, there were any number of highly salient Democratic political leaders making promises in an attempt to win the support of primary voters, and any of them could be targeted as the ones making meaningless promises. As the results outlined in chapter 5 show, many of the respondents could identify several of these Democrats: Hillary Clinton, Barack Obama, John Edwards, Dennis Kucinich, but none of them were named. Second, the obedience that we expect Republicans to exhibit extends only to those leaders that they see as legitimate: the "politicians" they're talking about are almost certainly not included.

Indeed, the young Republicans we spoke to seem to relate to politics through political leaders. Rather than issues and ideology, what are central to parties are charismatic leaders. Many young Republicans point to the similarities between the Republican and the Democratic Party in terms of issues, or hold that the stated differences between the parties are ephemeral. In terms of views, these two almost indistinguishable: what differentiates them are the leaders. Authoritarian, charismatic, and strong leaders are key components of politics for young Republicans.

Many of the young Republicans we spoke to defend authority. Lauren, an eighteen-year-old freshman says "I approve of how President George Bush is doing his job as president. I think it is wrong how many people put him down. I believe that everyone has their own opinions, but it makes our country look so weak when you hear someone talking bad about him." She believes that being in an authority position is a difficult thing, therefore it is important to respect that position. Even though, she admits, she does not always like the leaders, it is important to acknowledge the importance and difficulty of these positions and respect them even. She argues, "You will always have someone in government you do not like as much as the others, but everyone has to understand it is a very hard job." Despite the fact that Lauren, and all of the other Republicans we spoke to, say that they approve of Bush, none of them do so unequivocally, pointing, as Cynthia does, to the "hard position" he's been put in, and how "anyone would be criticized for making" decisions like he's had to. This is in sharp contrast to the reverence with which past leaders, like Ronald Reagan are held. Cynthia tells us that Republicans are in favor of lower taxes, but only since Reagan fought against the inheritance tax in the 1980s. Past leaders, other Republicans, like Steve, tell us, can't be compared to today's leaders: the situation, the war, is different.

In the absence of real differences between the parties—even on "easy" issues like abortion—these young Republicans seem to be relating to politics through the leaders. Bush and Reagan are good—or at least not deserving of the disdain that's heaped on them—and "politicians" or "people in the government" are generally bad.

STRATEGIC IMPLICATIONS

If Republicans wanted to increase their vote share among young people, it seems that they would be best served by increasing trust in political leaders. Young Republicans can be mobilized if they can trust and be motivated by their leaders. Assuming all young people are identical and could be mobilized during election time by employing cookie-cutter methods to include young people in the voting process fails to work effectively. Since Republican youth relate to politics through leaders, only through leaders that speak to them can they overcome political apathy and be mobilized to vote.

3
Democrats

[Democrats are] classy hippies, who listen to the Grateful
Dead and memorize the script to *Rent* and *Rocky Horror Pic-
ture Show.* They have good hygiene but you really can't tell.
—Simon, an 18-year-old Democrat

THE TWENTY-SIXTH AMENDMENT, GRANTING 18-YEAR-OLDS THE
right to vote, was expected to fundamentally change American
politics. In the first federal election after its passage, 25 million
young people were enfranchised; advisors to the Democratic candidate for president, George McGovern, believed that about 70
percent of them would cast ballots and that at least 70 percent of
those would be for the McGovern (*New York Times* 1973). As
McGovern found out, it didn't work out that way. Turnout among
young voters was far smaller than was expected (though still
higher than it is today), and the vote was almost evenly split
between McGovern and Nixon. The assumption then, as it is now,
was that young people are inherently liberal and Democratic: if we
want to explain something, we should try and explain why they're
not Democrats.

Moreover, the young people we spoke to still link the Democratic Party to the youth counterculture of the 1960s. Maybe
they've gotten older and wealthier, but they're the same people
who were hippies thirty or forty years ago. Those Democrats who
weren't alive in that era are thought to be doing about the same
thing, just with different brands inserted. Instead of memorizing
the songs in *Hair* or *Jesus Christ, Superstar,* they're watching
Rent (as Simon says, above). They may be getting high while
watching *Rocky Horror* instead of *2001,* but the activities remain
the same. Young respondents make frequent reference to this
sort of casual drug use, but it's only in a few of them that the drug

use itself seems to be the problem—not surprising, in a college environment. Rather, the problem seems to be that they haven't *stopped* using drugs as they became adults: in that way, among others, Democrats are people who just didn't completely grow up. This is, of course, a double-edged sword, as Democrats might be seen as immature, or unrealistic, but, on the other hand, much more in touch with young people and the issues that are important to them. All of it though, as with the other parties, is based on image, rather than reality. The bottom line is that our respondents don't know what the Democratic Party stands for, any more than they know what they Republican Party stands for, at least on an ideological basis. Moreover, while the image of the Democrats as being hip and cool may be more attractive to our respondents than the somewhat stogy image they have of the Republican Party, the Democratic youth don't seem to be any more active in political matters than their counterparts in the other partisan groups. The only thing that's different, really, is the source of this apathy, not its consequences.

DEMOCRATS' VIEWS OF OTHER PARTISAN GROUPS

The Democratic youth we spoke to see themselves as cooler, and more fashionable, than members of other political groups, especially Republicans. When we ask Kristen, an eighteen-year-old freshman who identifies herself as Democrat, how she differentiates herself from members of other political groups, we expected her to tell us the perceived differences between political parties: issues, leadership, or ideology. Instead, she described the differences between the parties based entirely on their branding and images. Democrats are "cooler" and more fashionable, according to Kristen. She describes Republicans as "strict" and "judgmental," "rich" and "stuck-up." Democrats, on the other hand are, "nice," "helpful," "laid-back," and "cool." Being a Democrat, for Kristen, is a distinction. It is a way to be a part of the accepted, in crowd. Independents, on the other hand, are not even conceivable for Kristen. "I don't even know what that means," she says. Independents, for her, are simply people who cannot make up their minds. Kristen's response makes more sense when we look at how loaded her conceptions of the parties are, and how at odds they seem to be. Are you laid-back or stuck-up? Are you cool or judgmental? For her, partisanship is so indicative of personality and life choices that there isn't social room for someone to be in the middle of the partisan spectrum.

Josh, a nineteen-year-old sophomore who grew up in suburban New Jersey, agrees that one of the reasons why he chose to be a Democrat is because of the image of Democrats is "nicer" and "favorable," showing more concern for others, an overall nice person. Carol agrees that the image of Democrats she has is one that is optimistic and positive. "They are more into fixing social problems" she says. Unlike other groups, Democrats seem to have agency: they can do something about problems. Susan agrees that for Democrats, "nothing is set in stone": they can change and update the system. The common thread is energy, agency, recognition that there are problems, and a desire to change to them. In this context, being nicer, and less judgmental, means caring about other people and their problems. It's important to note, here, that in our interviews, these references are universally general. Democrats want to fix social problems, but these aren't racial problems, or religious problems, or class-based problems: they're just "social problems."

Like Kristen, the other Democrats in our study seem to view Republicans and Democrats as almost polar opposites. Republicans, according to Susan, are "close-minded," "traditional," and "resistant to change." Josh associates being Republican with pessimism and old age, the opposite end of the spectrum from the youthful energy and problem solving associated with the Democratic Party.

Matt agrees with Josh and adds his own stereotype of Republicans as "right-wing nut jobs. They are ultraconservative and are close-minded. They feel that only the right wing part of the news story is the correct one. Most likely, they live in the South and are white and middle-aged. They tend to be extremely religious and attend a worship service on a regular basis. They like to attack other people's opinions, thinking that theirs is the only right one." Matt's vision of the Republican Party is drawn from what he sees of them on television, especially Fox News Channel. Among those respondents who said that they had seen the channel, and especially among Democrats who had seen it, the links between Republicans and commentators on Fox News are strong.

This association between Republicans and people like Bill O'Reilly or Sean Hannity goes deeper than references to their rhetorical style and intolerance. Oftentimes, Republicans are associated with "parents" and "older people," again drawing the distinction between the youth-associated Democratic and the older, judgmental, uncaring Republicans. In addition to being seen as older white males like those on Fox, as far as the Democrats are concerned, the Republicans are argumentative, aggressive, intolerant, not "nice" like the Democrats. As with the respondents in other groups, Democrats like Kristen and Simon don't know how the views of their group is different from the views or the Republicans—and don't understand independents at all—but they do know that the image doesn't fit them. Republicanism is, for them, something that older people, maybe their parents, would identify with.

LEADERSHIP

Like the other partisan groups, young Democrats complain about the lack of relatable leadership and voice their discontent with the current administration. Susan, a twenty-one-year-old college senior, complains that she is disappointed with the current administration. Politics, for her, is not just about the president: a viewpoint that may well have been reinforced by the results of the 2006 midterm election, in which a Democratic landslide was followed by little change in the policies that matter most to many Democratic voters. As Susan says, the president is almost symbolic, and political change has to come from changes in the content and issues that the political system is addressing.

"Just by changing the president," according to Susan, we cannot implement major changes, however, "voting for completely different issues and ideas can make a change." Unlike the Republican youth, who value strong authority and leadership, Democratic youth emphasize issues. "If you don't want to worry about issues, you don't have to," Susan says, "if you want to isolate yourself from politics." For Susan, and the other Democratic respondents, politics consists of the issues, even if the images of the parties don't include much about them. Susan, apparently, cannot imagine political involvement without issues, giving us a hint as to why she, and the other Democratic respondents, isn't politically involved. If politics is about issues, and the parties, as they see them, don't have anything to do with the real issues, there's no reason to worry much about the parties or the leaders.

In the same vein, Simon adds that politics is more about issues and less about the leaders. Leaders, to Simon, are just people who happen to occupy certain positions. As he describes it, political positions are not much different than corporate positions, where people move up gradually, often simply because they've been there for a certain amount of time. "Most people in government, politicians and low staff workers are just trying to get money and move up in the job ladder." The top of the ladder—elected political positions in the Congress and even the presidency—aren't much different than those in the lower levels: it's the organization that's important, not who's in any given position. By placing the blame on the institutions of government, the way things are set up, rather than the people in those institutions, the Democratic respondents are similar to the independents that we'll be discussing in the next chapter. There is, however, a difference here. As we'll see, independents blame these institutions for a lack of progress, implying that things would be fine if the institutions were better: if there were third parties, or fair elections, or clean campaigns. Among Democrats, the institutions themselves aren't the problem, and neither are the people in those institutions, rather, the problem is that these people and these institutions aren't focusing on the right things. The issues are what are really important, and people and institutions are just a way to get at them.

ISSUES

The focus of the comments made by the Democrats seems to be issues above all else. As Susan says, politics does not exist outside of issues, and the other Democratic youth we heard from have similar sentiments, even if they don't state them as succinctly. On the whole, they emphasize the importance of political issues in their political participation, but many downplay the significance of the differences between the issues stances taken by the parties. David says, "I don't believe there are big differences between the two parties. It seems like whoever takes office, whether a Democrat or Republican, the outcome will have been the same. David, like many others, thinks that political parties today use issues as tools to get elected, so their stances are often fluid and are direct responses to opinion polls. Now, this sentiment is not limited to the Democratic young people we spoke to: our respondents almost universally tell us that there isn't much difference between the parties, and perhaps with good reason. However, this opinion isn't as consequential for the other groups as it is for the Democrats we spoke with. Republicans, for instance, may not think that the parties are that different on the issues, but they seem to care more about the leaders, anyway. Independents may not see much difference in the issues, but to them, it wouldn't matter if there were a difference, as they are more concerned with how the structure of the political system prevents any real change from happening. The underlying message that the Democratic youth is that issues are the most important elements of politics, and if there's no difference in the issues, the parties don't matter.

This disdain for issues that Democrats perceive among political leaders and parties has a great deal to do with their low regard for those leaders. While they see issues as being important, they think that politicians are using issues just to get elected. As with their view that the parties aren't much different, the Democrats aren't alone in thinking that politicians are opportunistic and pragmatic, to put it nicely. However, there is a substantial difference in the roots of this disdain. Among Republicans, it is personal—the politicians, the leaders, aren't good people. Among Democrats, it isn't who the politicians are that's the problem, so much as what they do.

The relationship between the Democratic youth and political issues becomes even more interesting when we move from general feelings to specifics and ask what issues seem relevant to them. It seems that the mainstream political debate passes them by almost entirely and that none of the issues politicians argue about really resonate with the Democratic youth. David says that as important as issues and government policy are, they don't have any relevance to his life as it is today. He says, "I honestly don't know how much government policy affects me directly; I'm sure as soon as I get out of school and start working, policy I am aware of will affect me directly" (David 2007). There are two ways to look at a statement like this. The first is to see it as a justification for apathy: he doesn't think that what the government does impacts him, so there's no reason to worry about it. This may be the easiest answer, but it's belied by the second half of the statement, where he says that it will impact him more when he starts working. The debates over foreign policy and taxes and whatnot matter to other people, as they will to him, eventually, but they don't matter to him now. The debate, the issues, as he sees them in the media, don't matter to him because they're the issues that other people, older people, have to worry about, and the issues that are relevant to him just aren't in the mix.

Another of our Democratic respondents, Kristen, agrees that political issues don't relate to her life as it is today. She says that *theoretically* political issues and government policies are very important, but the current issues and policies aren't the ones that matter to her. The only policies of the government that she can actually relate to are "public transportation, garbage collection . . ." These are what politicians refer to as bread-and-butter issues, the things that impact your daily life. She can relate to these issues because she sees the concrete results of them; the abstract issues don't resonate for her at all. "It's all politics," she complains, another Democrat saying that the debates have nothing to do with her everyday life. And another: "I don't think that there are many issues I can relate to at this point, either," Carol says. She completes the thought by saying that she hopes that this will change with time and says that parties worry about older constituents rather than young people like herself.

If the issues that are debated in the political arena had more direct effect on them, many young Democrats say they would be more politically involved. Even the issues that politicians think young people would be interested in are not really the issues that relate to them. Issues like the draft are perceived as issues that young people would be interested in and they would relate to, however young people do not consider it a plausible issue. David says, "That's a scary thought, I have no idea. Is it possible, of course" (David 2007); however, even though it is possible, he does not find it plausible.

There is some scholarly evidence to suggest that the same focus on issues exists in adult samples of Democrats as well. Using a panel of respondents—so that respondents were sampled three times over four years—Martinez and Gant's (1990) analysis of partisan change during the 1970s shows that Democrats were more aligned with issues than other partisan groups. In all the three of the major issues categories of the time (New Deal programs, racial issues, and moral issues), issue positions within the Democratic Party were more consistent than they were within the other partisan groups. Democrats were uniformly in favor of New Deal programs, and in favor of liberal stances on racial and moral issues. In the other partisan groups, the views were mixed: Republicans may have been against liberal policies on race and moral issues, but didn't necessarily want to do away with the New Deal. Since then, the specific issues at hand have changed, but the general issue categories have not. Moral issues and redistributive issues are still the currency of the day, and while racial issues aren't as important as they were, they still represent an important second dimension in American politics. On these issues, Democrats are generally more united than Republicans, even if the complex nature of liberal rhetoric tends to hide that unity.

WORK TIME

Many Democratic youth feel that politic involvement means identifying relevant issues and gathering all relevant information on the issue. It is a very time-consuming experience. Keeping up with every piece of information, learning the different sides of the topic and debating different sides is required for political involvement. However, especially given the time constraints, many young Democrats do not want to invest that much time and energy into an activity for issues that do not relate to them. David, like many other Democratic young people, is overworked and overscheduled between going to college and working part-time in numerous jobs. Given the time constraints, he feels that the issues should be worthwhile.

Based on what we know about the differences between conservative and liberal adults, this would seem to be a more critical problem for Democratic young people than for their counterparts in other partisan groups. Conservatives (and, therefore, in the modern era, Republicans) are generally distrustful of complexity, while liberals tend to embrace it. As such, liberal youth would be much more likely to feel the need to seek out all sides of an issue before committing to an issue position: this sort of political activity requires a great deal more time and effort than the conservative strategy. Democratic youth, then, should feel much more keenly the time restrictions endemic to young people's overcrowded life when it comes to forming political opinions. In the absence of available time—and the interest required to make the time—it seems that they are simply avoiding issues for which they can't reach a satisfactory answer.

APATHY

Despite their political affiliations, the majority of the young people we have interviewed could easily be described as politically apathetic. Many Democrats we've described here don't plan on voting, nor do they know much about politics, nor do they see any compelling reason to learn. However, the reasons for their alienation are very different from other partisan groups. Republican youth choose not to participate in politics because they do not trust the politicians and feel there is a vacuum of political leadership. Independents on the other hand, choose not to be politically involved because they feel there are structural problems in the political system: particularly the bipartisan system. As our interviews here reveal, the Democratic youth are alienated from politics because of the issues at play in contemporary politics. This is not to say that there aren't issues that they do find to be important: just that they don't see those issues being addressed by the parties.

Kristen, an eighteen-year-old college freshman, tells that she wants to be politically involved because she is not happy with the ways things are. She believes that volunteering, especially in social and political organizations, is very important. "You can start a petition, write to your local authorities, or other things of that nature," she tells us. However, she adds, "I am not politically involved at all, yet." Despite her wish to be politically involved, she finds that the issues that are discussed politically do not really interest her. Given her limited time between being a full-time student, part-time work and her extracurricular activities, she feels that issues should be very important and relatable if she gives up her limited time. Yet, she is disappointed in the current issues that are politically discussed.

Josh agrees that the issues that are discussed politically do not relate to him at all. "Only a few government policies directly affect me," he says. "The only government policies that affect me are the handling of the War in Iraq and also the budgets given to universities by the government. The War in Iraq affects me because an enormous amount of my and my parents' tax dollars are being spent on the war that could instead be used for improving college education and cutting down tuition. I'm not sick and in position to rely on Medicare or any prescription plan, and I'm also not an illegal immigrant or an immigrant trying to obtain a visa." Because he cannot relate to the issues that dominate the political arena, he describes himself as "politically uninvolved." He would be more involved, he says, if there were issues that both attracted his attention and related to him. He checks the papers regularly for political articles, hoping he will relate to a topic, but he has thus far been disappointed.

Matt, on the other hand, points to the negative stereotype of people who are politically active. He says, "The typical person who is really interested in politics is junkie for the news. They will watch CNN and C-SPAN when they have nothing else better to do. If younger and more able to stay up later, they will read about upcoming Senate and House elections that will occur in two years on Wikipedia until three o'clock in the morning. Furthermore, the typical political junkie will vote in every single election there is, whether it be a presidential election or a local school board election." He sees politically active people as people who have nothing better to do. If the issues that are discussed in everyday politics are mundane, uninteresting, and not relatable, the types of people who are interested politically are boring, uninteresting people, who could not find something better to do.

Like the other Democratic young people we talked to, Matt and David relate to politics through issues, and lacking relevant issues, they simply opt out. The alienation caused by a lack of relatable issues is obvious from David's disinterest. He describes himself as not knowing much about politics. He knows enough to know that there aren't any real issues, and so doesn't see why he should spend time to learn anything more.

Dylan, a nineteen-year-old full-time student, echoes many of these same concerns. When he got to college, he tells us, he wanted to be politically involved. He started taking courses in political science, especially in American politics and government: but this interest was never reinforced outside of the classroom. As far as he could tell, no one in the real world actually cared about politics, or the concepts he spent so much time learning about: certainly, none of his friends had any interest. His main source of political information was the classes he was taking, and now that he is no longer taking them, his interest has waned. All of his friends, he tells us, are "watching *America's Next Top Model* or MTV's *Making the Band.*" If he wants to relate to his peers, he has a whole different world of information that he has to keep up with, and politics simply isn't a part of it. The other implication of his concern that he needs to be able to use whatever he learns to keep up with his friends is that if his peer group were interested in politics, if he felt that political discussions allowed him to relate to his friends, he'd be far more likely to participate in them. In this sentiment, as we'll see in chapter 5, Dylan is far from unique.

FEAR OF GOVERNMENT

Democratic youth, unlike the Republicans and independents that we spoke to, do not display a generalized fear of the government. This isn't to say that they entirely trust the government, or elected officials, but rather that they believe that the government can, and does, serve many important needs. Many of the young Democrats that we spoke to said that we need the government to protect minority rights, eliminate social inequality and preserve order, among other things. This is in sharp contrast to the statements of Republican youth, who tended to distrust any attempt on the part of the government to enact social change as meddling, or pandering to special interests.

David sums it up nicely, telling us that "We need government to keep everything running smoothly and keep fear in those who seek to do bad things. As much as government is intrusive it is needed to keep order." There is some fear of government intrusion—made especially relevant by concerns about erosion of civil liberties during the war on terror—but the government, in general, is both necessary potentially helpful. So long as individual rights and civil liberties are preserved, the Democratic young people we spoke to have no qualms with the concept of a strong government.

Susan similarly emphasizes the important role of government in preserving order and peace through laws and regulations. She fears that without a strong government, our society would be in "utter chaos." Josh, too, believes in the organizational power of the government, without which society would devolve to anarchy. He says: "If the government had just left us alone, we'd be unable to govern ourselves. Looters would appear out of no where, crime rates would increase, and the people would lose their sense of structure. We'd be like cavemen. Even animals and insects have leaders and pacts that are organized and structured. Without the government we'd lose a great deal of sociability with each other." In this respect, the Democratic youth distinguish themselves from the independents that we'll discuss in the next chapter. Unlike the independents, Democratic young people believe strongly that the political system can and does work in the broadest sense of protecting citizens from themselves. Carol adds that government is an important vehicle of equality, a central redistributive source to ensure taxes are paid and less privileged groups receive aid. Government is, once again, seen as a solution, while other groups tend to regard it as a problem.

Furthermore, unlike Republican and independent youth, Democratic youth believe that the individuals who are running the government are genuinely good people. David says "I believe that most low-level government officials are honest-to-god good people." He does understand there might be corruption and abuse of power; however, in general David believes people in the government are good. Like other Democratic youth we spoke to, he believes fundamentally in government as necessary to protect equality, even if he doesn't think it always does a good job at it. Carol complains about the negative portrayal of government officials as "money hungry" and "dishonest." Susan believes this is because the few bad cases are overly publicized. "There are a lot of good people in the government, and there are always a few bad seeds, but we have enough good that it cancels it out." Matt, too, believes that this is because the media focuses exclusively on the few negative outcomes and overlooks the majority of the good work that has been accomplished politically. As he puts it: "When elected to a post, these officials try to do a better job for the good of the country in the ways they see it constitutionally fit. While it's true the media only focuses on the bad apples like Larry Craig, William Jefferson, and Tom DeLay, you do not hear about the ones that do good. While it's also true power for some can corrupt them, for most they honestly try and do good for the better of the country. In the end, they work hard to get important bills passed, yet the media only focuses of the bad apples, and all the good ones, about 98 percent of them, are over looked, and forgotten about, even though they are doing good for the country."

Josh uses a similar metaphor, saying that while there might be a "few bad apples," overall, people in public and political offices mean well. "The majority of leaders and political figures don't have malicious intent," he says. They "aren't trying to hurt the people," even if they wind up doing so. The problem, as he sees it, is that there is often a disconnect between what people in government think is best, and what actually is best for the public. This optimism among Democratic youth is especially striking given the unpopularity of President Bush, and the rampant accusations of corruption and malfeasance at the time the surveys were taken: little, it seems, can dissuade these young people from their general optimism about their leaders.

Social Change

In many ways, the Democratic youth we spoke to differentiate themselves from their Republican and independent peers. They don't see government activity as something to fear; nor do they distrust the agents of government. Like the other partisan groups, however, the Democrats in our sample see little likelihood of the sort of sweeping social change that young people have traditionally been linked with. David sees little point in political activism: "Unless you're a blood relative," he says, of someone "with a lot of pull, of someone in charge of operations, no one will be able to just come in and change the way things work." As desirable as social change might be in the abstract, for the most part, they don't think that they'll personally be able to change very much.

Nonetheless, this still qualifies them as the most optimistic of the groups. As Simon says, in theory, even one person can change the whole system. "They have seen so many political activist parties started by single people," he tells us. "During the civil rights movement, many individual figures stood up and in gathered in unison to oppose the U.S. government." Therefore, in theory, there are no structural barriers against social change. Susan goes so far as to think that change may even come soon. "Everyday, we have more and more changes for the better and for the worse," she says. "There have been major changes. I think in the coming election, there will be the biggest change with so many different people running for office. They cannot prevent change if it happens on its own." They seem to be telling us that while change is possible, and even desirable, it happens as the result of broad social movements, individuals can play a role in it, as they did during the civil rights movement, or the peace movement of the 1960s, but individuals, unless they're in high places, don't play a critical role in that change. The potential for change may be embedded in our structural system, but as far as the Democrats in our sample are concerned, the practice of change is quite different. "Changes can happen if they go about in the right way," Carol says, the "right way" being through the legislative process, or through constitutional amendment. There is a difference, then, between theoretical and practical social change for young Democrats. Though many young Democrats believe that social change is possible on paper, in practice they are more skeptical. It is an arduous process: as Carol says, in a democracy, there isn't much one person can do.

While they are theoretically hopeful, in practice, many young Democrats feel powerless. They acknowledge that there are no structural barriers against changing the system, but they are not hopeful about it in practice. In that respect, they differ from the Democratic youth of the 1960s and 1970s, who believed in political activism and social protest as alternative and antiestablishment mechanisms of social change. The only acceptable way of social change is through the established channels, for many youth, and alternate routes are not as successful.

These responses are also important as they give us a clue as to what sorts of issues the young Democrats would find appealing. The prospect of broad social change excites them, as evidenced by their frequent mention of the protest movements of years past. While they tell us that there is little chance that one person can actually make a difference, they seem more than willing to be caught up in a social movement already underway. They are something of a reserve army of protest: ready to march once their issues of justice and equality become part of the political lexicon.

Information Sources

The main information sources of many of the Democratic youth we spoke to are programs that mix political information and entertainment: shows like *The Daily Show with Jon Stewart* and *The Colbert Report.* Many Democratic young people identify these shows as their main source of political information. Their alternatives are friends and family. Many report to not watching other news shows. They choose these shows mostly because they are "cool" brands that these young people want to associate with. Many young people, even those who identify themselves as Democrats, like David, find other Democrats "uncool" or "weak." Even though he identifies himself as a Democrat, if the Democratic party branded itself as a "cooler" party, he would be more involved in politics. However, David identifies these two shows as cool and fashionable brands that are consumed by attractive people, with a good sense of humor.

While NPR is identified typically as a Democratic source of news, few of the young Democrats we interviewed admitted listening to it, or even demonstrated a passing familiarity. While those that had heard of it said that they liked the ideological content, they characterized NPR as a channel for "adults," and "older people": presumably their parents. Some admitted not even knowing what NPR is and asked if they could Google it, and get back to us. One young Democrat, who did just this, informed us that it was a radio station, but looked like it was for older people. While the content may be closer to their ideological views and issue stances, it is the image that determines their involvement.

Shows like *The Daily Show* are attractive to many young people, because their audiences are characterized as "young," "fashionable," "cool," "attractive" people "with a good sense of humor." They are people, who "enjoy a good laugh. According to Susan, they could still be businesspeople but they need to be very intelligent with an understanding of politics and the news with a good sense of humor. Rather than the content of the show, the young, hip, fashionable image of the show makes them more susceptible.

How Are They Different and the Same?

Democratic youth are just as apathetic as their Republican and independent counterparts. However, the reasons why they are not involved politically are very different. Democratic youth predominantly relate to politics through issues. They feel like the open discussion or issues are central to politics. Issues that they find relatable and important to their lives are the core of political involvement. Often, they do not find relatable issues, therefore, they choose not to be involved politically.

Whereas the other youth fear the government or believe there are structural barriers against social change, Democratic youth do not fear the government, but seem to trust it as an important protector of rights and liberties. They also believe our political system is not set up to prevent social change, but they generally see little value in trying to bring about that change on their own.

DEMOCRATS AND VALUES

As before, we end by trying to determine what a Democrat *should* sound like, so we can see how the respondents in our surveys and interviews differ. It is more difficult, in this case though, as scholarly research on what makes someone a Democrat is surprisingly thin. In the chapter on Republicans, we were able to point to a large literature on the psychological predispositions that lead an individual to conservatism, and how perceptions of threat tend to exacerbate those predispositions. When we talk about independents, we can delve into realignment and dealignment theories to explain why people drop out of the partisan categories. Democrats and liberals, though, have been generally left alone. The reason for this seems to come from the ways in which the other categories have been problematized: conservatives can become repressive, independents don't participate, and so the remaining category of Democrats and liberals is the default. Unless something happens to you, the expectation seems to be, you'll be a Democrat.

The cynics among us may see this as a sign of the liberalism of academia:[1] after all, almost three in four professors identify themselves as liberal, compared to 15 percent saying that they're conservatives.[2] While the partisan ratios are a little more balanced—50 percent Democratic to 11 percent Republican—the direction is clear. However, the basis for the assumption that the default position is Democratic has deeper roots. We can see them even in William Buckley's (1955) definition of a conservative as someone who stands "athwart history, yelling stop." History, as it's been seen since the Enlightenment, is the process of society progressing in various ways: through the gradual build-up of scientific knowledge, through the increase in the standards of living of everyday people, through the recognition of rights belonging to all people, rather than just your family, or clan, or town, or nation. It's natural, according to the Enlightenment point of view, to want to continue this progress, and it's the people yelling "stop" that we should be trying to explain.

There is, however, some research that gives us an insight into the deeper reasons why someone may choose to support Democratic issue positions, rather than Republican ones. People's issue positions, survey researchers have long known, don't seem to hold together very well. Outside of political sophisticates with well-defined—and often partisan—belief systems, most Americans don't seem to put their beliefs about individual issues into coherent packages. What they do have, however, are values. These values are conflicting and often completely contradictory (as in Feldman and Zaller 1992), but they are there. In American politics, the most important of these values seem to be individualism, egalitarianism, humanitarianism,[3] and limited government.

Most everyone seems to endorse all three of these values to one extent or another. Relatively few people are willing to say that people shouldn't take care of themselves or that people shouldn't be treated equally. When an issue implicates only one of these values, people have a fairly easy time of resolving it. Volunteering to give blood, or perform civic duties only implicates humanitarianism, so people are overwhelmingly in favor of it (Wuthnow 1991). Guaranteeing lawyers for the indigent is a question of egalitarianism, and so is overwhelmingly supported (though support drops off once those indigent are actually in prison).

It's only when people are forced to make trade-offs between these values that things get interesting. Americans support homeless shelters, for instance, because of they believe in humanitarianism, and the benefit to the homeless isn't so great that it generally offends the belief in individualism. Welfare benefits, on the other hand, are humanitarian in that they provide for the poorest in society, egalitarian in that they redistribute income to reach a more equal state, but may offend the idea of individualism. Individualism holds that people are responsible for their own lots in life, and so giving people money that they haven't earned can be seen as offending this value.[4] A similar conflict can be seen over many controversial policies. Opponents of racial affirmative action, for instance, can find support for the beliefs in the individualism and opposition to big government: everyone should make their own way without government assistance. Those who favor the policies inevitably point to egalitarianism and humanitarianism: society has a responsibility to give everyone an equal shot at a good life and should do whatever is necessary to make up for past and current wrongs. In the American context, at least, it seems that Democrats are the ones who, when push comes to shove, value egalitarianism and humanitarianism above limited government and individualism (Rokeach 1973).

In the American National Election Study, two questions get directly at the balance between egalitarianism and individualism. One asks respondents to place themselves on a seven-point scale between a highly egalitarian viewpoint ("the government should see to jobs and the standard of living") to a highly individualist viewpoint ("the government should let each person get ahead on their own"). The second question deals with the same tradeoff in values, but adds a racial element, asking respondents to place themselves on a seven-point scale between "the government should help blacks" and "blacks should help themselves. The results for the highest and lowest categories on these scales, by the party of the respondent, can be found in Table 3.1.

In Table 3.1, with data from the 2004 ANES, we can see the vast gulf between strong Democrats and strong Republicans on these issues. Fully a quarter of strong Democrats placed themselves in the most egalitarian category for the general question, 23 percent did so in the racially tinged question. Among strong Republicans, only one to two percent placed themselves as such. Thirty-two percent of strong Republicans, though, placed themselves in the most individualistic category for the general question, with slightly fewer (28 percent) doing so in the racially tinged question. While the lines are not completely straight across the partisan categories—perhaps for reasons discussed in chapter 1—the trend is unmistakable. Overall, 49 percent of Democrats (strong and weak, not including leaners) place themselves as egalitarian on the general question, compared to 13 percent of Republicans. Seventy percent of Republicans place themselves in the individualistic categories on the same question, compared to 26 percent of Democrats.[5]

Despite the conflicts that arise when the issues are placed in opposition to each other as in the ANES questions, this dichotomy provides for agreement on a wide range of issues for which

Table 3.1: Egalitarianism of Responses by Partisanship, 2004 ANES

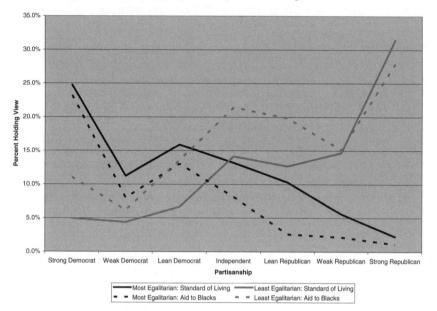

the values don't meaningfully conflict. Equality in the legal system, basic benefits for the homeless, opposition to *de juris*
racism, support for entrepreneurship and free public education
are all broadly agreed upon. Those policies likely to be contentious are those in which the values conflict, such as social
welfare. In these policies, government benefits are seen as going
specifically or disproportionately to one group. As with affirmative action, opponents of these policies point to limited government and individualism, while support is based on egalitarianism and humanitarianism. It is for this reason that the
Democratic Party has become, in recent years,[6] the Party of
minority groups seeking redress and representation. Homosexuals seeking the right to marry or protection from workplace discrimination, for instance, have natural allies in feminists and
blacks not because they want the same benefits, but because they
are all appealing to egalitarianism over individualism.

Americans may also be unwilling to express egalitarian sentiments because of the relative lack of support for egalitarianism
in an economic, rather than a legal context. Such views can be
traced back to Weber's (1958) Protestant work ethic. In this view,

hard work is a sign of God's favor, and material success is, therefore, a sign of virtue. If people don't have material success it can be attributed to their own moral failings. Any redsistribution from the wealthy to the poor is then giving to the undeserving and is, moreover, a violation of God's will. This stands in stark contrast with liberal views, epitomized by John Rawls's (1999) *Theory of Justice.* In Rawls's account, luck accounts for much of the disparity between rich and poor—morality has nothing to do with it. The role of society, according to Rawls, is to redistribute benefits in society so as to minimize the effects of luck to the greatest degree possible. In such a debate, Republicans strongly favor Americans the protestant work ethic, supporting a minimal safety net—as per the value of humanitarianism—but little more. This plays out frequently in political debate: Republicans talk frequently about "tax and spend" or "big government" liberals, who want to take your money and give it to the undeserving. Voters uncomfortable with Michael Dukakis's support of increased redistribution seem to have cost him the 1988 election (Gopoian 1993).

We can see this discomfort with economic egalitarianism in more questions taken from the 2004 ANES. In these questions, respondents were asked if the amounts that poor people and rich people pay in taxes is too little, too much, or about right. Those individuals wanting a more egalitarian, progressive taxation system would want the rich to pay more and the poor less. Those wanting less economic egalitarianism would presumably want the opposite. The results of these questions, again broken down by partisanship, are in Table 3.2.

The results are exactly what we would expect. 86 percent of strong Democrats say that the rich pay too little and taxes, and 61 percent say that the poor pay too much. In contrast, relatively few Republicans express economically egalitarian responses: 32 percent of strong Republicans say that the rich pay too little, and 27 percent say that the poor pay too much. Almost no strong Democrats expressed antiegalitarian views: only 3 percent said that the rich pay too much, and only 4 percent said that the poor pay too little. Meanwhile, 11 percent of strong Republicans want the poor to pay more in taxes, and an additional 3 percent say that the poor don't pay any taxes at all.[7] These results are rather more linear than those for the previously discussed egalitarian versus individualism questions, but the differences between partisan

Table 3.2: Views of Tax Burden by Partisanship, 2004 ANES

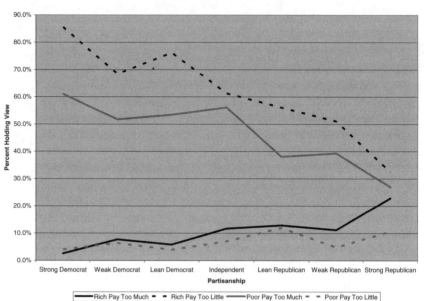

leaners and weak partisans are still blurred. Again, this is probably due to some confusion between them, as individuals try to
place themselves in the partisan category that they see as most
desirable.

Of course, even if people are willing to express such egalitarian views, we don't expect that everyone will be able to articulate them in a way that we would recognize. One of the reasons
that we do research on values, after all, is that survey respondents
are rarely able to offer any overarching reasons to support their
opinions on various issues. Because of this, Feldman and Zaller
(1992) argue that many humanitarian or egalitarian views will be
supported through references to past programs that proved successful. Many of the most popular liberal leaders of the past century, they note, presented themselves as pragmatists. Franklin
Roosevelt was just looking for ideas that would work; Lyndon
Johnson presented himself as a West Texas rancher who had
down-to-earth ideas. As early as 1955, Hartz argued that the
social welfare programs of the New Deal were justified mainly
from pragmatism: they worked, when the solutions proposed by

Republicans—even Herbert Hoover, known as one of the greatest humanitarians of his time—simply didn't.

This view of issues as being the results of essential values also gives us some traction on the tone of the Democrats statements. According to the analyses of liberal and conservative rhetoric performed by Phillip Tetlock (1986), liberals are more likely to see conflicts between these values. As a result, they have to use more complex reasoning to justify their issues positions when confronted with a conflict.[8] Tetlock shows that this added complexity—necessary to justify issue positions even when the undesirable results of the position are known—applies in a variety of situations, including the British House of Commons (1984) and the United State Supreme Court (Tetlock, Bernzweig, and Gallant 1985). Even in issues of war and peace, Wallace, Suedfeld, and Thachuk (1993) find that dovish leaders make more complex arguments than hawkish leaders.

Tetlock and other researchers looking at this phenomenon (such as Streufert and Streufert 1978; Ballard 1983) have developed a detailed system for measuring this complexity (Baker-Brown et al. 1992). At the lowest level, a score of one, there is no recognition that there's another viewpoint on an issue or that there is more than one dimension to be considered. By a score of four, the statement recognizes that there are multiple viewpoints or issues, but doesn't integrate them into a coherent whole. At higher levels—going up to seven—integration comes and increases.

In these rankings, liberals in almost every situation and around the world, and Democrats in the United States, rank higher than conservatives or Republicans. Only two exceptions to this trend have been established. The first involves arguments about abortion. Michele Dillon's (1993) analysis of the arguments made by groups on both sides of the abortion debate following the Supreme Court's decision in *Planned Parenthood v. Casey* finds that both sides use relatively simple arguments, though multi-issue groups (such as the American Medical Association and American Bar Association) were more complex than single issue groups (such as NARAL Pro-Choice America). The second has to do with conditions of stress. Leaders of aggressive states, and those that have been surprised, seem to use rather less complexity in their statements (as in Knorr and Morgan 1983; Wallace, Suedfeld, and Thachuk 1993).

In sum, we have a number of expectations about what statements from Democrats should look like. First, they should put values like egalitarianism and humanitarianism above individualism and a limited government. Second, their arguments should be relatively complex, noting both sides of an issue, and the trade-offs that are intrinsic to any governmental policy, with a possible exception for abortion issues. Third, with regard to issues that involve economic redistribution, they may well fall back on pragmatism to support their views, rather than espousing potentially unpalatable egalitarian sentiments.

BRANDING AND VALUES

Overall, the Democratic respondents in our interviews match some, but not all, of the traditional characteristics of Democrats. In terms of values, Democrats should put values such as egalitarianism and especially humanitarianism above individualism and limited government. We see this characteristic most clearly in their general optimism about government. They describe the government as being necessary to protect citizens, and tell us that it can serve to create a more just society through redistributive policies. While Republicans spoke about the need to protect individual initiative and property from the government, the Democrats were more worried about making certain that everyone had a reasonable standard of living.

This shared focus on the positive potential of government, and their optimism that the people in government generally have our best interests at heart, tells us that the Democratic youth are cut, broadly, from the same cloth as the adults with whom they share a party. However, the nature of young people's politics, its basis in image rather than substance, necessarily leads to substantial differences as well. Democrats are also expected to make use of much more cognitively complex arguments than Republicans or independents, but this simply wasn't present in our interviews. When asked about politically contentious issues such as the war in Iraq, we'd expect complex answers that, for example, recognize that removing Saddam Hussein was a noble goal, and that the troops are heroes, but takes issue with the way in which the war was described to the public. Rather, when our Democratic respondents talk about the war, their statements show very low complexity: the war is bad and the politicians behind it are corrupt. There's no recognition of multiple viewpoints or dimensions, and certainly no integration. Now, this could be an extension of the abortion exception. On the issue of abortion, representatives of liberal groups—especially single-issue groups—have about the same, low, complexity in their statements as conservative groups. If the issue of Iraq is the only issue for which Democrats showed this low level of complexity, it could be that they are simply so incensed about the issue that complexity goes out the window, as it does when people are under stress. However, the Democratic respondents don't seem to have a high level of complexity in any of the current political issues that they address.

Religion, for instance, would seem to offer a perfect opportunity for complex statements. Statements about the role of Islam in the attacks of September 11, for instance, tend to stress that Islam is a religion of peace, but that there are fundamentalists and extremists who distort that message. Therefore, the conflict isn't with Islam, but with those fundamentalists, and we should be allying ourselves with moderate Muslims against them. When it comes to American Christian leaders such as Jerry Falwell and Pat Robertson, and religious adherents in general, Democrats' responses were far less complex. Religious leaders are seen as hypocritical—especially on issues of sexual morality—and intolerant, and their followers are stupid, unquestioning, and as intolerant as their leaders. There's nothing positive about religion or the people that follow it.

Instead, they tend to focus on George W. Bush and members of his administration, and there's nothing complex about their viewpoints about Bush, his Attorney General Alberto Gonzales, advisor Karl Rove, or his Secretary of Defense Donald Rumsfeld. While several of the respondents expressed confidence that the majority of the people in government are good people doing a good job, they had nothing but disdain and venom for these four individuals, who were named most often in their responses. It's certainly possible to make a complex case against these figures. They could be seen as well-meaning people—like others in government—who overreacted to the war in Iraq or were given bad counsel from their advisors.[9] Instead, the Democrats' statements portray them as absolutely corrupt, completely incompetent, and entirely ill-intentioned.

In sum, the Democratic respondents to our surveys don't seem to be giving the cognitively complex statements that we would traditionally expect from Democrats. Rather, they seem to be approaching politics in the same way as the other respondents. Like them, the views of political groups and parties are based on relatively shallow evaluations of the images and brands associated with the parties and issues. The ideological content underlying these brands is almost entirely absent. This is by no means an indication that these young people don't make use of relatively more complex reasoning in general: indeed, when asked questions not directly related to the political sphere, their answers were rather more complex than those of other groups. There is no reason, as far as they're concerned, though, to apply the cognitive effort necessary to reach that complexity to political matters.

Their responses do, however, set them apart from the other partisan groups in an important way. While Republicans were most alienated from the images of political leaders, young Democrats seem most alienated from the political issues that they are presented with. As their responses indicate, they see the potential for political matters to be important, to be relevant to themselves, they just don't think that it is happening right now. Unlike Republicans, who would want a whole new crop of leaders before becoming involved, all that the system need do to engage the Democratic youth is speak to the right issues.

4

Independents

"Partisan politics [seem] to be an unnecessary distraction and most people who affiliate themselves with either party to be closed-minded, self-preserving, or annoyingly and incorrectly verbose in support of their party"

—Ryan, a 19-year-old independent

IMAGES OF INDEPENDENTS

WHILE TYPICAL STUDIES OF POLITICAL VIEWS OFTEN FOCUS ON PARtisan politics, a substantial group of young people proudly identified themselves as independents. Partisan politics often see independent voters as the "other": a category that remains outside the boundaries of the two major parties, or consider independents as voters who have not yet decided on a candidate, or set of issues positions, but will eventually. Indeed, research looking into the meaning of the term (Bastedo and Lodge 1980) shows that while individuals have a clear concept of what it means to be a Republican or a Democrat, the meaning of *independent* remains fuzzy. Even in the question normally used to define partisanship, the independent category is placed on step up from "or what."

However, in other ways, independents are more than just a residual category of those have yet to make up their minds. As discussed in the first chapter, and in more detail later in this chapter, there are real political indicators that lead to an increase in the number of independents, implying that they have made a political decision, on a political basis, just outside of the normal partisan system. While Republican and Democratic youth often describe independent youth as "shifty," "indecisive" and "politically ignorant," Independent youth have a very distinctive culture, ideology, and belief system. Many of the independent youth

111

we spoke to are aware of the negative stereotypes about themselves, but take pride in their political views. In this, they seem to be embracing the same view of independents that we tried to debunk in chapter 1: that independents know more about politics than partisans and choose to isolate themselves from the parties. However, it doesn't seem that they're being disingenuous. Rather, our interviews seem to show that the independent youth believe that they have acquired a deeper understanding of how the political system works than those individuals that align themselves with one party or the other. If, as discussed in chapter 1, this leads them to know less about, and participate less in, normal party politics, they don't seem to regard it as a loss.

Ryan, a twenty-year-old white student from suburban New Jersey identifies himself as an independent. While politically independent youth are typically seen as the "other" or as not belonging to the two major parties, Ryan insists on his political identity as an independent. As he says, "partisan politics [seem] to be an unnecessary distraction and most people who affiliate themselves with either party to be closed-minded, self-preserving, or annoyingly/incorrectly verbose in support of their party. I don't think there should be teams when governing America, people are born Americans not Republicans or Democrats" (Ryan 2007).

His decision to be politically unaffiliated with any party is also based on his conceptions of contemporary Republicans and Democrats. In his view, "A typical Republican is bullish closed-minded and aggressive against those who are different. They are not interested in hearing opinions that differ from their own and will argue their point even after they have been convinced that it's wrong." While Republicanism, to him, represents being close-minded and aggressive, he doesn't feel connected with the Democratic Party either. In his view: "A typical Democrat is flaky and argumentative. They stand for nothing and only highlight the problems in society, rarely offering a proposition for change and improvement. They live on their high horse but can't see past the end of their noses" (Ryan 2007).

In Ryan's view, neither political party addresses his concerns or reflects his political views. These views, he indicates, leave him with no choice but to be an independent. Note that the differences ascribed to the parties don't have anything to do with the policies of the two parties, but rather with images and personas associated with them. Many of the independent responses also indicated that the two major political parties are too similar in their views and ideologies. A common theme here is that the differences between the parties are somehow fabricated, and the dominance of the two parties leaves no room for alternatives.

Joe, a twenty-one-year-old part-time college student believes that there are no tangible differences between the dominant parties in the United States. "I think one of the major problems that we face today," he tells us, "is that there are no major differences between the Democrats and the Republicans. Therefore, most people don't care who wins because they feel like they are all the same and they stand for the same basic things. What America needs most is a candidate who comes out and is completely different and wants to deal with the real issues America is facing today." Because he does not see ideological differences between the two parties, he chose to be an independent.

Jim, a nineteen-year-old college student, agrees that there are few distinctions between Republicans and Democrats. He says that "The typical republican is a bald fat white man in a suit. He makes tons of money," and that "the typical democrat is a skinny white man in a suit. He makes tons of money too." In his view, an average Republican and Democrat are identical—except for a few extra pounds. Both are supported by established, affluent, while men with no ideological differences. The only difference he finds between these two groups is their consumption habits. What differentiates Democrats is that they eat "an all-natural soy-flavored energy bar."

Political ideology and issues do not differentiate the parties in these respondents' view. The minor differences between the parties are simple distractions according to many young people. As Jim tells us:

> Unfortunately, it's just a label. Oftentimes I find people agree with an issue "because I'm a Republican (or a Democrat)" rather than because that's just the way they truly feel about the issue. In other words, if someone is a member of one party, they agree with pretty much all their stances on issues regardless of personal opinion. This would make more sense if, for example, being Republican or Democrat meant having a specific mindset that governs all their actions. In actuality, however, I feel the grand scheme of Republican views doesn't follow a set pattern. For a short example, Republicans usually hate abortion because it is taking life. Conversely, they support the death penalty. I feel that Democrats do the same flip-flopping too.

In that respect the parties are the same: they are both arbitrary. What makes things worse is that's the way people vote in the senate. All the Republicans vote Republican and all the Democrats vote Democrat on every issue. Since I say the belief system is arbitrary, in my eyes it means that everyone is voting the way they are just because of the symbol on their nametag.

This inability—or refusal—to see distinctions between the parties is completely at odds with the traditional explanations for why individuals choose to be independents. Independents are expected to reject the parties because they are too ideological—as discussed later in this chapter—not because they aren't sufficiently ideological.

However, while independents fail to see any real differences between the political views of the parties, what they do see are vast differences in their consumption patterns, and hence their images and identities. It's not what they believe in and what issues they represent, but what brands they consume, what kind of food, music, and clothing they prefer and how they present themselves. Many of the independent youth that we spoke to describe Republicans and Democrats as if they were brands or products with images that are marketed to certain types of people. In our surveys, young people were asked to describe consumers and workers of prominent brands such as McDonald's and Starbucks. Many provided us with very detailed accounts as to what these people are like, projecting specific personality traits and making assumptions about the characters, daily lives and habits of consumers of and workers in these businesses. For example, a typical Starbucks employee is described by Billy as "a tree-hugging hippie. They (referring to Starbucks employees) enjoy playing their acoustic guitar or staring in amazement as others play their acoustic guitar," whereas, "a typical McDonald's employee enjoys smoking weed in their free time. They could care less if they mess up your order or spit in it." Even though these are, on average minimum-wage service-sector jobs, the employees are described in detail by the images and personalities are attributed to each person associated with respective brands. Similarly, young people attribute certain personalities and characteristics to the "consumers" of politics. Consumers of the "brands," Republican and Democrat, are also associated with certain images and consumption of other brands. According to independent youth, as Jim summarizes in a nutshell, Republicans have shotgun collections and Bibles, while Democrats have hemp-based products and soy foods.

REBELLION THROUGH INDEPENDENCE

This refusal to choose a party is often considered a strong sign of political apathy. Many political accounts consider strong party affiliation a prerequisite for political activism and involvement. The student movements and protests of the 1960s and 1970s were associated with young people with strong political party affiliations. Independent youth have rarely been considered as a source of political activism. While strong association with a party has been considered as a prerequisite for political involvement, social activism, rejecting authority and social change, independent youth have traditionally been thought to remain outside this equation. Because independent youth do not affiliate strongly with a major party, they are not traditionally believed to be the ones to advocate social change. However, the independent youth we spoke to show a very strong rejection of authority. Contrary to traditional belief, young people today do not show their nonconformity politically. While politics and political activism had been a medium for young people to show nonconformity and rebellion, young people today do not define politics that way. On the contrary, being politically independent is rejecting authority, being a nonconformist and rebelling against the traditional order. Jim, a nineteen-year-old college student, when asked what his party affiliation is, says: "Being the edgy nonconformist college student that I am: Independent." Young people see being politically independent as cool, edgy, and admirable. Being affiliated with a political party shows acknowledging, accepting and abiding by established rules. Being politically independent, on the other hand, is rejecting mainstream rules and established parties, hence it is considered to be rejecting the establishment. Jim sees partisan people as uncool, annoying, and unable to think outside the box. For him, these are people who side with the establishment and cannot challenge the existing order. Finn, a twenty-one-year-old college student agrees that he does not want to pick one party over the other and he does not want to side with one over the other. He says he realizes that this appears apolitical.

However, siding with one of the parties is almost like choosing between two limited choices offered by the established authority. Since the order in which politics operates and the choices presented to the young people are predetermined, opting out is a way to rebel, a sign of nonconformity. For example, he remembers that when he was young, he was "hung up on picking a party," as if he had to make a choice imposed on him by his parents and other authorities. He says that as he was growing up, in teenage years, instead of accepting these choices, he rejected this order and decided to be an independent. That is why becoming politically independent is a form of resistance and rebellion for young people and elicits cool images that young people wish to associate with.

APATHY

For the most part, the independent young people we spoke to showed the same apathy toward politics as the Democratic and Republican youth. Ryan says "a typical person who's really interested in politics is an enigma" to him. He does not understand why any young person would be involved in politics. The reason he is not into politics is because he believes people, who are actively interested in politics are typically "single-minded, dismissive of opposing views, and combative of their political opponents" (Ryan 2007). It is a certain "image" or a "label" he does not want to associate with. For Ryan, being involved in politics requires rigid partisan politics. He feels that being outside those party boundaries would not allow him to be fully involved in politics.

Being interested in politics is not only associated with being rigid and narrow-minded, but also with wealth. Like a consumption item such as going to the movies, taking up sports, or being involved in any other leisure activity, political involvement requires money. That is why Joe characterizes an average young person interested in politics as "wealthy." He tells us that wealth is the minimum requirement to at least consider being politically involved. Partly because being wealthy frees up enough time to dedicate exclusively to politics and partly because keeping up with politics requires economic investment. To be politically involved, keeping up with contemporary political news and literature is a prerequisite and that requires an economic invest-ment, according to Joe.

ISSUES

Despite their dislike for partisan politics, independent youth are very similar to Republican and Democratic when it comes to issues. Independents, too, rarely mention issues in their politics. For many independent youth, issues are not an inherent part of politics.

Ryan remembers many anecdotes from high school when his friends would complain: "What has the USA done for me?" He says, "It surprises me how much people in my generation take for granted the freedoms of living in our society." Because rights and freedoms are taken for granted, many of the youth we spoke to do not feel that they should be concerned with the already earned rights. For Ryan, many of the issues that political parties address seem outdated and not relevant to young people. They feel like issues such as women's rights and civil rights were earned decades before and do not require immediate attention. Furthermore, the issues that the two major parties address do not seem relevant to the young people. They feel like their concerns are not addressed and their issues not talked about.

Ryan does not even believe that the issues that the two major parties stand for are actually organic issues that stem from gen-uine concern of the parties. He says: "Both 'parties' often agree on things they view as popular zeitgeists, to which pledging will increase their likelihood of reelection, such as renewable energy." Issues, he believes, are just popular views that parties side with to attract votes.

The only "issue" that comes up in our conversations with, and surveys of, college students is the draft. Especially in a time of war, one issue of potential interest of young people is the possi-bility of reinstating the draft. While the draft was an important source of contention during the student riots of the 1960s and 1970s and remained at the core of major political activism at the time, young people today do not consider it to be a plausible option. While many youth identify it as a "relevant" issue, which would make them more politically engaged and active, they sim-ply do not believe the draft will be reinstated. Joe believes that if reinstated, it could mobilize many young people, but he still does not believe it will happen. He says: "I do not think that we will ever have another draft again. If Congress introduces a draft again people will rebel against the government and make sure no one goes to war against their will." This is why he does not consider it necessary to be politically active: the government is never going to do those really bad things that would make his activism —and that of his independent brethren—necessary.

At the beginning of the rise in the percent of voters identifying themselves as independent, several researchers argued that some independents were actually more concerned with issues than partisans. This was almost heresy at the time: the conventional wisdom, embodied in *The American Voter* (Campbell et al. 1960), and discussed in chapter 1 was that independents were far less sophisticated then partisans by any measure, and that the high-interest, low-partisanship voter was, at best, a deviant case. RePass (1971) argued for a distinction between "old" independents, like those in *The American Voter* and "new" independents, who had an ideological structure that was simply at odds with that presented by the two major parties. Rather then rejecting the two parties for whatever reason, as independents had previously been thought to do, these independents were focused on certain issues that neither party was adequately addressing (see also Pomper 1975 and Asher 1980): civil rights, the environment, Vietnam.[1] There is some reason to believe, though, that this spike in political awareness among independents, especially young independents, may have had more to do with the unrest of the end of the 1960s than with a shift in the way partisanship was conceived.

The independent young people in our surveys seemed to embody a combination of these old and new independents, in that they reject the parties, but do so on the basis of certain issues that they don't feel are being addressed. When Ryan talks about energy policy, he does so as an indictment of the major parties— no one is really doing anything about it—and as an affirmative statement of his political beliefs. However, unlike the partisan respondents, the independent respondents don't tell us what they would like to see done about these issues. Issues don't seem to be important in and of themselves, but rather as a tool to justify the negative feelings that the independents have toward the parties. They're discontented with the parties' issue stances, but not in the way that the "new" independents of the 1970s were. In this, our respondents are yet again defying the traditional model of independent voters.

SOCIAL CHANGE

Independent youth, too, are pessimistic about social change. They appear to be the most pessimistic of the three groups. While in the previous decades, particularly in the sixties and seventies, rebellion against the contemporary political climate and bipartisan politics was expressed through a desire to change the political system. However, independent youth do not transfer that disillusionment into political activism. Political independence in itself is a way to rebel against the system. This pessimistic attitude, among independent youth stems from structural obstacles.

Joe tells us that his disbelief in the ability of people to achieve social change stems from a structural flaw. He says: "it will be extreme[ly] difficult for a change in the political system because the process is so slow that it just dies out." The political system prevents social change, therefore the inefficiency and the inflexibility of the system discourages young people from attempting social change.

To some extent, these views accurately reflect the setup of the American political system. The legislative process is set up to have a large number of what are called veto points: ways to stop something from happening. In the Congress, a bill can be killed in committee, killed if the speaker decides not schedule it for a vote, killed if the rules committee decides to limit or add certain amendments, killed if the conference committee can't agree on the provisions, killed if the president decides to veto it. On the other hand, there's exactly one way that a bill can be passed and signed into law. Change in the political system, therefore, is difficult, and can be easily blocked by only a few people. Between the end of radical reconstruction in 1876, and the first—completely toothless—Civil Rights Bill passed in 1958, a small minority of southern Conservatives in the Senate were able to turn back literally dozens of bills seeking to improve the lot of blacks in the United States. In more recent years, the Kyoto Protocol was rejected by the Senate by a vote of ninety-five to zero,[2] and despite increasing support for actions on global warning, there is no sign that the issue will be revisited. In such situations, it's understandable that people like our independents could find fault with the pace, or even the possibility, of political and social change.

Ryan agrees that political and social change is not very easy in the United States. The rigidity of the system discourages Ryan as well as many of the other youth we spoke to from attempting social change. As they see it, only a very specific type of person could potentially create social change, described as "strong willed" with "strong conviction." Social and political activism, for the independent young people, is to be taken up by people with those specific personalities and is not the sort of thing just anyone—or, for that matter, they themselves—can do. Because the characteristics of a person who can potentially change the social and the political system are so narrowly defined, many young people do not feel that they could undertake this task.

These sorts of statements could easily be seen as indicative of a collective action problem. The independent youth we interviewed may all want some sort of social change, but want someone else to expend the efforts necessary to get it. Game theorists, in fact, would expect this sort of reaction when individuals want a public good, something that everyone would be able to enjoy, regardless of whether or not they put in the effort to get it. Clean air and military defense are classic examples of such public goods, as you can't get clean air for yourself without getting it for your neighbor as well. As such, people should be content to let others pay for the public good; in the end, this means that no one gets it. References to other people, who are more strong-willed, or have more time and money to put into political action, then, could be a sign that these independent youth are seeing such a collective action problem. However, in light of the other statements made by these same young people, it seems likely that these are more indications of the structural barriers that the independent respondents see in the political system. In a collective action problem, the issue is that other people, who want the change as much as you do, aren't willing to put in the effort to find a solution. We would expect that the object of frustration would be the people who are looking to enjoy the benefits without paying the price, what are often referred to as "free-riders." Instead, the frustration of the independents is voiced against the political structure, against the politicians who are content with the status quo, against the inertia in the political system. These aren't indicators of a collective action problem, no matter if one might be present, but indicators of a problem with the way in which the government is set up.

ROLE OF GOVERNMENT

Interestingly, image-wise, Republican, Democratic, and Independent youth consider themselves very different from one another. Often times, when we ask young people to describe themselves politically, they use consumerist tropes and tell us they are independent because they do not have brand loyalty to certain coffee brands or clothing shops or restaurant chains. Yet, when it comes to their image of the government, many young Independents share the similar views as their Republican and Democratic counterparts. Independent youth, too, have little confidence in the politicians and the government.

Joe says: "I have lost complete confidence in the politicians in government. These politicians are purely interested in themselves and how to make their pockets deeper. I think most of the politicians are corrupt and the only people they wish to please are the elites. The reason why I say this is because issues like health care are still a major topic in United States. We are a first-world country and third-world countries have better health care then we do."

He feels alienated from the politicians and the government. The issues he cares about, like health care, are not addressed by the government and the politicians. He also sees politicians as distant authority figures that restrict his rights, serve their own self-interests, and are often dishonest. It isn't that these views aren't shared by many, if not most, Americans: the public routinely rates the occupation of politician as among the most reviled in society. What is interesting about this is that *all* politicians are included in the condemnation.

Generally, opinions about politicians are subject to what is sometimes called "the dentist effect." People may feel that all dentists are corrupt, recommending unnecessary procedures and overbilling for the ones that they carry out, but they also reserve an exception for their own dentist. They may all be crooks, the thought goes, but mine is one of the good ones. Politicians fall into the same boat. They're all crooks, but the one who happens to represent me is one of the good ones. After all, the politician representing my district gets federal money for important projects in my area—in other areas, it's "pork," here, it's important—gets my grandmother her social security check, and holds town meetings to stay in touch with the district. As much as people may dislike politicians as a class, they like the ones that they know, or know of, but independents don't seem to. Like independents, Republican and Democratic respondents made reference to self-serving politicians, but also made frequent references to good ones, ones that were different: Ronald Reagan, Al Gore, John Edwards. These references were simply absent from the statements made by the independent respondents, indicating again that the independents are seeing a problem with the system as a whole. The people within the system are bad, but they're also irrelevant: the institutions themselves are the problem.

Independent youth also feel disillusioned by the fact that politicians are not paying enough attention to young people's rights. Joe complains that, in their attempt to solve short-term problem, politicians often defer current matters in order to get votes.

Referring to the Social Security issue, Joe says: "I think that if the government does figure out something my generation will not have any money left over for retirement. Another example is the education and federal loans; how the government chooses policies for education and federal loans affect me directly because if the government chooses to give out more grants it will benefit me." Because they feel, in political matters, young people's interests are often not prioritized, Joe is disillusioned by the political system.

Despite the consensus on their distrust to the government, many independent youth do not agree on the role of the government. Many believe that government should be a small force in American politics and should not be powerful, and some believe that the role of government is really important. Some, like Joe and Ryan, think that there would be "chaos" and "racism" if the government were weak.

TIME, WORK, AND MONEY

Independent youth explain their lack of interest in politics through time constraints. Joe believes that ". . . people are so caught up in their own lives that they really do not care what these politicians are doing. The average American works forty to fifty hours a week, supports their children, and is too busy stress-ing about the mortgage. As long as we do not have a war inside of the United States not a lot of people are going to care what the people on Capitol Hill are doing." However, time limitations are almost used as an excuse for not being involved politically. Even though it is true that young people work long hours, even when talking about time limitations, Joe mentions the triviality and irrelevance of political topics. Unless it's a civil war—Joe's term for anything that impacts youth's lives directly—people are not going to care. Political issues are simply not relevant to the daily lives of young people and cannot capture their attention amid many other things that are fighting for the attentions of young people.

These statements may seem to muddy the waters a bit. Up to now, our independents' statements have indicated that they don't see the point in political action, that the problem isn't with the people—either in Washington or in the public—but in the system. Here, however, there seems to be some indication that the problem is with the people. They're working too much, they're caught up in their own lives: if they weren't, maybe they could do something. Again, though, a closer look at the state-ments reveals that the problem the independents are seeing is with the institutions. It isn't that people are lazy, stupid, or igno-rant, but rather that that the institutions outside of government prevent them from taking action within the government. Aver-age Americans, as seen by Joe, are almost heroic, working too many hours, dealing with family problems, financially overex-tended. They may not be doing anything about the political sit-uation, but the blame for that is placed solely at the feet of the institutions, not the individuals.

Independents that we talked to, then, are discontented not only with political institutions, but with institutions in general. The common theme seems to be the corruption of institutions and the difficulty in changing them: individuals trying to operate within those systems seem to get off rather lightly in their view.

WHERE THEY GET THEIR INFORMATION

Most independent youth point to the problems in the media. Many are dissatisfied with the quality of political news and find problems with both conservative and liberal media outlets. Ryan says: "A typical Fox News devotee is uninformed and gullible. They sit in front of their television set with wide eyes and nod at every word from pundits like Bill O'Reilly or Ann Coulter. Brainwashed to hate liberals, they believe the divisive trash that is spewed into their living rooms." Similarly, Joe says that "the average Fox News viewers are Republican who is tuning in to listen how good of a job they are doing with the government. I think that these people are the types of people who tune to listen to what the Republicans want them to think. By now you can obviously tell that the Fox News channel is Republican own[ed]. I think that the people who view Fox News or either ignorant or they are brain washed."

Similarly, Jim describes Fox News consumers as people who don't "see the humor in the catch phrase they utter every day: 'fair and balanced news.' They are also the kind of person that waves behind the glass wall of the news room that views the street: a complete moron."

Conservative news outlets are biased and often polarize society, creating enemies out of the liberals. The people that follow these news sources as seen as badly as the parties that they are thought to adhere to: mindless at best. On the other hand, many voice their discontent with liberal news outlets as well. Many independent youth did not know what NPR was. Jim said: "I just Googled NPR, and it sounds like a radio station someone snooty would be really proud of listening to." Even though many of them did not know what NPR was and few were listeners, many voiced their discontent with NPR. This is due to the image and the perceived branding of NPR. A young person who doesn't know anything about NPR still attributed qualities and characteristics to the listeners. Because many perceive the audience to be "haughty" and "snooty," they do not want to be associated with the brand.

Overall, there is general discontent with both conservative and liberal news outlets. The main concern is the absence of non-partisan, unbiased news sources. Joe is concerned because he says: "I want to know about the news but I don't want someone to tell me what to think. The reason why I like this station is because it tells me the news and it lets me decide what to think about a particular topic."

Other relatively liberal news outlets like *The Daily Show* aren't necessarily seen as better, mostly because they do not take politics seriously and he complains about the absence of serious news shows for young people. Joe characterizes an average *Daily Show* viewer as someone with "a short attention span [who] is self-important. Many independent youth . . . find politics too ridiculous to take seriously and are a mob of rabble-rousers who worship Jon Stewart with reverence." While many independent youth like Ryan are not very happy with these shows, they still perceive it as a cool brand, hence are more receptive to its image. For example, Jim says, his mother often leaves Fox News on, but because he does not like their image he has a "mental block" against it, but he occasionally watches *The Daily Show,* which he finds more self-aware and irreverent. This self-conscious irreverence and acknowledgment of the absurdity in our political system appeals to many independent youth. Because shows like *The Daily Show* acknowledge the "absurdity" of politics, even though they may not agree with the message, young people are more receptive to it. By acknowledging that the system is absurd, shows like these defy established categories, and therefore are perceived as countercultural.

Like the other young people we spoke to, young independents relate to media outlets and sources of political information as brands. Many are not fully aware of the content of these outlets and in some cases not fully aware of the media outlets themselves. Despite this, they have strong convictions and stereotypes of people who associate with these outlets. Independent youth, specifically, are dissatisfied with traditionally conservative and liberal news sources. However, their discontent stems not from the content, but often from the perceived image of these news sources. Many are not receptive to certain media if they are prejudiced against the brand. They seem to be receptive to shows like *The Daily Show* because they find the image appealing, and hence seem to be receptive to their message. This pattern, as we'll see in the next chapter, is broadly applicable and plays a critical role in the success of Jon Stewart's program in informing young people.

REALIGNMENT VERSUS DEALIGNMENT

An understanding what traditionally makes individuals independents has to begin with Key's (1955) "Theory of Critical Elections." Key argued that American politics was characterized by what's called "punctuated equilibrium," in which there are long periods of stability followed by quick periods of rapid change that settle into another long, stable period. These long, stable periods are called party systems. The first party system ran from the founding of the country until 1816, with the collapse of the Federalist Party. This led to the period of one-party dominance in the Era of Good Feeling, where Democrats ran the country mostly unopposed. The second party system began with the advent of the Whig Party as opposition to the Democrats, and ended when the Whigs were replaced by the Republicans in the 1856 election. After this, the parties were set as they are today, with the later party systems referring mostly to changes in the bases of support and relative strength of the parties, with the third running until 1896, the fourth until 1932, and the fifth ending sometime— thoughts vary on when—after that.

The key here is how the transitions between the party systems happen. In the 1840s, the country underwent a period of great expansion, with much of the West being added to the country. This led to a resurgence of the debate over slavery, and whether or not the new states and territories being added should be free or slave. Even as this debate raged, with violence erupting throughout the country and even on the floors of Congress, neither the Democrats nor the Whigs wanted to deal with it. Both parties were afraid that any overt debate over slavery would lead to a civil war (which, of course, it eventually did), so both did their best to avoid any real debate or action. While this may or may not have been good public policy, it did little to appease the growing ranks of abolitionists in the North and Midwest, who were pressing for an end to the expansion of slavery, if not an altogether ban on it.

By the beginning of the 1850s, these forces were sufficiently tired of waiting for Whig action, and began to gravitate toward the many smaller parties that promised faster action on the issue, like the Free Soil Party and the Republican Party. The latter gained enough support—with the help of defecting Northern Democrats—to take one third of the popular vote in the 1856 election (the Whigs only gathered 22 percent), and win the 1860 election with 40 percent of the vote. What's remarkable about this is how quickly support for the Whigs evaporated. The Whigs had won the elections of 1840 and 1848, and took 44 percent of the vote in 1852. After the 1856 election, they were done. Both parties had previously been split between the North and South: after 1856, they were divided almost completely by section, with Republicans in the North, and Democrats in the South, a division that would last for almost eighty years.

A similar shift took place with the 1932 election, when Franklin Roosevelt's New Deal Coalition brought the Democratic Party into dominance by aligning African-American, Southern, and Labor interests. Again, the shift took place suddenly, and stayed in place for decades, and again, it came as the result of the inability of parties to deal with the issues at hand: this time, the great Depression. The Democratic Party went from winning a grand total of two elections in the period between the Civil War and 1932 to winning every election but two between 1932 and 1968. These shifts are known as realignments, and while they're jarring, they're expected.

Beginning in the 1970s, though, political researchers began to notice something new, which they referred to as dealignment. The number of individuals identifying with the two parties was decreasing rapidly, and the number of independents increasing. In 1952, the first year of the American National Election Study, only 5 percent of respondents categorized themselves as independents who didn't lead toward either party, as seen in Figure 4.1. This peaked in 1976, when 14 percent of respondents didn't identify with either party. While it had decreased to about 10 percent in the most recent surveys, this is still more than twice the level of fifty years before. When the total number of independents—including those individuals who initially say that they're independent, but then claim to lean toward one party or the other—is tabulated, the results are even more striking. The total number of independents increased from a low of 19 percent in 1958 to a peak of 39 percent in 2000. Even among those individuals who initially identify themselves with a party, the strength of attachment to that party decreased: the percent of people identifying themselves as strong members of a party decreased from 36 percent between 1952 and 1964 to about 24 percent between 1964 and 1976 (Norpoth and Rusk 1982).

Much of this dealignment comes from the decline in the number of Democrats in the South. Following the Civil Rights acts of the 1960s, conservative southern Democrats began to defect from the party (though they would generally continue to vote in

Figure 4.1: Percent of Respondents Identifying as Independents, by category, ANES

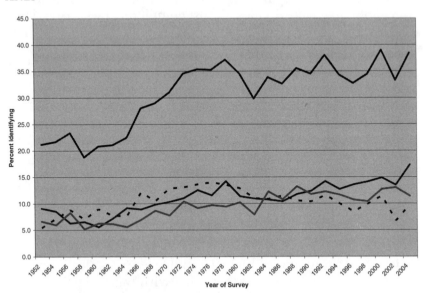

the Democratic incumbents that they had supported for years).
According to Stanley (1988), the percentage of Democrats in the
South declined by twenty-two points between 1952 and 1984,
while the number of Republicans increased by eighteen points.
Outside the South, the percentage of Democrats only declined by
five points, and the proportion of Republicans only increased by
three. All told, this means that in the South, at least, the percentage of individuals identifying themselves as independents
increased by at least nine points.[3] It has been argued that this
dealignment in the South was the precursor to a realignment:
that is, that southern conservatives were becoming independent
mostly as a way station on their way to Republicanism. While
this certainly happened to some extent—the solid South has
shifted from solidly Democratic to solidly Republican—the
increase in the number of independents has remained. Moreover,
changes in the South alone cannot explain the overall change in
the overall changes in the strength of partisan attachment.

This can be seen in Figure 4.2. While the number of independents (not including those who lean toward one party or the other)

Figure 4.2: Percent of Respondents Identifying as Independents, South versus Non-South, ANES

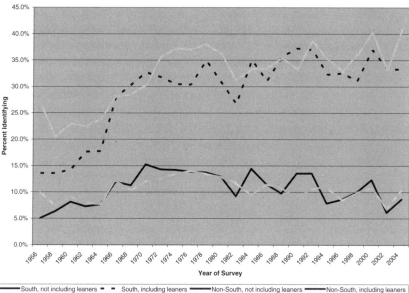

is higher in the South than in the rest of the country for a few periods since 1956, the overall trends in the South and the non-South are almost identical. Moreover, from both Figure 4.1 and 4.2, it's clear that the biggest part of the change doesn't come from people who identify only as independents, but in the increase in the number who lean toward one party or the other. In the past fifty years, the percent of individuals identifying as independents who don't lean toward either party peaked in the 1970s, and then decreased almost back down to initial levels in recent years. The percent of individuals who identify as independents including leaners, though, has steadily risen from about 23 percent in 1956 (14 percent among southerners; 27 percent among non-southerners) to a peak of around 39 percent in 2000 and 2004.[4]

So, traditionally, an increase in the number of independent voters has been seen as a sign of a coming realignment. Southerners turn independent in advance of switching to the Republican Party in the wake of Democratic action on civil rights. Whigs, no doubt, turned independent before joining with the Republican Party in the 1850s, and Federalists probably didn't identify with either major party before the Whigs came along. However, the recent increase in the number of independent voters seems to lie somewhere else: there simply aren't enough southerners switching over to account for the entire difference, and even among those who identify with a party, the strength of that identification has fallen off sharply.

TRUST AND IDEOLOGY

If we want to see if the young independents that we've interviewed are different than older independents, we have to isolate the nonrealignment factors that seem to have influenced older voters. Political scientists have come up with several explanations to explain the alienation of these voters from the major political parties. The first has to do with the long-term effects of the Vietnam War and Watergate and the decrease in trust in government that went along with them. The second has to do with the increased importance of ideology to the political parties, which may make it more difficult for people to agree fully with either party. It has been argued that these attitudes have led to an increasing amount of hostility toward the parties, as well as a substantial decrease in the attachment feel toward the parties (as in Dennis 1975).

The first explanation begins with the finding that the public attitudes toward the government have grown increasingly sour in recent years, reaching a low point in the early 1990s (Orren 1997). The percentage of people who say that they felt that they could trust the federal government dropped as low as 12 percent in 1994, from peaks as high as 35 percent during the early 1980s (Chanley, Rudolph, and Rahn 2000).[5] Partly, this drop has to do with the end of the cold war (Nye 1997). The long-simmering conflict with the Soviet Union led to increased trust in the government, and with its end, the bottom fell out of the measure. Trust was already low before the cold war ended, largely because of increased awareness of political scandals in the post-Watergate era (Nye and Zelikow 1997).[6] Chanley and her colleagues (2000) analysis finds that scandals such as the Keating Five and the House Banking scandal reduced trust in government by about four points each, painting, as they did, members of Congress as opportunists more concerned with financial gain than good government. People who grew up watching these scandals, and without the cold war to act as a cohesive factor, were far less likely to trust in the federal government than their forebearers. This distrust, in turn, led individuals to turn away from both political parties in disgust.

This decline in trust in the federal government was evident among young people even in the immediate aftermath of the Watergate scandal. In studies done during the 1960s, children and adolescents had very high regard for political figures in general, and the president in particular (Hess and Torney 1967). But by early 1974 (between the "Saturday Night Massacre" and the release of the transcripts of the Nixon tapes), schoolchildren were likely to say that Watergate was the most pressing problem facing the country, and fourth graders were saying that the scandal was leading Nixon to ignore other important issues (Hershey and Hill 1975).[7] As would be expected, this cynicism was most present among those children who were most politically interested, and therefore more aware of the issue. No follow-up studies were conducted on these children specifically, but the decrease in partisanship and trust in government that followed speaks for itself.

Between 1964 and 1974, the percent of people saying that they "just about always" trust the government fell from 15 percent to 3 percent, and never really recovered, bottoming out at 1.6 percent in 1982, and recovering slightly to 3.6 percent in 2004. While the proportion of ANES respondents who say that they "almost never" trust the government has remained low (hitting a peak of 4 percent in 1978), the number saying that they trust the government only "some of the time" has increased substantially over the last forty years. In 1964, 63 percent of respondents said that they trusted the government "most of the time," and 22 percent trusted it just some of the time. By 1974, these figures had almost reversed, and save for a brief time immediately after the attacks of September 11, more Americans have trusted the government some of the time than most of the time.

Alternately, an explanation for the decreased strength of partisanship can come from the increasingly ideological nature of the parties. When southern whites abandoned the Democratic Party after the passage of the civil rights acts under President Johnson, the long-term effect was greater than simply switching the vote of the solid South. The switch also aligned the two parties ideo-

Figure 4.3: "Do You Trust the Government?" by Year, ANES.

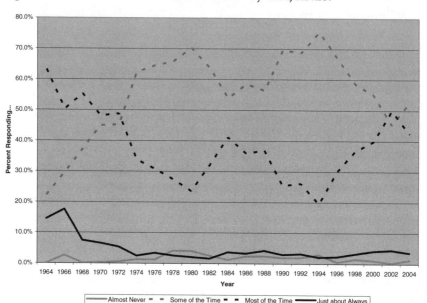

logically in a way that had never before happened in American politics. Once the shift in the South was over, conservatives and liberals, regardless of region, were each aligned in a single party. Liberals from the Northeast and Upper Midwest had long fought with southern conservatives for control of the Democratic Party: now, they won by default. Similarly, without the issue of race dividing them, state's rights united southern whites with laissez-faire libertarians and westerners untrustworthy of central government in an ideologically compact Republican Party. The shift in the ideological nature of the parties can be seen in their choices for presidential candidates. Once Democrat Lyndon Johnson—who had spent his career being all things to all people—declined to run for a second term in 1968, the race for the nomination came down to three liberals. Eugene McCarthy just narrowly lost the New Hampshire primary on the strength of student activists who cut their hair in order to knock on doors for him. Robert Kennedy ran on a promise to continue the struggle for civil rights. Even the choice of the Democratic establishment, Hubert Humphrey, wound up running against the war. The conservative wing of the Republican Party showed its strength in the nomination of Arizona Senator Barry Goldwater in 1964, and though Goldwater had little chance in the race against Johnson, his candidacy signaled the end of the struggle between the liberal and conservative wings of the party. In 1952, Dwight Eisenhower had been seen as a political threat upon his announcement that he was a "liberal Republican." In the fight for the 1968 nomination, Nelson Rockefeller, the leader of the liberal wing of the party, couldn't muster more than eleven percent in New Hampshire, and won only one state (Massachusetts) over Nixon. Today, even the phrase "liberal wing of the Republican Party" sounds absurd.

This increased ideological unity among the leaders of the party led to an increased ideological unity among the base,[8] but it had consequences. Ideologically, Americans are generally middle of the road. Since 1972, when the American National Election Study began asking respondents about where they place themselves on a liberal to conservative scale, fully a third (34 percent) of those who have an opinion rate themselves at the middle of a seven-point scale. Only 5.4 percent rate themselves as being extremely liberal or extremely conservative combined, with both those figures remaining relatively stable in the more than thirty years the question has been asked. Over the same period, though, Americans have come to regard the two major parties as being far more extreme.

In 1972, a nearly identical 23 percent of respondents regarded the Republican and Democratic Parties as moderate—four on a seven-point scale. At the same time, only 5 percent said that the parties were extreme: extremely liberal for Democrats, extremely conservative for Republicans. In 2004, only 17 percent viewed the Democratic Party as moderate, and only 11 percent regarded the Republican Party as such. More respondents, in fact, saw the Republican Party as extremely conservative (13.5 percent) than saw it as moderate. The situation is a bit better in the Democratic Party, with 11 percent viewing it as extreme, far lower than the number seeing it as moderate. While these numbers have fluctuated substantially over time, mostly in response to the perceived ideology of presidential candidates, the overall trend is clear, especially in the perception of the parties as moderate. The difference between the two parties on this, with the Republican Party being perceived as much less moderate in every poll since 1976 (before then, the perception of the two parties was almost identical),[9] is most likely due to the vocal positions of Republi-

Figure 4.4: Perceptions of Party Ideology by Year, ANES

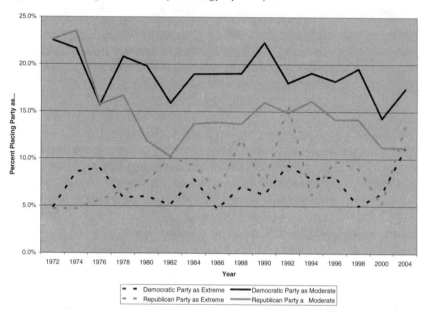

can candidates on highly salient culture war issues such as abortion, gay rights, and flag burning. The disconnect between the stable moderate views of the American public and their increasing perception of the parties as extreme could lead to the portion of the dealignment not explained by the changes in the South.

All told, then, we'd expect that independents would discuss politics through their objections to the current parties. None of our respondents are southerners, and it's unlikely that any of them would object to the civil rights acts of the 1960s (at least overtly), so that explanation for independents is out. What remain are concerns about the parties: distrust of the parties and the politicians running under their banners, or a belief that the parties are overly ideological.

THIRD PARTIES

So, as discontented as the independents seem to be with the two major parties, they would seem to be a prime recruiting ground for a third-party candidate. Their responses indicate that they don't see any real difference between the two parties, a major reason that someone would support a third party even if it doesn't have a chance of winning. However, their responses uniformly downplay the viability of third-party candidates: but why? While they don't provide an answer—other than to say that "other" parties are "a joke"—we can use their answers to related questions to draw some conclusions.

One reason may be that they recognize that third parties can't win under the current electoral rules. Many of the independent respondents to our surveys stress how the two major parties fail to address the issues that are important to them, and it seems likely that they would support a party that addressed those issues. The problem with the American electoral system in their view then isn't that there aren't good parties, but rather that the good parties can't win, either because of structural problems[10] or because other voters don't have what they see as the correct priorities and don't support them.

However, there is scant evidence in the interviews to support this. First, the third parties are a "joke" to the independent youth. If it were the case that they were avoiding the third parties because they weren't politically viable, we would expect that there would be some good words for the parties and candidates championing the issues that the independents want visible. Instead, there's the same response that most voters have toward the third parties: tolerance, as long as they don't waste too much of our time. Second, while there's frustration voiced at the structure of the legislature and the seeming inability of the two party system to address the real issues, there's no frustration at the factors preventing the third parties from ascending. While Democrats may be "flaky" and Republicans "lazy," there's no sense that they should be voting for someone else. Given the alienation that the independents express from the parties and politics in general, it's surprising that they don't voice any frustration with the electoral system itself, especially after the fiasco of the 2000 presidential election.

The other reason that our independent respondents disregard the third parties may have nothing to do with issues at all. Rather, the third parties may be dismissed out of hand as a "joke" because of the poor branding of the candidates that they field. While the independents may not care for the slick, commercial appeal of many Republican and Democratic candidates, they don't care for the candidates that lack it, either. In the past, third-party candidates may not have been an electoral threat to the major parties, but they were taken seriously, at least as signs of discontent in the country. Candidates like Strom Thurmond and John Anderson were rightly seen as the product of parties that had alienated parts of their base: serious, if misguided. The third-party candidates of recent years have not fared so well. Despite the appeal of his government-as-corporation message in 1992, Ross Perot is an object of ridicule for his appearance, his manner of speech, his choice of running mates, even his half-hour political informercials. Ralph Nader, the most successful third-party candidate since Perot, is seen as the embodiment of an out of touch liberal. Outside of them, nationally known third-party politicians are limited to Pat Buchanan, Jesse Ventura, and perhaps Lyndon LaRouche. While their issue positions may hold some appeal to the independents surveyed, their responses make it clear how the third parties are being judged: on their image. And without a public relations campaign to polish that image, and with the characters we've named being associated with them, it's little surprise that they're seen as a "joke."

5
The Daily Show

The Daily Show kind of reminds me of the newest punk rock scene. Just like punk rock, *The Daily Show* is the success of a previously failed marketing scheme. The MTV Rock-the-Vote campaign was a complete bomb, but now *The Daily Show* has at least intrigued kids enough to start questioning the political establishment. If there are older folks watching this show to obtain their news then they are completely lost. Although *The Daily Show* does shed light on some topics, its cynical jokes and comedic routines cloud the seriousness of certain subjects."

—Peter, a 25-year-old Republican

AT THE CONVERGENCE OF ALL OF THE FORCES DISCUSSED SO FAR comes *The Daily Show with Jon Stewart.* There can be no question that it's a brand and that the respondents to our surveys treated it as such, though much more positively than many of the other brands they mentioned. It is different than many of the other brands we have discussed, though, in that it has ideological content without being perceived as hypocritical. By and large, the Republican and Democratic Parties, as well as their representatives, are seen by the respondents to our surveys as being little more than "politicians," who will do or say anything to get elected. The messages that these politicians carry, then, can be safely ignored: they don't believe what they're saying, and neither should you.

Stewart and the producers of the show generally refer to it as "fake news," (despite the show's numerous Peabody awards)[1] but as Baym (2005) points out, it's a problematic label, as the show falls somewhere between comedy and journalism. The real contention of the "fake news" label, reinforced by Stewart's forceful statements in interviews, is that all of the news, especially cable news, is fake, and his program is actually more honest because it's the only one willing to admit it. In our surveys, respondents seemed to see this as a virtue, naming it trustworthy, even as they discounted or ignored other major sources of news and information.

In this chapter, we're going to go deeper into this phenomenon, first by examining exactly what our sample thinks of *The Daily Show*, as well as other news programs, and then through an examination of the cultural and political impact of the show. Finally, we'll use an experiment to measure exactly how much young people learn from watching Stewart's program rather than more traditional news broadcasts. In the experiment, young people are randomly assigned to watch an episode either of Stewart's program, or of NBC's *World News Tonight*, and we measure how much they learned in terms of objective facts, as well as in terms of general knowledge about how the political system operates.

Young People's Perception of News Sources

The young people in our surveys admit being extremely limited in their news sources. Rather than turning to newspapers, traditional evening news broadcasts, twenty-four-hour cable news many of our respondents admit to getting their news from primarily from informal sources like friends and family.

Regardless of their political affiliation, they feel alienated from news sources. In our interviews, we have asked about three major sources of political news. We have selected the National Public Radio (NPR) as it perceived as being more Democratic, or at least liberal; Fox News, as a more Republican news source; and finally, *The Daily Show*, as a source of political information that young people can relate to. We have asked college students not only about where they get their news, but also about their images of these different news media: what kinds of people they think get information from these sources. We wanted to explore the way young people see these different sources, the images they elicit and the stereotypes they have about these sources.

We did not, in the final survey, include broader sources, like the network evening news broadcasts, CNN, or *The New York Times*. Early versions of the survey did include these sources, but their wide appeal made it difficult for our respondents to identify their branding or imaging, beyond saying that viewers/readers are probably old.

Table 5.1: Political Media Use by Age, 2004 American National Election Study

Political Media Use Indicator	Age 18-25	Older than 25
Never Watches National Evening News	37.1%	20.4%
Always Watches National Evening News	8.7%	32.9%
Never Watches Local Evening News	37.0%	29.1%
Always Watches Local Evening News	7.9%	27.7%
Paid "A Great Deal" of Attention to TV News About Presidential Campaign	12.8%	32.8%
Watched programs about Presidential Campaign on TV	83.3%	86.4%
Watched "A Good Many" such programs	20.0%	33.1%
Watched "Several" such programs	38.9%	44.3%
Watched "Just One or Two" such programs	41.1%	22.6%
Didn't Read a Newspaper in the Last Week	29.7%	40.2%
Read a Newspaper Every Day	10.2%	30.1%
Read about Presidential Campaign in Newspaper	54.4%	71.4%
Read About Presidential Campaign in Magazines	26.9%	30.3%
Paid "A Great Deal" of Attention to Such Articles	13.8%	15.5%
Paid "Very Little" of Attention to Such Articles	27.6%	17.9%
Listened to Political News or Speeches on Radio	18.5%	32.9%

Among the sources that we did use in the final survey, many of our respondents pointed to the lack of relatable and trustworthy news sources: a fact that could only serve to exacerbate their political apathy and alienation from contemporary politics. Furthermore, as would be suggested by our findings regarding the importance of branding to our young respondents, the ideology of the news source seemed less important to them then their perceptions of the kinds of people that would turn to that media source. It doesn't seem to matter if they agree with the viewpoint that a particular media source is associated with: only if that media source is a cool brand.

The primary thrust of this chapter is to examine the impact of one of these brands, *The Daily Show*, in particular. But before we do so, we have to show that the branding of that program—and young people's awareness of it—differs substantially from that of other programs and media sources, each of which we'll discuss in turn.

*National Public Radio (NPR): "I don't know what
NPR stands for or what it is. I apologize."*

National Public Radio is well-known among many Democrats in the United States, especially in the relatively wealthy areas of the Atlantic seaboard where we carried out our surveys and interviews. However, the young people we spoke to had scarcely heard about it. An overwhelming majority of young people in our sample told us they did not know what it was or they had never heard of it. A few even asked if they could Google it and get back to us. "I cannot describe a typical NPR listener since I do not know anyone who actually listens to National Public Radio," Jim, a twenty year old told us. Many were not even sure what it was. Democrat David said: "I don't know what NPR stands for or what it is. "

Those young people who had heard about it had trouble identifying the content of NPR. One respondent described it as an extremely conservative channel that Republicans enjoy.

Though many did not know about the content and the ideology, one of the major stereotypes about NPR listeners was about their technological abilities. Many described an NPR listener as someone who does not have an Internet connection or a television. Because of their choice of medium—the radio—young people associate these listeners with old-fashioned technology. The only reason that you'd listen to the radio, the logic goes, is if you didn't have a choice in the matter or had grown up doing so. Listeners, then, should be older, and therefore more conservative. In a similar vein, it was also linked to older workers, especially commuters, who would have to listen to it on their way into the city.

Such expectations were only reinforced by the assumption that NPR listeners must be old. A few even described NPR listeners as extremely intelligent and educated, but added that it is primarily for older people. Many young Democrats said they do not listen to it because it is a brand for their parents, not them. As such, the fact that they don't want to be associated with the brand should come as no surprise.

As we've seen before, though, a lack of information about the content of something doesn't prevent the young people in our sample from holding strong views about it. Cynthia, for instance, a twenty-year-old Republican, told us that though she doesn't listen to NPR, she finds "the tempo slow and the voices boring," and that the people who do listen to it "tend to be Republicans and of the conservative mindset."

One of the few things that all of our respondents who had heard of NPR seemed to agree on was the lack of commercials. Often, this knowledge was unaccompanied by any actual exposure to NPR, but several of the respondents seized on it, saying that NPR was for "someone who does not like commercials." At least one of our respondents explained that news without commercials was tedious. To individuals who see the political world through the prism of branding, commercials and information about products seems to be desirable, as it gives hints as to what sorts of people should be associated with a program or network.

Fox News

While Fox News was better known than NPR, many of our respondents were confused about the content and the ideology of this network. Regardless of political affiliations, many of the respondents identified Fox News as being a liberal source. Nineteen-year-old Republican Steve told us that, "The typical Fox News viewer is a left wing, or a very liberal person. Fox News has always leaned to the left in their reports and opinions, so it would make sense for the viewers to lean that way as well." The most obvious explanation for this would be confusion as to what *conservative* and *liberal* mean—but the same respondent had no such difficulties in other answers. Rather, even a respondent with some degree of political sophistication doesn't fully understand the generally agreed-upon bias of the network.[2]

Despite the fact that the vast majority of our respondents had heard of Fox News and claimed to know something about it, for the most part, they hadn't watched it. They also tended to associate with "middle or upper aged people," just as they did with NPR: one described Fox News viewers as so "old or they can't find their remote." This aspect, the age of the viewers, was more salient to the respondents than the ideology, content, or format of the programming. Fox News isn't for them, even if they agree with the ideological content, because they relate the brand to older viewers.

Many of them also see Fox News as the voice of the establishment. A typical Fox News viewer is described by several of our respondents as "a middle- to upper-class businessman or woman." Therefore, many young people see it an established businessperson's channel and one that doesn't have anything to do with themselves.

Regardless of their political affiliation, the older and more established image of the Fox News brand is an important factor for young people in deciding to watch. While the widespread availability and the relatively more technologically advanced image of the network (it is, after all, on television rather than on the radio) may be incentives for watching, the perception that it's more for older viewers seems to be a deterrent.

The Daily Show with Jon Stewart

It's difficult to argue that *The Daily Show* doesn't have a relatively strong liberal bias. This is not necessarily an ideological bias, but rather a comedic one. Satire works largely by deflating those in power, and for most of the time since the change in format that brought Stewart to the show and politics to the forefront in 1999, Republicans have been in the best position to be satirized.

As such, we would expect that support for, and positive images of, Stewart's program would be correlated with partisanship. Republican young people would object to a program that mocked (mostly) Republicans, and Democratic young people would appreciate a program that mirrored their stances. However, as with Fox News and NPR, our respondents didn't seem to know enough about the underlying ideology of the program to embrace or reject it on those grounds.[3] Almost none of the Republican respondents noted any liberal content, and neither did the Democratic respondents. Rather, respondents who knew about it—and it was the best known of the three media sources included in the final study—discussed it in terms of the images they associated with it.

As with the other media sources, respondents put a premium on perceived age of the audience. Of those that knew about the program, the majority used words like *young, hip, teenager, college student,* or *right out of college* to denote a typical viewer. Whether they watch it or no, it is, as far as they are concerned, a show for young people like themselves. "Older people," Rachel, a Republican, said "just want the news flat out, and are not really into the whole satirical thing." In that sense, it's like the music or fashion aimed at young people: parents just don't get it.

While the content and the ideological stance of the show had little to do with how young people see it, the presentation of the material was an important part of the show's image. Many emphasized that it was fun or humorous element, both of which made the show attractive. This quality was mentioned across the board, among all partisan groups, and respondents emphasized that it was young, hip humor, targeted specifically to young people, college students, like themselves. This aspect was particularly important for the generally alienated pessimistic youth we spoke to, who see the satire as akin to their own views and the comedy as a kind of escape from reality. As Adrian, a nineteen-year-old independent, described the average viewer, "a teenager who is tired of all the government filtered news that is shown on every other network and want to hear the straight truth from someone who is as tired of our current government as they are."

These respondents may be alienated from the political process, but the show is seen as being just as outside of the system as they are, and is thus relatable. As another put it, "A *Daily Show* viewer is tired about hearing about the grim news all of the other stations report." They like to hear the lighter side of the news reports and hear the reporter make some jokes. As nineteen-year-old Steve, a Republican, put it, "*Daily Show* reporters like to remind viewers they are human too by the way they act, while other reporters just read the news and get off of the air . . . viewers like to be reminded that the reporter on the other end is also a human." Such viewers just "want to be entertained"; the news, therefore, "does not necessarily have to be true."

Perhaps most importantly, respondents noted that *The Daily Show* was more user-friendly than the other news sources mentioned in the survey. As we discussed in the first chapter, the complexity of political news stories, and the generally unfamiliar nature of the rhetoric and concepts employed there, make it difficult for relatively unsophisticated viewers to get a good understanding of the topic at hand. Traditionally, partisanship has been used to simplify these stories, making it clear which side is right, and which wrong, but among young people alienated from the parties, this isn't necessarily an option. While many of the respondents voiced this concern when describing other media sources, saying that they didn't understand them, or that they were talking about obscure topics, things that no one really cares about, or has time for, such comments were missing from descriptions of *The Daily Show* and its viewers. It was not uncommon for a typical viewer to be described as someone "that does not know anything about politics." This is a political news program that anyone can watch and understand. "This is because," a female Democratic respondent tells us, "Jon Stewart puts a comical view on real life events so it makes it easier for college students to be interested by it because they have political classes in school and this makes it perfect to relate the information they learned. They like to watch the news but they like the satirical view that he expresses and the opinions that he has."

THE IMPACT OF *THE DAILY SHOW*

Of course, the fact that young people like Stewart's program, and associate it with desirable traits such as youthfulness, humor, and approachability, does not necessarily mean that it's having any substantial political impact. After all, MTV's idiotic stunts-sans-helmets program *Jackass* probably has many of these same associations, and no one is claiming that it has a salutary impact on America's youth. There are, however, reasons to believe that

The Daily Show does have a positive impact on the young people watching. First, like other non–hard news outlets, it focuses on a very different kind of news, one that may be more relevant to the viewers. Second, this sort of program leads to increased chances that viewers will actually talk about politics.

The argument that people can learn about politics from something other than hard news outlets like CNN or network evening news broadcasts on the networks is not new. Moreover, it has become more prominent as mainstream hard news has become less focused on issues of policy, and more focused on what observers call the "horse race": who's winning, by how much, and what the strategies of the two sides should be (Hallin 1992; Farnsworth and Lichter 2003). Matthew Baum (2002) has argued that so-called soft news[4] can serve to teach people about foreign policy issues as well. Learning that Angelina Jolie is visiting Darfur means learning something about the situation in and around Sudan. Leonardo DiCaprio's Prius could lead to increased awareness of global warming, and Oprah's episode on female genital mutilation can bring up an issue that Americans wouldn't otherwise pay much attention to.

However, there are some caveats to these findings. First, these effects are only expected to incur for certain sorts of issues: those that directly involve major celebrities or those that can be framed as compelling human drama. The suffering of Zimbabweans due to hyperinflation, for instance, isn't a likely candidate for soft news coverage. Second, there is the assumption that these programs are offering a very limited amount of information compared with the traditional news outlets: seeing Brad Pitt talk about the impact of Hurricane Katrina on New Orleans is not the same as reading the report about it in *The Economist.* It may be the case, as in Baum (2002) that tabloid news show *Extra* mentioned Bosnia on as many episodes as the nightly news broadcasts, but that doesn't mean that *Extra* viewers were as well informed as they would have been had they been watching traditional news broadcasts. Media outlets other than hard news may be better than nothing, but that doesn't make them good.

Any benefit from *The Daily Show,* then, has to come from the fusion of politics and entertainment it embodies. The entertainment aspect makes it more likely that viewers will want to make use of the information, and the political aspect makes that information worthwhile.

Regardless of their feelings about the parties, the politicians, or the American political system as a whole, the respondents to our survey had an almost universally positive opinion of Stewart's program. When asked to describe a typical *Daily Show* viewer, respondents said that they were "cool," and, according to Jim, an independent, know how to laugh at the "miserable political system." By all appearances, it seems to be a brand that respondents want to associate themselves with: the description of *Daily Show* viewers was similar to that of Starbucks: generally positive, even if it wasn't their thing. In contrast, descriptions of Fox News had a great deal in common with what respondents said about McDonalds: brands associated with people who are in the way of everyone else, and are too dumb to realize it. As with any brand identity, it's pointless to have it if you can't communicate it with others. In Besen's (2005, 2006) research on youth employment, workers at a large, national coffee chain wanted others to know about their jobs, using it as a form of social currency, like clothes or musical tastes. In much the same way, people who watch *The Daily Show* are expected to want others to know about it, so they can benefit from the positive feelings their peers have toward it. Because they can't show off their brands by being at work, like the Starbucks employees, or through their clothing, like sports or music fans, their display should come in the form of actually talking about the show.

Empirical evidence for this expectation comes from Moy, Xenos, and Hess's (2005) analysis of the effects of soft news on political behavior in the 2000 presidential campaign. Controlling for all other factors, such as income, education, partisanship, and other media exposure, viewers of late-night comedy shows talked more about politics with family, friends, and coworkers by a significant amount. Among individuals with moderate levels of political sophistication, the increase was from about 2.6 instances of political conversation per week to 2.9 instances; among highly sophisticated viewers, the jump was from about 2.9 to about 3.4 instances per week.

This increase in the frequency of talking about politics is important for two reasons. First, there is an increasing emphasis in political science on the importance of deliberative democracy (see Guttman and Thompson 1996; Mendelberg 2002). The act of talking about politics is expected to increase the understanding people have of their own positions, and those of their fellow citizens, making them more likely to compromise in finding policy decisions, more knowledgeable, and more engaged in the political system (Chambers 1996). Exposure to all types of political and news programming on television has been shown to increase the frequency of political conversation (Kim et al.1999; Chaffee and Mutz 1988), and to the extent that viewers of *The Daily Show* are more motivated to show off their knowledge, this effect should only increase.

Second, there is strong evidence from political psychology that talking through your own issue positions and beliefs has a strong effect on those beliefs. Previous work by one of the authors (Cassino 2007) shows that the act of talking about a candidate leads individuals to stronger and more stable views regarding an election. In short, talking about what they like or dislike about a candidate leads people to better remember their own opinions, making those opinions more stable and more accessible in the future. These sorts of strong, accessible attitudes toward candidates are expected, in turn, to lead to higher levels of participation and involvement in the campaign. Talking about what Jon Stewart said last night, therefore, does more than just show off an association with *The Daily Show* brand: it forces people to examine their own attitudes and beliefs for consistency and makes them more likely to follow through on those beliefs. This effect may turn out to be as important as the effect of watching the show in the first place and will be one of the main variables we'll be looking at in our analysis of exposure to Stewart's show.

Of course, this is only politically important to the extent that the content of the program is political: and on this point, the evidence is overwhelming. Baym (2005) finds that two-thirds of the guests on *The Daily Show* in the months prior to the 2004 election were involved in government or politics, a proportion that has generally remained stable. Of the 112 guests who appeared on the program during the election off-year of 2007 through September of that year, 63 were directly involved in politics (64, including former White House Chef Walter Scheib), and an additional 10 were scientists talking about issues touching on politics. Seven were seeking their party's presidential nomination (Mike Huckabee, Joe Biden [twice], Christopher Dodd, Bill Richardson, John McCain [twice], Ron Paul, and Barack Obama). Of the 42 guests between August 2006 and the elections in November, 60 percent were politically oriented, as were 55 percent of the 160 guests on the show for the full year of 2006, including Pervez Musharraf and Bill Clinton. Nonpolitical guests included Microsoft founder Bill Gates, actor Peter O'Toole, and *Simpsons* creator Matt Groening.

Finally, the comedic approach to the political material may lead viewers to learn more about politics than they would from a straightforward presentation. There is evidence to show that negative information, especially when presented visually, tends to lead viewers to turn off their processing to avoid the information (Blanchette 2006). People, for instance, may not want to watch graphic violent images, and so ignore the content that goes along with them. Laughter, on the other hand, is highly positive, and so may lead viewers to pay more attention and be more likely to internalize the information presented (Fox, Koloen, and Sahin 2007).

We're not saying, like Steven Johnson, that "everything bad is good for you," (Johnson 2005) but rather that some bad things—like the popularity of *The Daily Show* among young people—may not be as bad as we think they are.

Is *The Daily Show* News?

Before we assign Stewart's program to the ghetto of soft news, we should see if the shoe fits. Patterson (2000) defines soft news as having several characteristics that distinguish it from hard news: less institutional, more sensational, human-interest themes, a focus on catastrophic events such as crimes and natural disasters, and a lack of public policy evaluations. In short, soft news tells us that something blew up and shows you the grieving relatives, but doesn't tell you in any real depth what should be done about it. This definition also makes clear what viewers who get their information from soft news are missing: important events that don't have dramatic footage and recommendations about what should be done to alleviate such problems in the future. While this definition is intended to separate legitimate news outlets from the lesser outlets that serve the people not interested or engaged enough to go to the real sources, we'll argue that in many ways, CNN and network news broadcasts are closer to this definition than the Comedy Central news programs are.

First off, coverage of politics in mainstream news has long been dominated by an emphasis on matters of image rather than those of substance (Graber 1976, 1980; Patterson and McClure 1976; Patterson 1977; Kovach and Rosenstiel 1999). In their analysis of the final two weeks leading up to the four presidential elections between 1988 and 2000, Fox and her colleagues (2005) find that the vast majority of the network news coverage is on the horse-race, rather than on substantive issues or candidate qualifications that might inform viewer's votes. While this last minute coverage is thought to be more important than earlier coverage of elections, as many voters don't pay attention until the last minute (Jamieson and Adasiewicz 2000), these result seem to hold throughout all stages of the coverage (Farnsworth and Lichter 2003).

We are far from being alone in making this sort of argument. *The Daily Show* has become successful enough that even the standard-bearer for journalistic integrity, *American Journalism Review*, has had to grudgingly admit that it's doing something right. As far as they're concerned, it isn't journalism because it isn't fact-checked and scrupulously balanced, but it is far bolder than mainstream media often is. As the *AJR* piece notes (Smolkin 2007), so much of what passes for news is spin that nonjournalistic approaches like Stewart's, or semi-journalistic approaches like opinion pieces, may be more informative than pieces that collect spin from both sides (Baym 2005).

Other sources—especially analysts of television news, who are typically less concerned with journalistic integrity than print news analysts—are more positive about the role *The Daily Show* plays in modern journalism. First off, entertainment media programs in general, and Stewart's program in particular, seem to offer more in-depth views of figures in government and their policies than hard news outlets: the interview segment is typically allotted about ten minutes of air time—nearly half of the program. When viewed in opposition to the "now this" style of broadcast journalism (Postman 1986), in which an anchor goes quickly from one story to the next and fails to provide context for any of them—a style appropriated by earlier comedy news broadcasts like *Saturday Night Live*'s Weekend Update—Stewart spends a remarkable amount of time on individual stories, sometimes as much as a third of the twenty-two-minute broadcast (Baym 2005).

The argument that *The Daily Show* is at least as good as the other news available was substantially bolstered by the aftermath of the terrorist attacks on the World Trade Center. As Hutcheson et al. (2004) note, most of the mainstream media aligned themselves with the White House after the attacks, uncritically accepting its version of events. Those commentators who didn't go along with this—such as comedian Bill Maher, then the host of *Politically Incorrect*—were considered unpatriotic. Comedy was considered inappropriate, and when the hosts of comedy shows came back on the air several weeks afterward, they typically apologized for trying to be funny. As Stewart said on his first night back on the air: "There were no jobs available for a man in the fetal position under his desk crying, so I came back here." Even so, the return of *The Daily Show*, the satirical newspaper *The Onion*, and comedy to *The New Yorker* were seen as milestones on the return to normalcy (Baym 2005). Reality, as Kuiper (2005) points out, had become almost too absurd to take seriously, and humor was a natural response. Moreover, while the mainstream media remained supportive and relatively uncritical of the White House up through the run-up to the war in Iraq in 2003, comedy programs turned against it much earlier. *The Daily Show* first began mocking President Bush a bit more than a month after the attacks, during his trip to China. While these jokes and attacks started out innocuous ("Mr. Bush, [Star of Martial Arts movies in the 1980s and 1990s] Steven Segal wants his jacket back," referring to the traditional Chinese garb given to the attendees on the China trip) and were masked with apologies, they quickly regained their previous venom. The incongruence between the mainstream media's continued lack of criticism of the White House and the increasing unease of much of the public with the direction that the country was taking may well have led viewers to comedic programs like Stewart's that allowed them to criticize the president and his advisors.

Fox, Koloen, and Sahin (2007) analyzed the content of Stewart's program, compared with network news broadcasts, during the 2004 Republican and Democratic conventions and the first debate between George W. Bush and John Kerry. While they found (unsurprisingly) that *The Daily Show* devoted more time to humor than the network news broadcasts and that the network news spent more time per story on substantive issues, Stewart's program, on the whole, had just as much substantive information about the election as the network broadcasts, largely because a greater proportion of each program was spent on election news. While news broadcasts often devote a considerable amount of time to natural disasters, soft news segments, celebrity features, and promotions for primetime news programs such as *Dateline* and *60 Minutes*, Stewart can focus just on the easiest targets for comedy: politicians and the media that covers them.

Obviously, then, *The Daily Show* isn't a news broadcast in the traditional sense—but that also means that it has managed to avoid some of the pitfalls common to news broadcasts. In doing so, it's gained a modicum of respect from media critics. The most important barrier between Stewart's program and the mainstream news seems to be the element of humor, and that, as we've seen, can have benefits of its own.

How Many People Actually Watch Them?

In terms of the sheer number of viewers tuning in *The Daily Show* and *The Colbert Report* on a nightly basis, the shows may seem overhyped. Neither of the shows regularly make the top programs on television in ratings, or even the top programs on cable, though ratings for cable television shows are notoriously skewed. In one week for which we have data, August 13 through 19, 2007, nine of the top ten (and twelve of the top fifteen) highest rated cable programs were on the Disney Channel, including three separate showings of *High School Musical 2*, which got as many as 17 million viewers.[5]

However, there is reason to believe that the Nielsen ratings are missing much of *The Daily Show*'s audience. For one, Nielsen tracks viewers on a household basis, excluding viewers who live in institutions—like college campuses. Nielsen began to try and fix this problem in the beginning of 2007, selecting several dozen dormitories to monitor, but the college-age audience is still severely underrepresented in the ratings system. This problem is compounded by Nielsen's normal recruitment techniques, which begin with a call to a home phone. The large number of young people using only cellular lines, are generally excluded from the get-go, even if they aren't living in a dormitory.[6] Even so, Nielsen's numbers show Stewart's program doing remarkably well for a late-night cable program. In 2004, an episode airing after the first presidential debate drew 2.4 million viewers, according to Niel-son, and averaged 1.1 million viewers per night that season. Cur-rently the show averages about 1.5 million viewers a night, with a ratings boost when an important guest is on, like Obama, or a January 21, 2004, interview with John McCain. In addition, about 800,000 viewers tune in to repeats shown the next day (Baym 2005).

How impressive these ratings are depends on what you're com-paring them to. Compared to the three network evening news broadcasts—which each get between 6 and 8 million viewers per night—they aren't much. Similarly, it doesn't do quite as well as the highest rated Sunday morning talk shows, like *Meet the Press*, which gets about 3 million viewers per week. But there are two factors to take into consideration. First, not everyone has cable, and second, not everyone is watching television at eleven o'clock. If we're to compare *The Daily Show*'s ratings with other cable news shows, things look a little better for it. Typically, it comes in the top three cable news shows, with ratings a bit below Fox News's *The O'Reilly Factor*,[7] and about on par with *Hannity and Colmes*. This puts it a step above CNN's top show, *Larry King Live*, and well above stalwarts like *Hardball* and *Lou Dobbs*. When compared to network late-night shows like *The Tonight Show*, Stewart is well behind, as Jay Leno and David Let-terman get between 4 and 6 million viewers per night. Among late-night programs on basic cable though, Stewart is well ahead of any competition: *The Daily Show*'s closest rival in the time slot seems to be the *Adult Swim* programming bloc on Cartoon Network, which averages about half a million viewers during its overnight run, from largely the same demographic as *The Daily Show*. *The Colbert Report* typically holds on to most of Stewart's ratings, averaging about 1 million viewers a night.

So, how many people are actually watching? Not nearly as many as watch network news broadcasts or the Disney Channel, but probably more than are watching any other cable news pro-gram. After all, O'Reilly's audience, with an average age of sixty-three, isn't nearly as likely to be underrepresented in the ratings as Stewart's, with a median age of thirty-five,[8] is. The real key to the importance of the show isn't in the number of people who are watching, but rather in their age. According to data from a 2004 Pew Research Center poll, the percentage of respondents under the age of thirty who said that they got most of their news from comedy programs such as *The Daily Show* was statistically indistinguishable from the percent that said they got their information from broadcast news outlets (21 percent for the comedy programs; 23 percent for evening news broadcasts). At least 1.5 million people are watching, and a disproportionate number of them are young enough that their political views are still subject to change. O'Reilly's sixty-year-old viewers have strongly ingrained partisan habits, so while his show may matter to people within the Republican Party, they're not expected to do much to get more voters for the Republicans. Stewart, however, may well be changing minds.

INDIRECT PERSUASION

In the psychology literature on persuasion, attempts to convince someone of something are generally divided in two types. The names of the types vary by the theory, but they generally correspond to "direct" and "indirect" forms of persuasion. Direct persuasion is the hard sell—like a television commercial or a salesman at your door. You know that they're trying to persuade you of something, and so your defenses are up: you evaluate claims critically and look for any sign that you're being deceived. Indirect persuasion is more akin to product placement on a television show. It is like an episode of *Friends*, where a character buys new furniture at Pottery Barn or competitors on *The Apprentice* trying to piece together a new ad campaign for Crest. This sort of indirect persuasion is thought to be more effective, because your defenses aren't up, and you're more likely to accept information uncritically. Advertisers, of course, know this: thus the change between ads that repeat the name of the product as many times as possible to ads that are supposed to be funny or engaging, even if they're only peripherally related to the product. The idea is that ads playing on indirect persuasion techniques can get you to think good things about the product being advertised and be more likely to buy it, even if you never hear the hard sell.

Not surprisingly, political consultants are playing this game as well. The early years of political advertising followed the same rules as all advertising at the time: repeat the name of the candidate as often as possible and lay out the reasons for voting for him. In time, the ads moved away from the hard sell, using emotional appeals and images, and limiting mention of a candidate's name. Political advertising has even developed its own version of product placement: putting candidates on nonpolitical television programs where they don't do the hard sell of their policies that would be expected on a political program. Candidates on *Meet the Press* can expect to be grilled about their issue positions and to be confronted with anything embarrassing that they've ever been quoted as saying. Candidates on *Oprah* or *Martha Stewart*, on the other hand, can talk about their childhoods, their relationships, their hobbies, and all sorts of things that may get viewers to like them without the defenses that go along with the direct persuasion route going up (Benoit et al. 2003). As Oprah Winfrey explained her decision to invite the 2000 presidential candidates on her show, "Over the years, I have not found that interviewing politicians about the issues worked for my viewing audience. I try to bring issues that people understand through their hearts and feelings so they can make decisions" (*Chicago Sun-Times*, September 1, 2000: quoted in Baum 2005).

Matthew Baum's (2005) analysis of candidate appearances on talk shows that candidates gain more than simply additional exposure by appearing on such programs (Oprah's audience far exceeds that of even network news broadcasts, the highest news shows on the air). The viewers of political news programs like *Hardball* or *Meet the Press* are rather more politically sophisticated than the audience of a show like *Oprah*. As such, there's a much greater ability to persuade these viewers by increasing the likability of the candidates as an indirect way of getting them to vote for them. Even when the host of a non-news program like David Letterman asks pointed questions, Baum finds that they're nowhere near as pointed as those asked on traditional news programs.[9] These hosts don't ask the hard questions because their audience doesn't really expect them to and doing so might well alienate future guests. Their job is to be entertaining, and confrontation adds little to that. As Stewart said in an interview in which Tucker Carlson, then the host of *Crossfire*, accused him of being John Kerry's "butt boy"[10] in a 2004 interview, because his questioning was too soft, "You're on CNN. The show that leads into me is puppets making crank phone calls."

The Daily Show certainly meets most of Baum's criteria for an entertainment show that's likely to have a persuasive effect on viewers. First, the main audience for the show—males and females eighteen to thirty-nine—are generally among the least politically knowledgeable, leaving them open to persuasion. Second, humor may well have a disarming value, bringing down people's normal barriers against persuasion. We will argue, however, that even if it doesn't have much of an effect directly persuading viewers to change their minds about political issues, it may have a deeper effect on the way in which the viewers think about politics. To the extent it shapes the ways in which viewers think about political information, it doesn't have to directly persuade them. Rather, they will apply the show's viewpoint to novel political information, and persuade themselves.

We first discussed this effect in chapter 1, when describing why independent voters may have more difficulty learning about politics than partisans. The idea is that people don't remember separate facts as well as they do stories, especially stories in which there are clearly delineated good and bad actors. This clear delineation makes it easier to understand what's going on, as it allows us to simplify motives and actions: good people do good things because they're virtuous; bad people lie and cheat because they're evil. Partisans know who the good guys (us) and the bad guys (them) are, and so have an easier time making some sense of the political world than independents, who don't have the benefit of a clearly divided world.

For political novices, like many of the young people we're interested in, raw information of the type that's found on many politically oriented news and talk programs is probably useless. While they may be able to retain some of the facts they don't have an easy way to categorize those facts, and come to a conclusion about what implications they should have for issue and candidate preferences. Programs that have partisan and ideological content, therefore, should be much more informative for young audiences. Bill O'Reilly and Rush Limbaugh have no trouble identifying who the good guys and bad guys are, and, therefore, the stories that they're telling are going to be more memorable, and, arguably, more persuasive.

If this is the case, then the ratings strength of Fox News Channel should be a major cause for concern among Democrats. Stewart's show may get ratings similar to those of O'Reilly's program, but there are a number of other Fox News shows on the top of the cable news ratings before the next top-rated show that could be considered at all liberal, MSNBC's *Countdown with Keith*

Olbermann, averaging about 800,000 viewers per night.[11] Indeed, a desire to counterbalance Fox News and perceived conservative dominance of talk radio was one of the major factors behind the introduction of liberal radio network Air America Radio.[12]

However, the highly partisan nature of Fox News may actually make it less effective at persuasion. Remember that persuasion is most effective when it is able to work indirectly, when people have their guard down. Viewers of the O'Reilly Factor or Hannity and Colmes can scarcely fail to understand that there is a persuasive message at work: in effect, it becomes a hard sell. On Stewart's show, this simply isn't the case. While there is a great deal of ideological and partisan content to the show—as is clear from the episode described in the appendix—it isn't obvious enough to be a hard sell. Criticisms are levied at both Democrats and Republicans, and representatives of both parties are portrayed as being inept and often hypocritical. On Fox News programs, the criticism of Democrats is unrelenting, and the biggest criticism levied on Republicans comes when they side with Democrats or are in other ways not sufficiently orthodox.

THE COLBERT REPORT

Less attention has been paid to *The Colbert Report* than to Stewart's show—perhaps because it has yet to cover a presidential election, as it only began in October 2005. In that limited time, though, *The Colbert Report*, too, has shown itself to be influential. In June 2007, Colbert broke his wrist while warming up the audience before the show and was not about to let the event pass without comment. He immediately began aggrandizing his injury, putting together mockumentaries interviewing the members of the cast who saw the accident, and comparing his suffering to any pain or disappointment seen in the news or with his guests. He went so far as to issue red "wriststrong" bracelets, selling for $10, with proceeds to benefit a veteran's charity. His guests—especially those with their own programs—were asked to start wearing the bracelets on the air and a remarkable number complied. So much so that in August of 2007, two out of the three network evening news anchors wore them on the air during broadcasts. In the *New York Times* article noting their acquiescence (*New York Times*, August 27, 2007), the media editor of the Huffington Post blog, Rachel Sklar was quoted as saying it was a "test" to see how "funny and cool" the anchors were: if they didn't wear the bracelets they were showing themselves to be "stiff and boring." The spokesman for the anchor who didn't pass the test, Charles Gibson, tried to play it down, saying that they had an exclusive agreement with Jon Stewart instead. The message, though, was clear: Gibson wasn't as cool as the other anchors, he didn't understand the appeal of these shows, was perhaps even threatened by them. By not being in on the joke, in effect, he became the joke.

Experimental Procedures

Past survey research has shown that viewers of *The Daily Show* are more politically informed than viewers of other political shows such as *The O'Reilly Factor,* and this has been used by defenders of the program to argue that their viewers aren't the drug-addled teens that critics have made them out to be.[13] Indeed, the message seems to be that Jon Stewart does a better job of informing people about politics than the "real" news shows. However, there are plenty of reasons to doubt this evidence. Most importantly, any such survey is necessarily correlational. The people who watch Stewart may know more about politics than the people who watch O'Reilly, but that isn't necessarily what caused them to be more informed, and is what we normally refer to as a selection effect. This argument is bolstered when we look at the education levels of viewers of both shows: Stewart's viewers are 78 percent more likely than the average adult American to have four or more years of college, while O'Reilly's viewers are only 24 percent more likely than an average American to have spent that many years in college. Given that watching either program is unlikely to have caused people to go to college, it seems likely that the difference in political knowledge is the result of past education, rather than the relative informational content of the programs.

If we want to determine the effect that watching Stewart's program has on political knowledge, we'll have to do so through a randomized experiment. In this experiment, fifty students, with either high or low degrees of political knowledge, were first given a questionnaire to measure their basic political knowledge, then asked to read an article from that week's *New York Times* dealing with President Bush's surprise trip to Iraq's Anbar Province in early September 2007. Then, they were asked to fill out a questionnaire relating to the article (discussed in more detail later). Afterward, they were randomly assigned to watch a twenty-two-minute broadcast of either the NBC *World News Tonight with Brian Williams* or *The Daily Show* from the previous evening. The programs covered many of the same stories, but, as we would expect from previous analyses, *The Daily Show* had more political content than the NBC broadcast. This could be seen as a confound: perhaps participants in the experiment might learn more about politics from Stewart's program because there's simply more politics on the show. First, remember that we're trying to understand if *The Daily Show* does more to teach viewers about politics than conventional news broadcasts, and the larger portion of the program devoted to political matters is a part of why that might be the case. Second, on the episodes in question, the amount of time devoted to national politics on the Stewart's program and the corresponding episode of *World News Tonight* were very similar: 15 minutes, 20 seconds on *The Daily Show*, 13 minutes, 58 seconds on the NBC broadcast.[14] Both of the programs devoted the majority of their time to a discussion of General David Petraeus's testimony before Congress in support of maintaining the surge of troops in Iraq. Detailed summaries of the programs can be found in the appendix.

After this exposure to the programs, the participants were given one of two new questionnaires, each different from the first. All of the respondents were given both of the questionnaires: only the order of the two was experimentally determined. In one, which we'll refer to as the first, students were asked to read an article from the *Times* related to a news story that they had seen in the broadcast, as well as to the article that they had read before answering the previous questionnaire. This one dealt with a report made by an independent military commission regarding the training of Iraqi troops. While the initial article didn't specifically deal with the training of Iraqi troops, it did deal with the debate over how much progress had been made, with some of the same political figures holding similar positions in both articles. Similarly, while neither of the broadcasts dealt with the issue of training troops in Iraq, both dealt with the military situation there in different ways: through the Petraeus report in both of the broadcasts, and the situation on the ground in *The World News Tonight* program.

In the second questionnaire, they were asked a series of factual questions about the Petraeus report and the situation in Iraq. Answers to some of the questions were present in both of the broadcasts (the name of the general testifying, for instance), some were only present in one of the broadcasts (the number of American troops currently on the ground), and some were in neither of them (the name of the fortified zone inside of Baghdad). The answers to still other questions were not directly stated in either broadcast, but were implied in both, such as the likelihood that President Bush will follow Petraeus's recommendations.

These different kinds of questions allow us to test different facets of what participants assigned to the different conditions learn from the broadcasts. The extent to which they learn facts from the broadcast they saw demonstrates their recall of the material. The extent to which they can answer questions just implied in the broadcasts demonstrates their comprehension of the material. Finally, the extent to which they can answer questions not in the broadcast demonstrates their ability to integrate the information in the broadcast with preexisting information, if present.

The two questionnaires completed by participants after watching the news broadcasts test different potential effects of exposure. The first article, unrelated to the information in the broadcast, but similar to the first article, tests if the participants are better able to store and recall political information in general. If it is the case that watching *The Daily Show* leads to better developed ideological memory structures, they should do better, in certain ways, at answering questions about the first article. The similarity to the first article, given before exposure to the broadcast, ensures that the comparison is a fair one. By asking factual questions, we see how much they learned, independent of how strong their ideological structures are.

All of the findings on these points come from the three questionnaires, all of which are included in the appendix. The first two questionnaires ask the respondents to summarize and recall elements from the *Times* articles, and each contains two parts. The first part of the questionnaire simply asks the participant to write a brief summary of the article and offers some prompts to aid in the process. For instance, the instructions for the summary of the first article, dealing with President Bush's surprise trip to Anbar province in Iraq, reads: "In a few sentences, summarize the article you just read. What was President Bush doing in Anbar province? What's going on with the benchmarks?" The second part of the questionnaire given after each of the articles, presents fifteen statements in three categories, and asks them to circle exactly eight of those statements that came from the article. Five of the statements are taken from the article, and ten are not. Half of the statements are congruent with the positions taken by actors in the article, and half are not. As an example, in the first article, President Bush is said to have praised local leaders in Anbar province as a way of diverting attention from the progress made by the government in Baghdad. A congruent statement would be, "The president declined comment on whether progress had been made by Iraq's central government." An incongruent statement might be, "The president praised the progress made by Prime Minister Nuri Al-Maliki's government in Baghdad."

Statements from the three categories (included in the article, not included but congruent, not included and incongruent) were matched on several dimensions, including the average length of the statement, references to specific individuals and places, and the complexity of the sentences. For instance, all of the statements were between fourteen and twenty words long, all had one or two references to specific people or places, and had a maximum of two sentences clauses. Matching the statements in this way helps us to ensure that some statements aren't chosen simply because they seem more complex, more specific, or contain more information.

Overall, this design allows us to test a number of our expectations about the effect of *The Daily Show* on political knowledge and on young people's political belief structures. Increases in political knowledge should be evident from the summaries respondents offer of the current situation in Iraq. If it is the case that exposure to *The Daily Show* engenders more learning than exposure to the *Nightly News* broadcast, participants assigned to watch Stewart's program should offer more detailed summaries, use more facts to support their view, and simply have more to say about the situation.

Second, we want to see if *The Daily Show* actually does allow young people to better develop political belief structures. The expectation is that the combination of ideological content with humor to shut down viewer's normal defenses against persuasion will make it more likely that viewers will internalize the program's rather liberal ideological structure. Participants with better developed ideological structures should be more able to recollect facts from the article and better able to make sense of those facts and their implications for other political issues. Some of this should be evident in the article summaries, but it will be most clearly expressed in what statements the participants in the experiment remember as having been in the article.

To explain why this is, we have to go back to early research on categorization and groups. Suppose that you're given a list of words, all of which have something in common, like this:

Balloon	Cloud	Mosquito
Kite	Sparrow	Helicopter
Frisbee	Bat	Bubbles

After I ask you to learn the list, I give you a distracter task, like trying to add or multiply a series of large numbers. Then, I ask you to decide if a word was or was not on the list. Some of the words you can choose from represent objects with the same characteristic that linked the previous list—they fly. Some of the words represent objects that don't fly. All else being equal, you'll be more likely to choose a word that represents a flying object. Even if you don't remember the specific words from the list, you'll be likely to remember that they were all flying things, and something from that category will seem more likely to have been on the list. Put simply, the brain is always looking for patterns, and it's a lot easier to remember the pattern behind the list then it is the individual items on the list.

In the experiment, we're applying the same logic to political items. If the participant in the experiment sees a pattern to what's going on in the articles, they'll use that to remember what was said and done. Therefore, they'll be more likely to say that something fitting that pattern was in the article, or in the broadcast, even if it wasn't. This requires, by and large, that the participant has an understanding of the underlying motives and values of the political figures and groups involved. For instance, no political sophisticate who read the article on President Bush's surprise visit to Anbar province in Iraq would say afterward that Bush was calling for a partition in Iraq, even though both of the concepts are brought up frequently in the article. Someone who doesn't understand why Bush went to Anbar, though, could easily make such a mistake.

The two articles are long enough that it's unlikely that participants will be able to remember all of the statements that were actually included, though those with a better developed political knowledge structure should have greater recall. The key measure, though, is in the number of congruent statements and noncongruent statements chosen as having been in the article, though none of them actually were. Because respondents are being asked to choose a total of eight statements, they will have to choose *at least* three that were not actually included. Ignoring the correctly identified statements, a respondent who chooses only congruent statements is demonstrating a much better developed political knowledge structure than someone who chooses several incongruent statements.

In one sense, this may make it seem like they're remembering the article incorrectly, as they're mentioning things that weren't actually in it. What it really demonstrates, though, is that they've formed connections between what was said in the article and their preexisting political knowledge: a sign of highly structured political views.

We also expect that there will be substantial differences in the effects on participants with high and low degrees of political interest. As is obvious from the interviews described in the last three chapters, most young people are politically apathetic: politically engaged and interested young people are a rarity. However, it's important to have some of them in our study so that we can test the conditionality of the effects. We're hypothesizing that exposure to *The Daily Show* should lead young people to have a greater capacity to understand American politics as they internalize the program's ideology. If this is the case, it shouldn't have any effect on young people who already have a coherent ideological structure. If we find that these high-interest participants are benefiting from exposure to the program as much as their low-interest counterparts, we will have to reevaluate our models.

RESULTS: POLITICAL KNOWLEDGE STRUCTURES

The two questionnaires filled out by participants after the randomly assigned media exposure measure very different aspects of what they took away from the short broadcast, and so we'll treat the analyses separately. Together, though, they paint a unified picture of how the different media sources affect participant's political knowledge.

We'll begin with the analysis of the questionnaire designed to measure sophistication of the post-broadcast political knowledge structure. Remember, respondents were given fifteen statements and asked to choose the eight that were most likely to have been in the article that they had just read. Five of the statements actually were contained in the article; five were not, but were consistent with the article; and five weren't included and were inconsistent with the article. The number of each of these statements chosen by a participant (correct, congruent, and noncongruent) were each subject to a separate ordered logit analysis.[15] The results of these analyses can be found in Table 5.2.

The first analysis, modeling the number of correct statements selected by the participants, seems disappointing: none of the three explanatory variables have a significant effect. The first, the experimental condition the participant was in (*Daily Show*, 1, or *World News*, 2) shows that respondents in *The World News* condition chose more correct statements, but not significantly more. At median levels of pretest political knowledge (identifying five of the ten political figures correctly), there is about an 11 percent chance that a participant in *The Daily Show* condition chose just one correct statement, and a 6 percent chance that a participant in *The World News* condition did. There is a difference there, but not a significant one.

The second explanatory variable is the control for the respondent's pretest knowledge. Participants who know more about politics before going into the experiment should do better at identifying correct and congruent statements; but there is no such effect in the first analysis.

Our final explanatory variable in our simple model is an interaction between the two. We expect that the experimental condition should have different effects on people with high and low levels of political knowledge, but, again, there is no evidence of this in the initial analysis.

Things change, though, in the models for the number of congruent and noncongruent statements chosen. In both of these, all three of the explanatory variables are significant or very nearly so at conventional levels of measurement. Given a sample size of only fifty respondents, these results are indicative of something significant. In both of the models, the variable for

Table 5.2: Ordered Logit Analysis of Experimental Political Knowledge Structure Results

Predictor	Correct Statements Chosen			Congruent Statements Chosen			Noncongruent Statements Chosen		
	Coefficient	Std Error	Z	Coefficient	Std Error	Z	Coefficient	Std Error	Z
Experimental Condition	0.48	1.34	0.36	−3.84	1.69	−2.28	3.00	1.54	1.95
Pre-Test Knowledge	0.06	0.33	0.19	−0.69	0.38	−1.83	0.74	0.38	1.92
Condition × Pretest Knowledge	0.04	0.23	0.19	0.67	0.26	2.56	−0.64	0.26	−2.45
Cut 1	−1.26	2.18		−8.36	3.07		−0.40	2.52	
Cut 2	0.03	2.11		−5.54	2.68		1.29	2.38	
Cut 3	2.10	2.15		−3.62	2.58		3.93	2.44	
Cut 4				−2.25	2.59		5.53	2.55	
Cut 5				−0.32	2.71		7.21	2.77	

experimental condition is significant: being in *The World News* condition leads participants to choose fewer congruent statements and more noncongruent statements relative to the participants in *The Daily Show* condition. Also, the interaction variable is significant in both, and in the opposite direction of the main effect of the experimental condition. Finally, the variable representing participant's pretest political knowledge is significant, and in the expected direction, with more knowledge leading respondents to choose more congruent statements and fewer noncongruent statements.

As with the other logit analyses we've carried out, it's difficult to estimate exactly what these effects mean without translating them into percentages, as we've done in Figures 5.1 and 5.2.

In Figure 5.1, we can see the number of congruent statements chosen by participants at the twenty-fifth and seventy-fifth percentile of pretest political knowledge.[16] The regression results show that those randomly assigned to *The Daily Show* condition chose more congruent statements, but that the effect is conditional on political knowledge. As seen in Figure 5.1, the net effect

Figure 5.1: Number of Congruent Statements Selected, by Pretest Knowledge and Experimental Condition

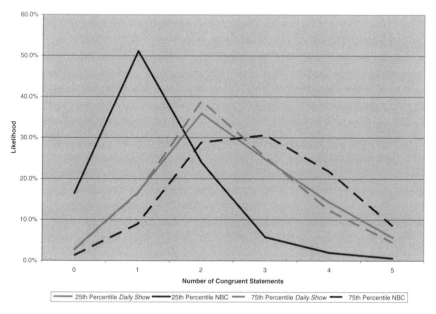
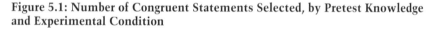

is that individuals assigned to *The Daily Show* condition chose about the same number of congruent statements regardless of their knowledge level. Participants at the twenty-fifth percentile of political knowledge had about a 36 percent chance of choosing two congruent statements, compared with a 38 percent chance among those at the seventy-fifth percentile of knowledge. At all other levels, the difference between the twenty-fifth and seventy-fifth percentiles is even smaller.

This is in sharp contrast to the participants in *The World News* condition. Participants at the twenty-fifth percentile of political knowledge have a two in three chance of choosing either zero or one congruent statement, while those at the seventy-fifth percentile have about a 10 percent chance of the same, and have a 60 percent chance of choosing three or more congruent statements.

There are also substantial differences within the individuals at the twenty-fifth percentile of political knowledge, based on the condition that they were assigned to. Participants with low political knowledge assigned to *The World News* condition pick significantly fewer congruent statements than those assigned to *The Daily Show* condition. In *The Daily Show* condition, low knowledge participants had a 55 percent chance of choosing two or fewer congruent statements; participants with the same level of knowledge assigned to *The World News* condition had a 92 percent chance of the same.

The differences between individuals at the seventy-fifth percentile based on the experimental condition were smaller. As would be expected from the regression coefficients, participants at the seventy-fifth percentile of political knowledge did better at identifying congruent statements when they were put in *The World News* condition. The difference is significant, but only marginally so, and is most obvious at the extremes. For instance, participants in *The World News* condition had a 30 percent chance of choosing four or five of the five congruent statements, while those assigned to *The Daily Show* condition had about a 17 percent chance.

Based solely on these results, however, we can't be sure that being assigned to *The Daily Show* condition is actually strengthening the knowledge structures of participants with low levels of political knowledge. While the results are consistent with participants being better able to identify what parties and representatives of those parties think and do after watching *The Daily*

Show, we have to remember that participants assigned to *The World News* condition did better at identifying statements that actually were in the articles, even if the effect was not significant. All participants chose eight statements, so if participants in *The World News* condition chose more correct statements, on average, than participants in *The Daily Show* condition, they would necessarily choose fewer congruent statements. This is why we have the second measure of the strength and consistency of the participant's political knowledge structures: the number of noncongruent statements that they chose. If it is the case that participants in *The World News* condition chose fewer congruent statements solely because they had chosen more correct statements, they should also choose fewer noncongruent statements. On the other hand, if individuals with low levels of political knowledge chose more noncongruent statements when in *The World News* condition, the attrition explanation—that they simply had fewer statements to choose—goes out the window.

As seen in Figure 5.2, the results of the analysis of the number of noncongruent statements chosen strongly support the strength-

Figure 5.2: Number of Noncongruent Statements Selected, by Pretest Knowledge and Experimental Condition

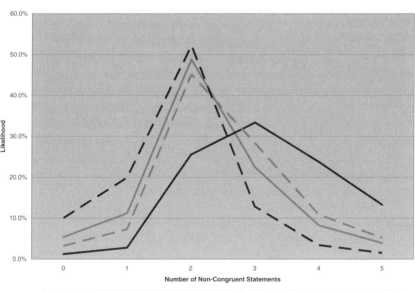

ening of political knowledge structures explanation. Among participants in the twenty-fifth percentile of political knowledge, participants assigned to *The Daily Show* condition chose far fewer noncongruent statements than participants randomly assigned to *The World News* condition. Participants at the twenty-fifth percentile in *The Daily Show* condition had a 65 percent chance of choosing two or fewer noncongruent statements, while those in *The World News* condition had only a 30 percent chance of doing so. There is a 37 percent chance that low-knowledge participants in *The World News* condition chose four or five noncongruent statements and only a 12 percent chance that a participant in *The Daily Show* condition did so.

In the seventy-fifth percentile, the difference between the two experimental conditions was rather smaller, though participants in *The World News* condition chose marginally fewer noncongruent statements. Fully 30 percent of respondents in *The World News* condition chose either zero or one noncongruent statement, compared with only 11 percent in *The Daily Show* condition.

Looking at the differences between participants at high and low levels of political knowledge within the same experimental condition, the results are similar to those of the analysis of the congruent statements. In both, political knowledge made little difference in the number of statements chosen by participants in *The Daily Show* condition, but had a substantial effect on those in *The World News* condition. In *The World News* condition, participants at the twenty-fifth percentile of political knowledge had a 30 percent chance of choosing two or fewer noncongruent statements. In contrast, participants at the seventy-fifth percentile of political knowledge assigned to *The World News* condition had an 82 percent chance of choosing two or fewer noncongruent statements.

From these two analyses, the larger results are clear. Prior political knowledge, as measured by the political figure identification items, has little effect on the ability of participants in *The Daily Show* condition to pick out congruent and noncongruent statements. Watching *The Daily Show* seems to level the playing field between high- and low-knowledge participants in a way that's entirely absent in *The World News* condition. High-knowledge participants in *The World News* seem to get far more information out of the broadcast than those participants with low levels of prior political knowledge.

If we're to ask which of the broadcasts does a better job of informing political knowledge structures, these results would seem to be a draw. Participants with low levels of political knowledge learn more when they're assigned to *The Daily Show*; those with high levels do better when they're assigned to a traditional news broadcast. However, there are other factors that have to be taken into consideration. First, the difference between participants in the two conditions with low levels of political knowledge is substantial, the difference between participants with high levels of political knowledge is not. As such, both broadcasts do about equally well at informing those who already have high levels of knowledge, but *The Daily Show* does much better among those with low levels of knowledge.

Second, it can be argued that informing individuals with already high levels of political knowledge simply isn't as difficult. Once an individual has a highly developed knowledge structure about some topic, be it politics, comic books, or quantum physics, they can leverage their existing knowledge to make sense of even fragmentary information. Individuals lacking such knowledge structures have a much more difficult time of it. For instance, a man reading the entire *Encyclopaedia Britannica* (as in Jacobs 2004) is going to learn a lot about subjects he already knows about, but learn very little about those things he doesn't know about, no matter how many pages he reads about chemistry or ancient history. The key is to establish the basic level of fluency that will allow for future learning, and *The Daily Show* seems to be doing a better job of that.

Third, young people, on the whole, are likely to be in the low-political-knowledge condition, so *The Daily Show* is expected to better serve their needs. All of the participants in our experiment were university undergraduates, and half of them were, necessarily, in the "high" political knowledge group. However, many of the participants were political science majors, and many of them were enrolled in upper-division courses on Congress or the presidency—making them far more knowledgeable about politics than the average young American, and, perhaps, Americans in general. Evidence about the ignorance of the American polity, relative to voters in other nations, is monumental (Hyman and Sheatsley 1947; Berelson, Lazarsfeld, and McPhee 1954; Delli Carpini, and Keeter 1991, 1993; Bennett 1996), so the ability to impart information to low-knowledge audiences is critical.

RESULTS: POST-TEST KNOWLEDGE

While the results of the second questionnaire, in which we measured how much participants had learned from the broadcasts, are very different from the results of the first, they complement each other well.

To begin the analysis, we've divided the ten questions on the posttest knowledge questionnaire (available in the appendix) into three categories. First are items that were included in the broadcast that the participant watched, second are those items that were not included, and third are the items that were implied, and we have very different expectations for each. For included items, the best predictor should be the participant's existing political knowledge, as measured in the pretest questionnaire. Those participants who know more about politics should be more able to make links between existing knowledge and that knowledge presented in the broadcast, and so should be more likely to remember it.

The number of not-included items answered correctly is analyzed mainly as a control. Again, the number of correct answers should be best predicted by the participants' preexisting political knowledge, but there is some reason to believe that experimental condition (especially as interacted with preexisting political knowledge) should have some effect. From the previous analyses, we know that exposure to *The Daily Show* leads participants to do better at tasks requiring integrated political knowledge structures. Individuals with better developed political knowledge structures should, in turn, be better able to recall knowledge that they have previously been exposed to, including information that was not actually present in the broadcast that they just saw.

A more direct test of the strength of participant's political knowledge structures comes from the number of implied questions that they are able to answer correctly. These implied items are two questions whose answers were not directly stated in either of the broadcasts, but could be deduced from either of them. The first was a factual question: "Which party currently controls Congress?" If they did not previously know the answer to this question, it could be deduced from the broadcast by noting the identity and demeanor of the individuals questioning Petraeus: someone aware of the stances of Republicans and Democrats on Iraq issues could easily tell that Democrats were

Table 5.3: Ordered Logit Analysis of Experimental Knowledge Results

Predictor	Included Items			Not Included Items			Implied Items		
	Coefficient	Std Error	Z	Coefficient	Std Error	Z	Coefficient	Std Error	Z
Experimental Condition	0.68	1.05	0.65	0.29	1.19	0.24	-2.27	1.34	-1.69
Pretest Knowledge	0.40	0.26	1.54	0.27	0.27	0.99	-0.15	0.31	-0.48
Condition × Pretest Knowledge	-0.08	0.19	-0.40	0.16	0.21	0.76	0.41	0.25	1.65
Cut 1	-0.23	1.42		-0.96	1.56		-3.35	1.74	
Cut 2	0.71	1.43		1.87	1.56		-0.35	1.66	
Cut 3	1.89	1.44		3.67	1.63				
Cut 4	3.11	1.46		5.03	1.68				
Cut 5	5.43	1.60							

in charge. The second of the implied items was a predictive question, on the likelihood that the president would follow General Petraeus's recommendations. While neither of the broadcasts came out and said that the White House would certainly follow Petraeus's recommendations, the strong endorsement of both Republicans and conservative media groups was clear in both.

Results from each of the three categories were analyzed using the same procedures as the analysis of the political knowledge structures (ordered logit) as in the previous set of analyses.[17]

As before, the raw regression coefficients are relatively difficult to parse. What's clear, however, is that the effects are much weaker on this set of dependent variables. In the first two analyses, only one of the predictors has even a marginally significant effect: individuals who knew more about politics in the pretest scale did better remembering items that had been included in the broadcast that they were exposed to. Even if it were treated as being significant (and it falls just short) it's hardly earthshattering.

What is striking, though, is the effect of the experimental condition and its interaction with pretest knowledge on the number of implied items that the participant was able to answer correctly. Both coefficients were significant, and in the expected direction. Their relative magnitude—the main effect is about five and a half times as large as the interaction effect, and in the opposite direction—implies that at low levels of knowledge (below five on the pretest knowledge scale) participants assigned to *The Daily Show* condition do better, and at high levels of knowledge, participants assigned to *The World News Tonight* condition do better: exactly the relationship seen in the previous analyses.

To understand the magnitude of these effects, however, we'll again turn to Monte Carlo simulations to translate the coefficients into percentages, as presented in Figure 5.3.

By looking at the solid lines in Figure 5.3, we can compare the results for individuals with low levels of knowledge assigned to the two conditions. The most obvious difference is in the proportion of respondents expected to get none of the implied items right. Almost half of participants in *The World News* condition missed both of the implied items, while a bit less than one in five of those in *The Daily Show* condition did the same. A full 21 percent of low-knowledge participants assigned to *The Daily Show* condition answered both of the items correctly, while only about

Figure 5.3: Number of Implied Questions Answered Correctly, by Pretest Knowledge and Experimental Condition

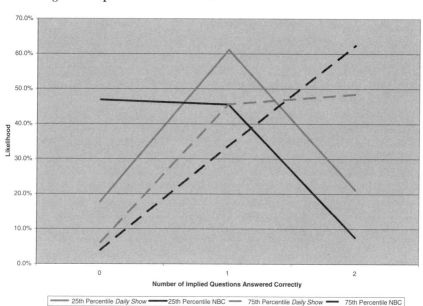

8 percent of those assigned to *The World News* condition were expected to.

Results for participants at the seventy-fifth percentile of pretest knowledge ran in the opposite direction, but with lesser magnitude, just as they did in the previous analyses. Few individuals at high levels of knowledge assigned to either condition were expected to get neither of the implied items correct, but high-knowledge participants assigned to *The World News* condition were expected to be more likely to get both of them right. A bit less than two in three of individuals at the seventy-fifth percentile assigned to *The World News* condition were expected to answer both of the implied items correctly, compared to about half of those in *The Daily Show* condition.

While the magnitude of this difference is smaller, it's important for what it tells us about the results. Rather than being a fluke—perhaps due to *The Daily Show* implying the items more strongly than the NBC broadcast—the results are due to the same mechanism that we observed in the previous analyses of political knowledge structures. Those participants who already knew a great deal about politics got more out of *The World News* broadcast, and those who didn't know much going in got a great deal more out of *The Daily Show*. Moreover, the fact that these differences came only in one of the three types of questions actually adds to our understanding of the first set of analyses. The increase in participants' ability to tell things that could have happened from things that could not have happened in the political arena wasn't increased because they learned more facts about the political figures and parties, but rather because they got an idea of their issue positions and viewpoints. As demonstrated by the results among the seventy-fifth percentile, Brian Williams and NBC do a better job of communicating facts than Jon Stewart, but that doesn't mean that they do a better job of communicating information about politics. The ideological nature of the broadcast, as hypothesized, makes it easier for participants in *The Daily Show* condition to identify trends and make predictions about political figures and parties: certainly a more valuable skill than the ability to recite facts.

CONCLUSION

Critics of *The Daily Show* are right, in some sense: it isn't journalism, in that it doesn't communicate discrete facts about the events of the day as well as traditional broadcast news outlets do. However, as our results have shown, it does serve a substantial educational purpose: giving viewers an idea not of what political groups and figures have done, but of what they are prone to do.

In the first chapter, we laid out some of the reasons why it's difficult for political independents to learn about politics, and they mostly stem from the inability of independents to bootstrap themselves into political knowledge. Partisans are able to learn about events by simplifying the political world into black and white. Political sophisticates can leverage their existing knowledge to make sense of things whether they're partisan or not. Nonpartisan political novices, however, don't have either of these options, and so don't get any information from watching traditional news sources: they simply don't have the level of existing knowledge necessary to make sense of what's being presented, much less the ability to put it in context. After watching one twenty-two minute episode of *The Daily Show*, a third of which didn't even deal with political matters, political novices had significantly stronger political knowledge structures than those viewing a traditional news broadcast. They were able to make judgments about what parties and individuals would and would not do in a given situation, and that's the sort of knowledge that they can leverage in the future.

In essence, the fact that they've formed expectations about what political figures would or would not do shows an understanding of their underlying motives. They were more likely to know, for instance, that Republicans would resist a firm deadline for withdrawal from Iraq, and that Democrats would want to put pressure on the Iraqi government. Now, it doesn't seem likely that this sort of understanding functions as well as more overtly partisan coverage, like that provided by Fox News. After all, parsing motives isn't as easy as identifying good guys and bad guys— but it does seem to work, and a relatively nonpartisan way of making the political world comprehensible is something we should certainly be interested in.

By no means is the audience of *The Daily Show* completely comprised of individuals with relatively little political sophistication. As we noted earlier, the median age of Stewart's viewers is thirty-five, and they're more likely to have a college degree than the average Fox News viewer. Being older, or having a college degree, doesn't guarantee that an individual is politically sophisticated, but it does mean that many of the viewers are turning to Stewart for entertainment, rather than for news. In doing so, as our results show, these sophisticated viewers are getting less information than they would from watching standard news programming. However, this isn't really a fair comparison: a better one would be to compare how much these viewers learn from other entertainment oriented programs on at 11 PM on weekdays. By that metric, Stewart certainly comes out on top.

We should also address the question of whether or not *The Daily Show* actually changes anyone's mind about political issues. We don't have any direct evidence that participants in the experiment who were put in *The Daily Show* condition change their minds about political issues, but there is substantial evidence for indirect persuasion. The experiment showed that watching even one episode of Stewart's program significantly affects participants' expectations about political figures and parties. Now this, by itself, may or may not change anyone's mind: but it certainly makes it more likely that they will change their mind in the future. In social psychology terms, we would say that the success of *The Daily Show* in creating expectations has framed the issues in such a way that viewers will tend to understand new political information in a way consistent with the way past information has been presented by Stewart. Viewers learn to think about Republicans and Democrats, Bush and Pelosi, in a certain way, and use those expectations to understand their actions in the future. If anything, this sort of indirect persuasion is more powerful than direct persuasion techniques, which can be easily identified and rejected by the recipient of a message.

Most important, though, is not the success of Stewart's program as an informational source, or in persuading viewers to adopt a certain political viewpoint. All of this only matters to the extent that it succeeds as a brand that young people are willing— even eager—to associate themselves with. Unlike nearly all of the other informational sources we asked about in our surveys and interviews, respondents generally knew about *The Daily Show*, and, regardless of their political beliefs, held generally positive views of it. Our respondents had never watched Fox News, and didn't even know what NPR was, but Stewart's program was "cool." This is the real paradox of *The Daily Show*. The entertainment aspects of it mean that it isn't as good an information source as traditional newscasts, but it is those same aspects that make it acceptable as a brand. It doesn't directly endorse a partisan point of view, but its indirect persuasion is more effective than partisan messages. It's not the best information source for all of its viewers, but for the young, relatively low-information audience that we're concerned with, it is by far the best.

6
What Does Tomorrow Hold?

MAJOR THEORIES OF POLITICAL SOCIALIZATION—HOW YOUNG people learn to function in the political sphere—have pointed to the critical role of events in young people's political development. David O. Sear's work on this point (Sears et al. 1974) argues that young people's learning about politics is a discontinuous process, spurred on by a desire to understand what's going on in the political events they hear discussed by family and friends and in the media. These events, therefore, can have a disproportionate impact on the political views of those young people going forward. To the extent that today's events are informing the political views of the next generation of voters, we can leverage what we know about the effect of those events to give us some idea of what is going to happen years from now. To use the terminology that we've developed over the past five chapters, the political figures and events of the present day have the potential to become a permanent part of the brand associated with a party, and if we know how a party's brand is perceived, we can draw conclusions about that party's future success. While we're not going to attempt to predict the outcome of any particular election—only a few political scientists are brave enough to do that[1]—we can use what we've uncovered in the previous chapters to make more general predictions about the nation's political direction.

We can do this by combining two key insights into how individuals change their minds about politics, and, especially, the key to their political behavior, party identification. The importance of partisanship in understanding political attitudes, behaviors, and outcomes is such that any glimpse into what the partisanship of tomorrow will look like can tell us an enormous amount about who will control the Congress, the presidency, and where the country is going.

177

The first of these insights comes from macropartisanship. We briefly mentioned macropartisanship theory in chapter 1, but it's worth revisiting now. Like so much other recent work in political science, macropartisanship begins with the understanding that voters really don't know very much about politics. Representative democracy requires that voters at least be able to remove bad incumbents from office, but voters often don't even know who the incumbents are, much less whether they're doing a good job or not.

Macropartisanship takes an interesting tack on the problem. Rather than assuming that people know more than they can tell us—like Milton Lodge's online processing model,[2] or Marcus's affective intelligence theory—it assumes that the public can respond rationally without knowing very much. All people really have to know is whether things are going too far toward one extreme or the other and adjust themselves accordingly. So, if the country seemed too liberal during the 1960s, with the sudden expansions in civil rights and social programs, enough individuals would become more conservative to throw the balance the other way. If society became too conservative in the aftermath, we would expect the pendulum to swing back. This isn't necessarily the result of any individuals having huge changes in their views or attitudes, though it could be. Rather, it could simply be the result of an accumulation of small changes over time. So, even if individuals don't really know what's going on in politics, small shifts based on the general tone of the country can be enough to create a responsive *public*, if not responsive individuals.

According to macropartisanship theory, these changes should be visible in the balance of the parties in the public. Too much liberalism should lead to more Republicans and fewer Democrats, and vice versa. While the originators of the theory have provided substantial evidence for these swings in the public as a whole, individual-level evidence is harder to come by. First off, this is essentially a hypothesis that things change over time, so individual-level evidence requires that we follow individuals for multiple surveys over the course of months or years: an expensive proposition. Second, if we were to ask them the same questions again and again over time, it would be difficult or impossible to tell the difference between the sorts of meaningful changes that macropartisanship theory is talking about and random, meaningless changes. This problem of measurement error means that we're going to have to follow those individuals for even longer, and we still won't even be sure that we have meaningful results.

This doesn't mean, though, that we can't test the macropartisanship hypothesis. To do it, though, we'll need to bring in another concept central to how political scientists understand people's reasoning about politics: Bayesian models. Generally, Bayesian models of behavior are derived from a mathematical formula credited to Reverend Thomas Bayes (it's been suggested that mathematician Nicholas Saunderson developed it first, but "Saundersonian reasoning" just doesn't have the same ring to it), which details how to determine the probability of something happening, given what has already happened. While this is directly applied to statistical models, where Bayesian approaches are favored over the more common frequentist approaches of conventional statistics, its indirect application to models of thinking and behavior is no less important.

A Bayesian approach to information processing would hold that new information is more valuable to someone who doesn't know very much than it is to someone who already knows a lot about the issue in question. Suppose you go to a restaurant have an awful experience—bad service, you have to send back your food—whatever annoys you most. Will you go back? Well, it depends on your previous experiences at that restaurant. If it's your first time there, you'll probably figure that any future trips are going to be like the bad one and avoid the place. If you've been there a dozen times before without any problems, you may very well go back.

Using the same logic, a young person might be more likely to change his or her party than an older person with similar political views. An older Republican, for instance, might not like the way the Republican party is going now, but has seen enough bad times come and go to hold on to their partisanship even in the bad times. A younger Republican who hasn't been so inoculated might well be more likely to become independent, or even a Democrat.

So, if people are changing their partisanship in response to new political information, those individuals with less prior information about the parties should be most likely to change, and we can identify two such groups. The first is people who don't pay much attention to politics: since they don't have much information to begin with, any new information that they're exposed to should have a bigger effect. This would be something along the lines of "Oh, *that's* what Republicans are." The problem, of course, in looking for changes in the partisanship of people who don't know much about politics is that they're not—by definition—very likely to be exposed to new information. Unless we can bring them into a lab, make them to take a class, or by some other means force them to be exposed to politics, there's no reason to expect that they'll be doing any updating at all. On top of this, people with relatively little political information are also the most likely to be subject to the measurement error problem mentioned earlier. Because they have less full notions of what it means to be a member of a party, and less attachment to the parties, they're more likely to change their announced partisanship without a real reason.

We'll focus our attempts on the second group that's most likely to be subject to macropartisanship effects: young people. While they're not necessarily any less interested in politics than people who have been following it for some time, they do have less political information at their disposal. There is substantial empirical evidence that young people are more likely to change their political views than older individuals and that highly salient events have a greater impact on them than on adults (see Hershey and Hill 1975; Sigel 1965; Converse 1966; and Sellers 1965). Additional support for this view could come from politician's frequent reports that a particularly dramatic political event during their childhood or adolescence instantly crystallized their political views, though it isn't clear how much credence should be given to such stories.[3]

So, if macropartisanship theory and theories about young people's political socialization hold, young people should be more likely than their older counterparts to change their partisanship (Converse 1969 and Campbell et al. 1960 reach the same conclusion, though for different reasons). Additionally, since older people are less likely to change their partisanship, changes made when an individual is young have the potential to be very longlasting. If we can see how current events are changing young people's partisanship today, we may be able to get a good idea of what their views will look like in the future.

Of course, this doesn't resolve the already mentioned problems that arise from any test of macropartisanship. If we want to see how people are changing their partisanship in response to political events, we have to somehow introduce new political events. Outside a laboratory, there isn't much way to do this. Inside a laboratory, there's no guarantee that the task will be realistic enough to give us applicable results. Since we also can't just sit and wait for events to change, we have to change them ourselves, and do so in the field, outside a controlled laboratory setting. To do this, we'll make use of an experimental priming survey.

We'll get into the process of how this works shortly. First though, we should explain what these surveys are like. We use a standard telephone survey, in which people are contacted randomly, and all of the respondents get the same questions. However, some of the respondents get the questions in a different order. About half of the respondents, chosen randomly, are asked questions about national issues like the war in Iraq and President Bush's job performance at the very beginning of the survey, while others are asked the same questions toward the end, just before they're asked standard questions about their party identification. Those people who are reminded about their views on these national issues should be more likely to bring their views on these issues to bear on the partisanship question. For instance, when someone says that they are against the war in Iraq, and is then asked about their partisanship, they should be less likely to say that they're a Republican, and more likely to say that they're a Democrat, solely because they've been reminded of their view of the war. We can see how big this difference is by comparing the partisanship of people who were asked about Iraq, and other issues, just beforehand with those who feel the same way about the issues, but weren't reminded of them just beforehand.

How Does the Priming Work?

Before we can trust the results of this sort of priming experiment, we should understand exactly how it works. We have to start with the understanding that the human brain—at least the prefrontal cortex—is designed to be a mind-reading device. It's generally very good at looking at other people and predicting what they're thinking, and what they're going to do. So, if someone smiles at you, you can tell that they're friendly. If they're scowling, you know to watch your back. This skill is so vital to humans that those people with a deficiency in it—those with autism, Asperger's, and related disorders—often have severe problems fitting into society.

Our own understanding of why we do what we do ourselves is based on this same skill. It's been proven pretty conclusively in experiments by psychologists like Benjamin Libet that we understand our own motives and actions in much the same way that we understand other people's motives and actions. We observe our actions and emotions and make inferences about how we feel. It's been shown, for instance, that people who are asked to hold a pencil in their mouth, without the pencil touching their lips, think a cartoon is funnier than those people who aren't holding the pencil in such a way. Apparently, the brain notices that the mouth is mimicking the shape of a smile and so thinks the cartoon must have been funny. In a similar experiment, Stanford psychologist Robert Zajonc showed that while people prefer Chinese ideograms based on how often they've seen them in an experiment, they're more than willing to offer up detailed reasons for their liking that have nothing to do with having seen it before. All the subjects in the experiment know is which of the ideograms they like. When they're asked why, all they can do is make up a plausible story, in the same way that they'd make up a story to explain why someone else might like or dislike it.

While it may not seem like it, this has a lot to do with how people answer questions about their partisanship. The bottom line is that people don't have privileged access to their own thought processes. There is, in essence, no correct answer to questions like partisanship. People with more political expertise and knowledge are likely to be more stable in their responses over time and weather the ins and outs of everyday politics because their partisanship is important to them: they talk about it, and think about it, and remember what they said. It isn't that they "are" Democrats, or Republicans, or whatnot, but rather that they know that they have been a member of that party in the past and should probably continue to be so unless there's a good reason not to. Like any piece of factual knowledge, it's easy to forget if it isn't relevant or it doesn't come up for a while.

Really, all that people can do is tell you, when pressed, is what sorts of things Republicans and Democrats should think or do, vote for or support. They can then look at themselves, and decide whether their thoughts, or actions, their vote choices or issue positions are consistent with one party or the other. If they've got a lot of political savvy, they can explain any inconsistencies away, making appeals to higher principles or past leaders—libertarian Republicans who may be in favor of drug legalization or Reagan Democrats who support a stronger military. If they don't have that savvy, or a strong history with one party or the other, then an inconsistency between what they've been before and what they think a member of a party should do now may lead them to change positions.

In essence, when people are answering questions about their partisanship, they're doing just that, answering questions.[4] So, if we want to analyze their answers to these questions, we have to bring to bear everything that we know about how people respond to surveys. Our understanding of how people answer questions is based on two concepts: considerations and affect.

First, let's talk a little bit about how memory works. *Memory* can refer to two different things. The first is long-term memory, often abbreviated LTM. Long-term memory is the storage space for all of the information that we've built up over a lifetime and is pretty close to infinite in storage capacity. In computer terms, this would be the hard drive.

Of course, as any computer tech would you tell you, it doesn't matter how big the hard drive is if there isn't the RAM to access it. In the brain, that RAM—short term, rewritable storage—is short-term, or working memory (WM).[5] This represents the amount of information that we can access at one time, and is generally thought to be limited to about seven discrete chunks of information. So, for instance, you can generally hold a phone number (sans area code) in mind by just repeating it to yourself—until something distracts you, pushing one or more of those numbers out of working memory. The size of one of these chunks of information is also pretty variable: "seven," "386," and "the Constitution of the United States," could each easily be one chunk.

Inside long-term memory, we represent each of these chunks of knowledge as nodes in a vast network, connected to each other like Kevin Bacon in six degrees of separation. When one node[6] gets fired up for any reason, all of the nodes that are connected to it get fired up as well. It doesn't really matter why that particular node was fired up: the node representing "Hillary Clinton," for instance, could get fired up when you see a picture of her, hear her name mentioned, or even see something about her husband, Bill. Once that node gets activated, all of the nodes that are associated with it get a lower level of activation, with the exact degree of that activation depending on the closeness of the nodes. If, in the past, two things have almost always gone together —like "Bill Clinton" and "Hillary Clinton"—the activation of one will activate the other to an almost identical degree. If the two aren't that closely associated in someone's mind—say "Bill Clinton" and a lesser known associate like "Donna Shalala"— the activation of the linked node will be markedly less. On the macro level, then, we can say that the association between Bill Clinton and Hillary Clinton means that Bill is a necessary component of Hillary's brand, and whatever he does will necessarily reflect back on her. These sort of links are also self-sustaining: even if Hillary decided to divorce Bill, the association between the two would remain strong among those people for whom it already existed.

This sort of connection between two nodes is called semantic linkage, because it's based on the meanings of the nodes, but it isn't the only type of linkage between the nodes. There's also a network of associations between nodes that runs parallel to he semantic linkages, based on how good or bad the node is considered to be. That is, if the node representing something really bad gets activated in long-term memory—say "cancer," "poison," or "cockroach,"—the activation spreads to all of the other bad things in LTM. So, hearing about a friend being diagnosed with cancer will activate the nodes representing "death" and "poison," but also negative nodes that have no semantic association with cancer, like "Hitler," "war," or, depending on your political persuasion, "Bill Clinton" or "George Bush." As with semantic associations, the extent to which the affectively connected nodes are activated depends on the degree of similarity. Hangnails are bad, but not quite on the level of cancer, so the activation of "hangnail" would be less than that of "death" or other *really* bad nodes.[7]

We call this process—for both semantic and affective associations—spreading activation, and it doesn't stop with one node activating all of the related nodes. Once those nodes are activated, they necessarily activate all of the nodes associated in any way with themselves, including the node that initially fired. Which then fires again, at slightly reduced strength. In such a way, a node that's activated doesn't stop being so immediately;

instead, the level of activation decreases slowly over time. This particular characteristic turns out to be very important, as it means that a node that was previously activated is more likely to be brought into working memory than one that has not been recently activated.

Now, we're constantly being bombarded by information, so long-term memory is a cacophony of nodes firing up and spreading activation to related nodes and that activation colliding with the activation spreading from other nodes. Those few—again, about seven—nodes that, at any given time, have the highest level of activation are pushed into working memory. It is these chunks, and only these few, that reach the level of our conscious awareness. We are, on some level, thinking about all of the other nodes that are activated, but we're simply not aware of it. It should be clear, though, that the nodes that make it into working memory are the result of an enormous—and enormously complex—process that regulates and biases that information.[8]

The major source of that bias is the affective association network. While affective connections between nodes in LTM are far weaker than the semantic associations, they ensure that the chunks that make it into WM will generally be on the same side of whatever it is we're thinking about. While the affective and semantic association networks run parallel to each other, their effects are additive. So, suppose there are two nodes semantically associated with "Bill Clinton": "nineties economic boom" and "Lewinsky scandal." The concept represented by each of these semantically associated nodes could be reasons to like or dislike Clinton: what we refer to as considerations. Which of these consideration is more likely to come into working memory? If they're equally associated semantically, then depends on the affective associations of "Bill Clinton." If the person likes Clinton, the addition of the activation due to the semantic association with "Bill Clinton" and the affective association with "Bill Clinton" should make "nineties economic boom" (a positive node) more likely to make the jump into WM. If Clinton is regarded negatively, the negative node "Lewinsky scandal" would be more likely to enter consciousness. So, when someone thinks about Bill Clinton, the things that come to mind are likely to be things that agree with how the person thinks, generally, about him. For people who like Clinton, the economic boom, or decline in crime rates, or social security reform are likely to come to mind. Among those who don't like him, the Lewinsky scandal or the Mark Rich pardon are more likely to come to mind. Of course, people aren't going to go through this process every time they're asked about Bill Clinton. People who've thought about it before are likely to have learned that they like him or dislike him, and their responses to the question "Do you like Bill Clinton?" are more likely to elicit declarative responses, with "I like him" being shorthand for "I know that I like him." Even if we were to ask them to really think about why they liked or disliked him, it wouldn't change anything: affective connections would ensure that people who like him would think of positive things and people who dislike him would think of negative things. No one, in the end, changes their mind.

When it comes to a less familiar question, though, things are a bit different. In the absence of a learned answer, people have to go through process of tallying up considerations. So, the unfamiliar object of evaluation—New Mexico governor Bill Richardson, for instance—is activated, and the seven or so most highly activated nodes come into WM. These considerations are tallied up, and if they're generally positive, then the person reports liking Richardson. If they're generally negative, the person reports disliking Richardson. As we've seen, the considerations that form that evaluation in working memory are not necessarily representative of all of the relevant considerations in long-term memory. They're biased by a number of factors, with affect being chief among them. If Richardson is more related to positive than negative things in the affective association system, then positive nodes semantically related to Richardson are more likely to be brought into working memory. When people who like Richardson think about him, more positive things come to mind, and the more they like him, the stronger the bias will be, and the less likely that anything that comes to mind will contradict the existing affect. The respondent averages out everything that's in working memory and reports liking or disliking Richardson, then proceeds to remember that response, which will be stored and recalled later.

Left unchecked, this leads to a snowballing effect. Those that like a candidate come to like him or her more, and those that don't like a candidate come to like him or her less. It is, however, possible to check this process. If, for some reason, a node that is at odds with the affect associated with the node being evaluated is activated for some reason other than their semantic connection, the evaluation can change. For instance, new information could change someone's evaluation. If the individual in our example learns something new about Richardson—say a sex scandal, or something equally memorable—that information will almost certainly come to mind when he or she is asked to evaluate Richardson, regardless of the esteem in which Richardson is otherwise held. With this new, presumably negative, information in the mix of considerations brought into working memory, the overall evaluation of Richardson will be more negative than before. This evaluation will then be stored in LTM, and negative affect nodes will be more likely to be activated the next time Richardson is evaluated.

New information isn't the only reason that a node might be more likely than usual to be brought into WM. Remember that when a node is activated, the level of activation falls off relatively slowly, rather than shutting off all at once. So, a node that's semantically related with the one being evaluated but has been recently activated is likely to be brought into WM for the evaluation despite any discrepancy with how much the object of evaluation is normally liked or disliked. So, no matter how much you like Bill Clinton, having a discussion about the Lewinsky scandal will lead, at least temporarily, to a more negative evaluation of him.[9] This property of evaluations—especially relatively unlearned evaluations that have to be constructed on the fly— means that we can change evaluations simply by reminding individuals of some consideration semantically related to the object being evaluated. However, it's important to be subtle about it. When people know that their evaluations are being pushed up or down by some factor that may not be relevant to them, they can easily correct for it.[10] Responses to the question, "How do you feel about Bill Clinton?" will be almost identical to responses to, "Given the Lewinsky scandal, how do you feel about Bill Clinton?" Respondents can recognize that their evaluation of Clinton is temporarily more negative because of the mention of Lewinsky, and correct for it. We can expect responses to change when we remind respondents of something only when they don't know that they've been reminded.

All told, this isn't actually very difficult. Respondents tend to forget what questions they've been asked pretty quickly: far quicker than the activation of the nodes brought into play by those questions dies down. So, asking people their opinion of the Lewinsky scandal—or any question that activates the node representing "Lewinsky scandal"—then, a little later, asking them about Clinton will make it more likely that the Lewinsky scandal will come to mind in their evaluation of Clinton, without giving them the opportunity to correct for the temporarily increased salience of the Lewinsky scandal. As such, their responses will be equivalent to what they would be if the Lewinsky scandal were chronically salient, if it were one of the things that always came to mind when the respondent was evaluating Clinton. If half of the people in the sample were subtly reminded of the Lewinsky scandal in such a way, and the other half were not, the difference between the two groups would tell us the minimum impact the Lewinsky scandal has on people's evaluations of Clinton.[11]

We can do the same with questions about party identification. For people who haven't thought about it too much, who don't have an answer without having to construct it on the fly, a subtle reminder can lead them to treat a consideration as if it were always present. By reminding people of President Bush and the war in Iraq, we can simulate what their party identification would be if Bush and Iraq always came to mind when answering the question.

WATERGATE AND IRAQ

This lasting association between a scandal and a party is far from unprecedented in American politics. For decades after the Civil War, Republicans were able to maintain control of the presidency by "waving the bloody shirt." Democrats were the party of the Civil War and the South, and reminding voters in Northern and border states was enough to keep the Republican Party in the White House almost continuously from Lincoln's election in 1860 until Wilson's victory in 1912. Even that victory came as the result of a split in the Republican vote caused the entry of Teddy Roosevelt as a "Bull Moose" Progressive. For a large segment of the population, it seems, the Civil War had become part of the brand of the Democratic Party, who thereafter rejected it out of hand.

More recently, there's evidence that the Vietnam War had a lasting impact on the likelihood of people identifying themselves with the Democratic Party. Before Vietnam, the Democratic Party was more trusted on issues of foreign relations and war than the Republicans. It was, after all, Democratic presidents who had led the country through the two world wars, and Democrats who represented internationalism against the isolationism of old-line Republicans.[12] Since the debacle of Vietnam, for which Democrats shouldered most of the blame, the situation has reversed, as voters trusted Republicans on matters of defense and foreign relations far more than Democrats until very recently.[13]

Perhaps the biggest effect of an event on partisanship in recent years, though, comes from the Watergate scandal. It may seem as though the effect of the scandal on the electorate was clear: in 1974, Democrats gained forty-nine seats in the House and four in the Senate, the biggest loss for the president's party since the deep recession of 1958 when Eisenhower was president. Even within the Republican Party, it was conservatives (according to *Congressional Quarterly*'s 1974 election postmortem) and Nixon supporters[14] who were most likely to suffer from the scandal at the ballot box. However, scholarly analyses seemed to show that the Republican's losses in the 1974 midterm weren't the result of Watergate, or even the rapid deterioration of the economy, but rather the candidates who chose to run for office. Jacobson and Kernell (1981) argue that when the situation looks grim for one party, as it did for the Republicans in 1964, candidates who have been waiting in the wings to run for that party typically postpone their entry into higher elective office, preferring to stay on as a city councilman or district attorney to losing a race for Congress.[15] The qualified candidates waiting in the wings for the opposite party, on the other hand, jump at the chance to enter a race with favorable national conditions. Fundraisers, too, tend to sit out elections that look unfavorable, making it difficult for these less qualified candidates to raise money, resulting in a campaign death spiral that would be difficult for anyone to transcend. According to this model, voters didn't turn to Democrats because of Watergate, but simply voted for the better qualified candidates, who happened to be Democrats. The only real punishment of the Republican Party came not from the hands of voters, but from the candidates who chose not to run, and the contributors who chose to wait for another year.

While Jacobson and Kernell's candidate selection theory certainly explains some of the reason why Democrats did so well in the wake of Watergate, it's important to remember that the absence of evidence is not evidence of absence. In this case, it isn't surprising that we'd have difficulty finding effects of Watergate on vote choice. Uslaner and Conway (1985) point out that 52.7 percent of voters in the 1972 congressional elections voted for Democratic candidates. If these voters wanted to punish Republicans for the Watergate scandal, their only option was to vote for Democratic candidates again. Since voting is a dichotomous outcome—the ballot box doesn't ask how strongly someone feels about their candidate—we could easily be missing the real effects. To address this, Uslaner and Conway separately examine the vote choices of individuals with stable party identifications versus those with unstable party identifications: what Key (1966) referred to as "switchers" and "stand-patters." Not surprisingly, they find that Watergate had very little effect on the stand-patters: if you're a Republican, and you've been a Republican, you keep voting for Republicans, and the same for Democrats. However, Watergate had a much greater effect on those individuals with unstable party identifications. For these voters, the effect of the Watergate on vote choice was a bit more than three times as great as it was for those voters with stable party identifications. Trust in government, and feelings toward Richard Nixon, too, had much stronger effects. According to these results, Watergate's effect on the electorate was largely indirect. People for whom party identification was unstable were more likely to become Democrats and Republicans during this period, so Democrats picked up seats.

Additional support for this can be found in Helmut Norpoth and Jerry Rusk's analysis of the increasing number of independents in the wake of the Watergate scandal (Norpoth and Rusk 1982). While they find that the partisanship of individuals who had been voting for some time remained largely unchanged by the uncertainty and scandal of the 1960s and early 1970s, there was a substantial impact on the partisanship of younger voters, who were more likely to identify themselves as independents or Democrats than voters in older cohorts.

These findings fit in nicely with our cognitive model of how people answer questions about party identification. People with strong, stable party identification remember how they answered questions about party identification before and aren't likely to change for anything, even something like Watergate. Those with less stable party identifications are more likely to have to construct their answer from whatever comes to working memory at the time, and it's difficult to imagine that Watergate wouldn't be on the mind of someone answering questions about politics in 1974.

We want to know, though, about the lasting impact of something like Watergate on partisanship in the electorate. After all, if the effects of the scandal are mostly on the switchers—the people with less stable political views to begin with—who's to say that they won't switch back soon afterward, perhaps in response to the OPEC embargo or the Iran hostage crisis? We've already made the case for why this shouldn't happen. Every time people answer a question about their partisanship, the position should become more stable, and the more people learn about politics, the more stable their answers should become. For an individual with any exposure to political information, the simple passage of time should be enough to create greater stability.

Sorting out the long-term effects of Watergate on partisanship requires the use of time series models. Such models are similar to those we presented in the first chapter, in which we isolated the baseline levels of partisanship to determine the impact economic factors on young people's political views. Mackuen, Erikson, and Stimson's (1989) initial article on macropartisanship does just this, controlling for all of the factors that we know lead to changes in partisanship, like the economy and presidential approval, then determining the size of the fluctuation in that expected level that coincides with Watergate and can't be explained by other factors. All told, Mackuen, Erikson, and Stimson's analysis finds that Watergate reduced the expected number of Republicans by about six points compared to what it would have been otherwise.[16] More importantly, unlike factors such as consumer sentiment and presidential approval, the effect of Watergate did not fade quickly. While the effect of today's economy on partisanship seems to go away in about six months and the effect of today's presidential approval in about six weeks, the effects of Watergate seem to be permanent. Now Mackuen, Erikson, and Stimson don't attempt to separate out the differential effects of Watergate on partisanship by individual characteristics like age or stability of partisanship—indeed their dataset is incapable of making such divisions—but the point is the same. There were six points—around 20 percent—fewer Republicans in the wake of Watergate than there would have been had the scandal not happened, and that six point drop didn't simply fade away, but almost certainly contributed to the Democratic domination of Congress (if not the presidency) that continued for twenty years afterward.

In this permanent effect, the Watergate scandal stands almost unique in recent history. Other events that have altered people's partisanship have had far shorter impacts. For instance, Lebo and Cassino's (2007) analysis shows that the effect of the first Gulf War—which pushed George H. W. Bush's approval to over 90 percent—only lasted about three months. While it may be too early to fully assess the long-term impact of the attacks of September 11 on American politics and partisanship, preliminary evidence from the same study seems to show its effects disappearing in advance of the beginning of the war in Iraq. Again, we can understand how this works by going back to our cognitive model of the partisanship question. As important as the Gulf War was as it was going on, it ceased being a political issue shortly thereafter. The war itself was over with quickly, and the both the politicians and the polity moved on to other issues, most notably the economy. Despite President Bush's increasingly desperate attempts to draw attention to his success in the Gulf, it seems that it simply wasn't what came to mind when people who had to think about their answers were asked about their party identification. Similarly, while the country rallied around President George W. Bush after the attacks of September 11, the political aspect of the attacks shifted from our response to the attacks to the broader war on terror, an issue that quickly soured with much of the public.

The difference between these events and Watergate—and, we'll argue, the current war in Iraq—is the duration of the relevance of the event. The nodes representing events like Watergate and September 11 become associated with a party through a process called "wire by fire." That is, the more often two nodes are simultaneously activated, the closer the semantic association between the two nodes becomes. This means that the duration of the event is of critical importance. An event that is politically relevant for a few months—like September 11 and the first Gulf War—simply isn't around long enough to become closely associated with the node representing the party. As such, it's easily pushed out by the next issue to capture the public's attention.

An issue that's relevant for years at a time, on the other hand, is going to gain a very tight semantic association with the party, be more likely to come to mind when voters think about the parties, and thus have a permanent impact on those voters that have to think about the question. This is the critical difference. The Civil War created a generation of Republicans, the Depression a generation of Democrats, and Watergate—to a lesser extent—a time of Democratic dominance because of the duration of the event. Several years of intense media coverage and public interest came between the initial revelation of the break-in and the end of the scandal with Ford's pardon of Nixon—an action that then itself became the subject of debate and scrutiny. The first Gulf War, on the other hand, stopped being politically relevant once it was over, and people returned to thinking about the economy. This isn't to say that there's some critical point—six months, a year, five years—past which a political event will have a permanent effect on the partisan balance. On an individual level, the length of time that the association has to be reinforced before becoming self-sustaining will depend on how many other associations there are. As before, the more someone knows about politics, the harder it is to make partisanship change. By any standard, though, the war in Iraq is at, or near that point. As of this writing, we are nearing the fifth anniversary of the invasion, meaning we've been in Iraq longer than the duration of the Civil War or our involvement in the Second World War. Of course, the War in Iraq is not as immediate a reality to the majority of our citizens as either of those two conflicts were, but Watergate makes for a good comparison. Both had little direct impact on everyday life—there was no rationing due to the scandal—but dominated the news cycle and political debate of the time. At the very least, we can expect the war in Iraq to have the same sort of long-term impact on partisanship that Mackuen, Erikson, and Stimson (1989) find for Watergate.

The biggest potential problem with this argument is the increasing fragmentation of media, which was simply not as much of an issue during the Watergate era. The effects of Watergate on partisanship could be larger than what would be expected from any scandal today simply because people can now choose to consume the information that matches what they want to believe. Republicans who want to believe that everything is going swimmingly may be able to turn to Fox News, while Democrats can turn to Daily Kos for a pessimistic view. If everyone is simply choosing the media source that fits them, there should be no reason for people to change parties. However, it must be remembered that not everyone can choose media in this way. Selecting the programs and arguments that will fit in with an individual's preconceived notions requires some degree of sophistication. The people that are most likely to be able to reinforce their own views in such a way are those who already have some degree of knowledge, and these aren't the people that we think should be affected by these events in the first place. The effects—to the extent that they occur—should be among those individuals who, for whatever reason, are just now learning about the parties and forming their associations. By the time someone knows to get all of their news from Fox News, they're not going to be changing their minds regardless.

The Impact of Iraq

So far, we know that we can determine the impact of an issue like the war in Iraq by subtly making that issue temporarily more likely to be brought into working memory. This simulates the effect of that issue being chronically accessible—in other words, a permanent part of a party's brand. If we randomly remind half of a sample about the war, and don't remind the rest, we can determine how much people's views would change if the war was chronically accessible to everyone. Finally, there is good reason to believe that this impact will be longlasting, as the duration of the war as a political issue makes it much more similar to Watergate than to events with a fading impact, like the Gulf War or the attacks of September 11. What remains now is to estimate this impact, and see what conclusions can be drawn about the long-term effects of the war on the parties.

The priming study took place over the course of four separate polls taken of likely voters in New Jersey in advance of the 2006 midterm elections.[17] For our purposes, New Jersey makes a good testing ground because of the hotly contested Senate race then underway. While Democrats had long dominated state politics, there was every indication that Republicans stood a chance at winning the Senate seat. First, while Democratic Bob Menendez was an incumbent, he had never previously won statewide political office. Rather, he was appointed to his seat just months earlier by Jon Corzine, who had decided to give up a seat in the Senate for the governorship. Second, what voters did know about Menendez wasn't at all positive. Menendez was associated with Hudson County machine politics and had done little to differentiate himself from them. Hudson County was the site of some of the most rampant corruption in a state known for shady politics, to the extent that the federal government stopped accepting documents issued by the Hudson County government as proof of anything in 2004. Third, even if Menendez's challenger, Tom Kean Jr. wasn't well known of his own right, he was the son of a popular former governor who had recently achieved national prominence through his service on the blue-ribbon commission investigating the attacks of September 11, 2001. All told, New Jersey was a bright spot for Republicans nationwide during the debacle of the 2006 midterm elections, and the national party poured millions into advertising in an effort to help Kean gain the seat. Finally, there was some concern that Menendez's Hispanic ethnic background and ties to the Cuban community in south Florida could alienate both white and African American voters.

It was thought that Kean's biggest obstacle to gaining the Senate seat was his support of the war in Iraq. While he made some effort during the campaign to differentiate himself from the president—calling for the resignation of Secretary of Defense Donald Rumsfeld, for instance—he remained an advocate of the war and of the president's strategy in it. Menendez, on the other hand, was a strong critic. While in the House, he had voted against the authorization for the war and frequently referred to it as one of the most important votes of his career.

Politics and the war in Iraq were very much on the minds of New Jersey voters, and, as we'll see, increasingly so as the election grew closer. Half of respondents, randomly chosen, were asked questions about President Bush and the war in Iraq[18] at the beginning of the survey, approximately ten minutes before being asked about their partisanship, and half were asked a series of questions about Bush and Iraq just before the questions on partisanship.[19] The group that was reminded of Bush and Iraq should have views equal to what their views would be if the Republican Party were chronically linked to Iraq, in the way that they were, in the past, linked to Watergate.

RESULTS

Typically, experiments require only minimal statistical analyses. After all, in an experiment like the priming experiments being discussed here, the difference between the two groups should be a result solely of which condition the respondent was put into. Since the groups are assigned randomly, the demographic factors that are generally so important to predicting people's views shouldn't matter.

However, we're not predicting a difference between the groups based solely on the assignment to being primed to think about Iraq or not. Rather, we expect that the condition that a respondent is put into should have a different effect depending on certain preexisting factors. For instance, someone who thinks that everything in the country is going well and approves of President Bush and the war in Iraq should be more likely to identify with the Republican Party when primed. On the other hand, an individual who disapproves of Bush and the war in Iraq should be more likely to identify with the Democratic Party when primed. We also have to take into account the age of the respondents, as young people should be far more susceptible to these priming effects than respondents who don't have to think about their responses because of sophistication or identification. Because of this, we'll make use of a regression model, in which we model an individual's response to the party identification questions based on their views on a series of national issues questions, demographic factors such as ethnicity and age, and whether of not the respondent was primed to think about Bush and Iraq. Critically, we'll also include a number of interaction effects between views on national political issues, age, and priming condition.

In the model, we include all five of the national-issue questions, though we don't expect that all of them will have independent effects. The first of the questions is the most general, asking if the country is moving in the right direction. Two of the national-issue questions deal with Bush's performance, one asking if the respondent approves or disapproves of him, and the other asking the respondent to rate his job performance on a four-point scale, from "poor" to "excellent." Two more deal with the war in Iraq, one asking if invading Iraq was the right thing to do and the other asking about progress in the war on another four-point scale (from "not well at all" to "very well"). We don't expect all of them to have independent effects because they're all so tightly related: there are relatively few people who think that President Bush is doing an excellent job, but that the war in Iraq is not going well at all. We can think of all of these questions as being different expressions of the same thing, the place in the affective network held by Bush and Iraq. Each of the questions is going to measure a slightly different aspect of this, making the evaluation a little more positive or a little more negative. For instance, general approval or disapproval of Bush might be more related to Bush's perceived personal characteristics than the question about job performance. As such, we'd expect that the most general of the questions—"Is the country moving in the right direction?"—would have the strongest effect, as the confounding factors like affection for Bush personally or a desire to support the troops are far fewer. The position of this question in the survey as the first of the national issues also supports the idea that it would be the purest measure of what we're interested in, as answers to later questions can be expected to be contaminated by responses to the prior question(s). Finally, this question fits in nicely with the overall theory of macropartisanship. In macropartisanship theory, people don't necessarily respond to individual events or figures, but rather to the general trend of the country: if they feel it's becoming too conservative, they lean toward liberalism, and vice versa. The direction of the country question comes closest to measuring this perception. Despite this, we include all five of the national-issue questions, as well as all of the interactions for each of them, to ensure that we don't miss anything that might be there. It is, after all, better to be too inclusive than not inclusive enough.

For each of these national questions, the model includes two interaction effects. The first is an interaction between the answer to the question and the priming condition. This will tell us about the differential effect of the priming on people who feel differently about the direction of the country, Bush and Iraq. For instance, we wouldn't expect the respondent's feelings about President Bush to have a direct impact on their partisanship, as some people who like him will be primed and others won't. However, if feelings about Bush make those respondents who were primed to think about him more Republican or more Democratic (depending on *what* they think about him), this predictor will be significant, but the main effect (without any interactions) of Bush's approval will not be.

The second interaction effect is between the respondent's views of the national issues, their priming condition and their age. This sort of three-way interaction is rare in political science, and it's easy to see why. In this case, we're not only predicting that views of national issues will have an impact on partisanship only in certain priming conditions, but also that the impact of those views in that priming condition will be conditional on the age of the respondent. For reasons we explained before, in general, younger respondents should be more susceptible to these priming effects than older ones, as they're expected to have less political experience. While such effects can be difficult to uncover, and difficult to interpret,[20] they are critical to our understanding of how the perceived failures of the current administration will impact tomorrow's political balance.

Results of this regression can be found in Table 6.1.[21]

As expected, the variable representing the respondent's view on the general direction of the country had the strongest impact. While it was not a significant predictor of partisanship as a main effect—nor was it expected to be—it *was* significant in both of the interaction sets. Moreover, the effects are strong in both cases. While the coefficient attached to the interaction of the right track/wrong track question by age and experimental condition is far smaller than the interaction without age, remember that age, here, is measured by the respondent's year of birth. This means that the coefficient on the three way interaction is being multiplied by, on average, 1950, giving a result that is, on average, about equal to the coefficient for the two-way interaction. None of the other variables representing views on national issues are significant for either the two or three way interactions, though the respondent's views on Bush's job performance come close in both cases. In fact, the only other significant effect of national issues on party identification is a main effect of Bush's job approval, unsurprisingly indicating that respondents who disapprove of Bush are rather more likely to be Democrats (though the inclusion of the interaction effects makes the interpretation of the coefficient rather more complex than that).

Because of the difficulty in fully interpreting these coefficients, we turn again to Monte Carlo analysis to create percent-

Table 6.1: Regression Model for Party Identification by Experimental Condition

Predictor	Coefficient	Std. Error	Z	P>Z
Condition	–0.045	0.447	–0.1	0.92
Views on National Issues				
Right Track/Wrong Track	0.454	0.560	0.8	0.42
GWB Job Performance	–0.294	0.307	–1.0	0.34
GWB Job Approval	–2.230	0.651	–3.4	0.00
Iraq Progress	0.072	0.219	0.3	0.74
Iraq Right or Wrong Thing	–0.834	0.515	–1.6	0.11
Interactions with Experimental Condition				
Right Track × Condition	23.428	11.700	2.0	0.05
GWB Performance × Condition	–11.595	7.280	–1.6	0.11
GWB Approval × Condition	–4.457	15.444	–0.3	0.77
Iraq Progress × Condition	5.440	5.439	1.0	0.32
Iraq Right × Condition	–2.029	12.268	–0.2	0.87
Interactions with Experimental Condition and Year of Birth				
Right Track × Condition × Age	–0.012	0.006	–2.0	0.04
GWB Performance × Condition × Age	0.006	0.004	1.6	0.12
GWB Approval × Condition × Age	0.003	0.008	0.4	0.72
Iraq Progress × Condition × Age	–0.003	0.003	–1.0	0.30
Iraq Right × Condition × Age	0.001	0.006	0.2	0.87
Demographic Factors				
Year of Birth	0.008	0.009	0.9	0.36
Education	0.111	0.046	2.4	0.02
Gender	–0.221	0.099	–2.2	0.03
Race: Non-White?	–0.760	0.143	–5.3	0.00

age estimates.[22] The effects of the respondent's views on the right track/wrong track question on their party identification are shown in two separate figures, one for individuals at about the mean age (fifty-five), and at the tenth percentile (twenty-five years of age). As the effects are generally linear, any age in between can be extrapolated from these two. It should also be noted that the exact percentages reported here are for white males, and while women and non-whites are expected to have different overall levels of identification, comparisons between categories are unaffected.

Figure 6.1: Estimated Effects of Priming on 25 Year Olds

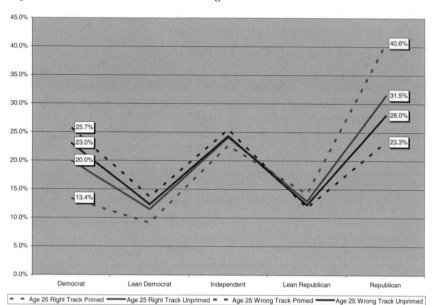

The most immediately striking feature of the results is the enormous difference between the effects of priming on young and old respondents. At age fifty-five, the difference between the dotted lines representing the primed condition and the solid line representing the unprimed condition are minimal. For instance, an unprimed fifty-five-year-old who feels that the country is on the right track has about a 19 percent chance of being a Democrat, and a 31 percent chance of being a Republican. Reminding him or her of the current state of the country changes those results, but only slightly: the primed equivalent is expected to have a 17 percent chance of being a Democrat, and a 34 percent chance of being a Republican.[23] The results for twenty-five-year-olds are dramatic in comparison. A young respondent who feels that the country is on the right track has about a 20 percent chance of being a Republican, and a 32 percent chance of being a Democrat, little different than his or her older counterpart. However, while priming a fifty-five-year-old had little effect, priming the younger respondent leads to a 6 percent decrease in the likelihood of being a Democrat, and a nine point increase in the like-

Figure 6.2: Estimated Effects of Priming on 55 Year Olds

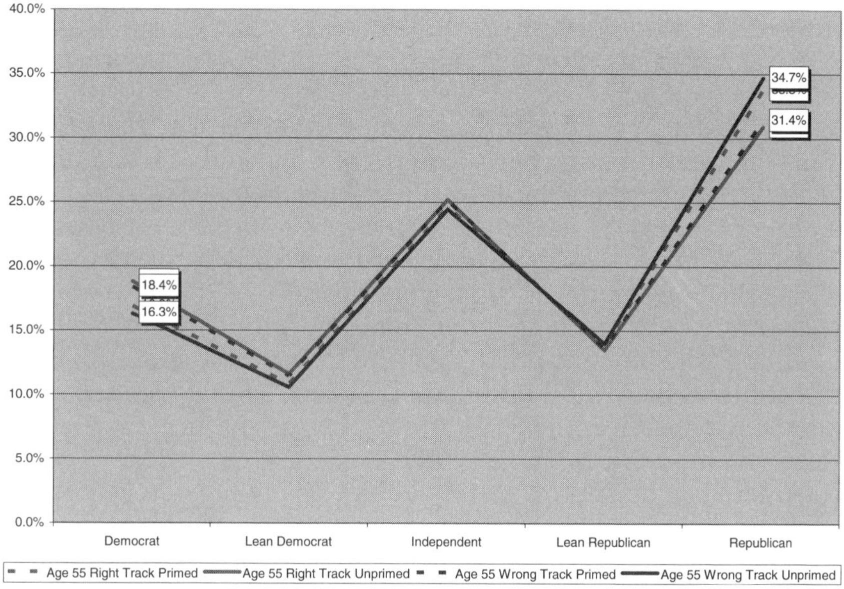

lihood of being a Republican. Among those who feel that the country is on the wrong track (a far more likely outcome: 24 percent of respondents said that the country was on the right track, while 66 percent said that is was on the wrong track), the results are similar. A primed middle-aged respondent who says that the country is on the right track is little different from an unprimed one: the likelihood of being a Democrat increases by about 2 percent, and the likelihood of being a Republican drops by about 3 percent. For the younger respondents, priming an individual who says that the country is on the wrong track reduces the likelihood of being a Republican by about five points, and increases the likelihood of being a Democrat by about three points.

BARACK OBAMA AND THE ANTI-BUSH BRAND

These results suggest that if Bush and Iraq were chronically accessible—coming to mind whenever voters thought about politics in general or the Republican Party in particular—the political playing field among young people would be slanted in favor of the Democratic Party and recent evidence seems to strongly support that contention.

In the 2008 Democratic Primary, junior Illinois senator Barack Obama was able to leverage his early statements against the war in Iraq to defeat establishment candidate Senator Hillary Clinton, whose nomination had seemed like a lock only a few months before. In trading on the Iowa Electronic Market—a pool used mainly by political scientists to guess the outcome of political events—Clinton was predicted to have a 78 percent chance of taking the nomination as early as October 2007. Obama's chances at the time were given at about 10 percent, roughly equal to the likelihood of someone other than the major candidates winning the nomination. The likelihood of Obama winning spiked after his victory in Iowa, then fell after Clinton won in New Hampshire: even on Super Tuesday, the odds of either winning were considered to be approximately equal. His win, even according to those that should be most in the know, seems to have been a surprise.

So, what happened? As of this writing, political scientists have yet to complete the quantitative research that will be necessary to pinpoint the causes of Obama's come-from-behind victory. That does not mean, however, that the media have not already decided on a cause: his strong support among young people. After his wins on Super Tuesday, newspaper stories about young people pressuring their parents to support Obama (even former President Jimmy Carter implied that he was feeling the heat) abounded. He filled stadiums and drew record crowds on college campuses. Turnout in the Democratic primary exceeded any in recent political history. The level of engagement and excitement that Obama generated seems to argue that the young people are not, in fact, disengaged. However, Obama's success arguably stems from the same sort of branding that we've been discussing throughout. It isn't that Obama is different from other politicians, but rather that, by chance or design, he became a far more potent brand than the other contenders for either nomination and so was able to mobilize young people's support.

What are the components of this brand? We can't ignore his personal image: he's young, multiracial, wearing Hugo Boss suits, and sneaking the occasional cigarette. He's also a skilled orator who's able to adjust the tempo and rhythm of his speeches to match the audience, and almost inevitably builds to a rousing crescendo. But that alone does not a movement make: the Gary Hart of 1984 was young, smart, sexy—maybe too much so—and a great speaker without generating a youth movement. The success of Obama's brand—and the proliferation of T-shirts and buttons, bumper stickers and bobbleheads, both those made by the campaign and by those seeking to capitalize on its popularity mark it as a brand—comes from his message. He was the one major candidate for the Democratic nomination who had always been against the war in Iraq, who hadn't been seen to compromise with a disliked president, and it's on the basis of these strengths that he was able to take the nomination. As we would expect from our exploration of Democratic young people, issue positions came to dominate the race for the nomination. Obama's brand was desirable enough to draw young people in, and his issue positions appealed to Democratic young people. Disconcertingly for the GOP, young people in the 2008 primary election seemed to act as though Iraq were a chronically accessible issue —almost as if it were the only issue—and threw their support to the strongest antiwar candidate.

PARTY POLARIZATION

At the same time that Obama was coming from behind to win the Democratic nomination, another underdog, Arizona senator John McCain, took the Republican nomination. While he had been a favorite to win early on (in March, 2007, he and Rudolph Giuliani's were tied for first in the Iowa Electronic Market odds), McCain's campaign had nearly run out of money in the summer of 2007, and his IEM odds of winning the nomination fell to about 10 percent. His greatest appeal, too, is in accord with what we would expect from our interviews: leadership. Unlike his rivals for the nomination, he had a remarkable biography and a reputation for strong, principled decision-making, even if it went against the demands of his party.

As of this writing, Obama holds a small advantage over McCain in national polls and seems to do better state by state. Referring again to the IEM, Obama is expected to win about 52 percent of the national vote and is given just shy of a 70 percent chance of winning. Still, given all that we've said about the centrality of

Iraq and President Bush to young people's partisanship—and thus their voting decisions—this seems like it's a bit *too* close. Fifty-two percent of the national popular vote would be the largest majority won by a Democratic presidential candidate in decades, but it's still nowhere near the sort of sweeping victories won by Lyndon Johnson in 1964, or Ronald Reagan in 1984. The reason for this may have to do with the secondary effects of the salience of Iraq and President Bush. While our data tells us that it seems to shift support to the Democratic party overall among young people, it has a much larger effect of polarizing the parties. That is, the continuing salience of national issues tends to reduce the number of antiwar Republicans or pro-Bush Democrats. More-over, the smaller number of Republicans who are pro-war and pro-Bush seem to become more Republican than the antiwar, anti-Bush crowd becomes Democratic, muting the Democratic advantage.

In Figure 6.1, representing the views of young respondents, the lines representing the unprimed condition are very close through-out. This represents a rough balance within each of the partisan groups of those who feel that the country is on the right track and those who disagree. Remembering that the simulation represents the views of white males—in our simulation, for instance, about 46 percent of Democrats feel that the country is on the wrong track, and about 47 percent of Republicans feel that it is on the wrong track—at least for the simulated group, there is real diversity of opinion even among partisans. In the primed condition, though, this falls away. While the absolute number of Democrats remains the same, the proportion feeling that the country is on the right track declines from 46 percent to about 34 percent. Similarly, the percent of Republicans who feel that the country is on the right track increases from 53 percent to 63 percent.[24]

REPLICATION

Before moving forward with these results, it's important to make sure that they're not overly specific to the time and place from whence they came. After all, the surveys on which the previous analyses are based stem from a hotly contested Senate election receiving national media attention and one in which the war in Iraq was a central issue. While the cognitive underpinnings of the results aren't any different when there isn't an election at hand—

associations between nodes are associations between nodes, regardless—it remains important to run a wider test of the model. For this purpose, the same priming experiments were used on a national survey in the spring of 2007, well after the hotly contested 2006 elections, well before most people had begun paying attention to the 2008 presidential election, and including all of the states in which highly salient elections had not recently taken place. While there were a few differences between the studies—the national poll omitted the second question on Bush's job performance in favor of a question asking about candidate choice in the 2008 election—the structures of the two were almost identical. In total, the national study included 1,204 respondents, including a downweighted oversample of New Jersey voters.

Results for the national replication can be found in Table 6.2.

Table 6.2: National Replication of Party Identification by Experimental Condition model

Predictor	Coefficient	Std. Error	Z	P>Z
Condition	0.109	0.799	0.1	0.89
Views on National Issues				
Right Track/Wrong Track	0.525	0.892	0.6	0.56
GWB Job Approval	−3.662	0.929	−3.9	0.00
Iraq Progress	0.259	0.311	0.8	0.41
Iraq Right or Wrong Thing	−0.647	0.684	−1.0	0.35
Interactions with Experimental Condition				
Right Track × Condition	41.030	21.204	1.9	0.05
GWB Approval × Condition	−8.827	21.484	−0.4	0.68
Iraq Progress × Condition	−0.321	0.222	−1.4	0.15
Iraq Right × Condition	−31.658	17.740	−1.8	0.07
Interactions with Experimental Condition and Year of Birth				
Right Track × Condition × Age	−0.021	0.011	−2.0	0.05
GWB Approval × Condition × Age	0.005	0.011	0.5	0.64
Iraq Progress × Condition × Age	0.000	0.000	1.0	0.34
Iraq Right × Condition × Age	0.016	0.009	1.8	0.08
Demographic Factors				
Year of Birth	0.000	0.000	−0.9	0.38
Education	0.051	0.062	0.8	0.41
Gender	0.035	0.144	0.2	0.81
Race: Non-White	−1.189	0.205	−5.8	0.00

Once again, only one of the national views had a significant impact on partisanship when the interactions were included: the general right track/wrong track question. Also again, the coefficient attached to the two-way interaction of this indicator with priming condition was larger than the three-way interaction of right/track wrong track by priming condition by age by a factor of about 1,950, indicating that the two cancel each other out at median levels of age (as measured by year of birth). In order to make the comparison between the national and New Jersey results easy, both sets are included in Table 6.3.

As shown in Table 6.3, the results from the New Jersey surveys more than hold up in the national survey. Rather than the priming having a greater impact during a hotly contested partisan election, the electoral environment actually seems to have muted the results. For instance, in the New Jersey surveys, priming a young respondent who said that the country was on the right track reduced the likelihood of being a Democrat by seven points and increased the likelihood of being a Republican by about nine points. In the national study, priming the same group led to an eight-point decrease in the likelihood of being a Democrat, and a seventeen-point increase in the likelihood of being a Republican. In fact, nearly all of the effects in the national survey are larger than in the New Jersey surveys.[25]

These results tell us three important things about the New Jersey results. First, the New Jersey results were not a fluke. The coefficients—even ones as complicated as three-way interactions—fell in exactly the same pattern in the national poll. Given the vanishingly small likelihood that such patterns would occur by

Table 6.3: Comparison of Effects of Priming by Age

| | | Age 55 | | | | Age 25 | | | |
| | | Right Track | | Wrong Track | | Right Track | | Wrong Track | |
		Primed	Unprimed	Primed	Unprimed	Primed	Unprimed	Primed	Unprimed
New Jersey	Democrat	16.9%	18.8%	18.4%	16.3%	13.4%	20.0%	25.7%	23.0%
	Lean Dem.	10.8%	11.6%	11.5%	10.6%	9.1%	11.5%	13.7%	12.4%
	Independent	24.6%	25.2%	25.1%	24.4%	22.7%	24.1%	25.5%	24.3%
	Lean Rep.	13.9%	13.5%	13.6%	14.0%	14.2%	12.9%	11.8%	12.3%
	Republican	33.8%	30.9%	31.4%	34.7%	40.6%	31.5%	23.3%	28.0%
National	Democrat	17.6%	24.0%	18.0%	19.7%	10.6%	18.9%	29.4%	25.3%
	Lean Dem.	10.7%	12.9%	11.0%	11.6%	7.4%	11.3%	14.0%	13.3%
	Independent	21.5%	22.7%	22.0%	22.3%	17.3%	22.0%	22.3%	22.8%
	Lean Rep.	13.3%	12.3%	13.4%	13.1%	13.0%	13.2%	11.1%	12.0%
	Republican	36.8%	28.1%	35.6%	33.2%	51.8%	34.7%	23.3%	26.7%

chance, twice, this gives us a great deal of confidence in the results. Second, the results of the New Jersey analysis aren't contingent on a contested election to make the issues more relevant to voters. Third, proximity to an election may very well work against these effects. In the heat of an election, parties become identified with candidates. In New Jersey, respondents who felt that the country was going in the wrong direction may have been reluctant to identify with the Democratic Party if they were uncomfortable with Bob Menendez. In the national survey, taken long enough before the general election that the parties were not necessarily identified with any one candidate, such issues didn't yet exist. However, this also raises the possibility that the effects will fade as the 2008 election nears and the parties get a human face that not everyone will be happy with.

Perhaps most importantly, these results extend the conclusions drawn from the New Jersey survey. Once again, the results lead us to expect that if Bush and Iraq were always associated with the Republican Party, the balance of the parties would be about the same but the polarization within the parties would increase dramatically. In the national survey, respondents were quite a bit more pessimistic about the direction the country was going in than in the New Jersey surveys: fully 80 percent of those with an opinion said that the country was on the wrong track. This means that absent any priming, about 24 percent of our simulated white males would be Democrats, and about 28 percent would be Republicans, giving a party balance of about fifty-five to forty-five, in favor of the Republicans. Among primed white males, the party balance is almost identical, with Republicans holding an advantage of about fifty-three to forty-seven. Again, while the Republican Party can be expected to lose some people who hold negative views of Bush and Iraq, the gains it makes among the smaller group of individuals who have positive associations for these almost offsets the losses. The extent of these losses can be seen in the expected levels of polarization. Currently, among the simulated twenty-five-year-old white males, approximately 43 percent of each party holds views at odds with the general beliefs of that party: 43 percent of Republican say that the country is going in the wrong direction, and 43 percent of Democrats say that it is on the right track. If Bush and Iraq were chronically accessible, we would expect that only about 8 percent of Democrats and 36 percent of Republicans would hold views contrary to those of their party.

POLARIZATION AND PARTY BALANCE

At first glance, these conclusions about the likely impact of the continued association of President Bush and the war in Iraq with the Republican Party in the minds of young voters may seem unimportant. Counterintuitively, it doesn't seem as though constant reminders of Bush and Iraq are going to add much to the rolls of the Democratic Party, and polarization is certainly nothing new to any student of the last twenty years of American politics. However, there is a lot more to these results, and they serve their purpose of painting a picture of American politics as today's young people grow to dominate the political scene.

The finding that, on the whole, the issues of Bush and Iraq don't help the Democratic Party seems at odds with both reason and recent experience. However, the finding is not that Democrats will not find these issues useful in elections against Republican candidates—only that the rolls of the Democratic Party won't get any bigger because of them. In fact, it can be shown that making national issues like the war in Iraq accessible in evaluations of candidates does have an impact on their vote choice. In the same New Jersey surveys discussed earlier, the first poll was taken the summer before the election, and before many voters had begun to study the race. In that poll, unprimed respondents gave the Republican candidate a small lead, one that was reversed in the primed condition. As New Jersey voters came to identify the candidates with their views on the war, Kean's lead dropped away. In an election in which candidates and parties spent millions of dollars, Iraq was the main issue, and the final tally from voting booths across the states matched the priming result from July almost exactly. In the end, it seems, the other issues simply didn't matter, and Menendez's opposition to the war won him a full term in the Senate.

Similarly, results from national exit polls in the last few elections, compiled by the Pew Research Center, show that support for Republican candidates among young voters has decreased as the war has dragged on. Among voters eighteen to twenty-nine, Democrats held a small lead in 2002, forty-nine to forty-seven. In 2004, this had turned into an eleven-point advantage for Democrats, fifty-five to forty-four. In the 2006 elections, nationally, young voters favored Democratic candidates over Republicans by a margin of sixty to thirty-eight (Keeter 2006).

None of this means, though, that the issues created more Democrats in the aggregate. More likely, the issue of the war served to increase turnout and fundraising for Democratic voters, decrease it for Republican voters, and encourage those independent voters who came to the polls to cast ballots for the Democrat: all trends that seem to have helped Obama in his fight for the 2008 nomination. All of these, however, are temporary effects, lasting only as long as the war is a salient issue. None of them lead us to expect substantially more Democratic victories five, ten, or twenty years down the line.

Also, even if the war doesn't have a substantial impact on the long-term partisan balance in the electorate, it may easily impact the partisan balance of the Congress. Individual congressional seats, especially in the House of Representatives, can be held for a very long time. The exceptionally high reelection rate of incumbent representatives means that many of them elected on the strength of their opposition to the war can be expected to maintain their seats for decades afterward. Even in the 2006 midterm elections, often regarded as a landslide victory for the Democrats, the antiwar party only picked thirty-one seats—about 7 percent of the 435 seats in the House. Overall, reelection rates for incumbents in the House of Representatives in recent years have generally exceeded 95 percent. Therefore, even a short-term increase in voting for Democrats could yield long-term legislative majorities. Typically, these gains in seats are expected to follow a pattern of surge and decline. After the issue—in this case, opposition to President Bush and the war in Iraq—recedes in importance, seats that had been won by the insurgent party in districts that typically favor the other party will be slowly picked off, and the partisan balance in the legislature will return to that predicted by demographics and partisanship. As such, we'd expect that the current Democratic majority in Congress should increase so long as Iraq is an issue, then slowly ebb until another issue upsets the balance. This process can be slowed substantially by gerrymandering in the state legislatures, but, as suggested by the House reelection rates, is slow to begin with.

The fate of the Senate is rather more difficult to forecast. Unlike the House, in which enough seats are in play every election year to allow for generalizations, Senate elections are almost always idiosyncratic. In almost any state, a well-heeled challenger from an opposing party can present a serious challenge to an incumbent, and it's impossible for Senate incumbents—elected by the entirety of a state—to protect themselves with gerrymandering. We would expect that, as in the House, the Democratic advantage should increase so long as the war is an issue, but the extent of that increase, and its duration, is anyone's guess. Overall, even without a change in the overall partisan balance, the advantage given to individual Democratic candidates because of the war can be expected to translate into a substantial advantage in the legislature for the foreseeable future.

However, the expected differences in polarization between the parties can be expected to have an even greater impact on the future of American politics. Already, researchers in political science have documented an increase in polarization over the past twenty years, especially in the Congress. As recently as the 1970s, there was a substantial overlap between conservative Democrats and liberal Republicans in the House and Senate. Today, no Democrat in either house of Congress is more conservative than any Republican, and no Republican is more liberal than the most conservative Democrat.[26] In the public, too, researchers have noted the increased polarization of Americans. Whether it is due to increasingly homogeneous suburbs, the increasing importance of religion in predicting political views, or the increased ability of individuals to choose their media influences, Americans today are less likely to socialize with people of different political views, and the composition of the parties reflects this. In recent years, this polarization has been most evident on what are referred to as "culture war" issues such as abortion, civil rights, pornography, and gun control (Lindaman and Haider-Markel 2002; Carmines and Layman 1997), but the war in Iraq is a likely candidate for similar effects.

For an issue to result in party polarization, three things are necessary. First, there must be a clear division between party leaders on the issue. In many cases, this is a slow process: in the case of abortion, for instance, it was nearly ten years after *Roe v. Wade* that a clear consensus developed within each of the parties on the issue (Adams 1997). Second, the issue must be highly salient to voters: there's no reason to base your choice of parties on an issue if it simply isn't that important to you. Third, the issue must be easy to understand (Carmines and Stimson 1980; 1989). An easy issue is symbolic rather than technical, has a clear line from processes to outcomes, and is familiar to voters, having been on the political agenda for some time. Abortion is among the most commonly cited examples of an easy issue (Abramowitz 1995): if you think abortion is murder, ban it; if you think it's a woman's right to choose, don't. If all of these requirements are met, the parties tend to divide along the issues, either through conversion of individual's issue positions to match that of their preferred parties, or through attrition.[27]

The war in Iraq satisfies all three of these requirements. The positions of party leaders on the issue have become increasingly polarized as the war has dragged on, casualties have mounted, and the public has become increasingly impatient with the limited progress in reconstruction and security. As of this writing, Democratic leaders are calling for a gradual withdrawal of troops, while Republican leaders, including the president, press for an extension in the "surge" of American forces. Second, the issue is highly salient. Even after five years, news about casualties in Iraq continues to dominate the news cycles, with attention to the conflict increasing even further during periodic congressional debates over funding and strategy (which also serve to highlight divisions between party leaders). Third, the question of staying or going is relatively easy, even if the implications of either policy are substantially more muddled.[28] Despite the potential complexity of the issue, it has been reduced to a simple, dichotomous choice.

Like the electoral success of the Democratic Party due to the war, the immediate impact of this polarization can only be expected to last so long as the war is an issue. Once the troops end major combat operations in Iraq, whether because the country has been pacified or because of a withdrawal, individuals can be expected to cease joining or leaving parties because of it. However, those individuals who joined the party because of that polarization can be expected to stay with it. As we've seen, the more political information an individual has, because of either political interest or age, the less likely that individual is to change parties. Also, identifying with one party tends to increase political interest and exposure to political information, speeding the process. When today's young Americans join one party or the other largely because of their views of the war and President Bush, they're likely to stay there, and the longer the war is an issue, the more of them there will be.

Our results suggest that the relatively small proportion of the Democratic Party that has positive views of President Bush and the war can be expected to abandon the party, if they have not already. In the national sample, remember, it is expected that the proportion of Democrats who have positive views of the war will decrease from about 47 percent now[29] to about 8 percent when the war is chronically associated with the partisanship decision. The polarization in the Republican Party, while also substantial, is not quite as extreme: a drop from about 47 percent opposing the war to about 36 percent opposing it. This implies a Democratic Party that is far more united on certain issues than it has been in the past and more united than the Republican opponents will be. This unity, of course, will only extend to certain issues, most likely those with a semantic association to Bush and Iraq.[30] This would most obviously include issues of war and peace, but could be easily extended to intelligence gathering and international multilateralism. While reducing the diversity of opinion within the Democratic Party, this sort of unity can be expected to increase the ability of the Democrats to dominate political debate on these issues, especially when faced when more than a third of the Republican Party can be expected to have the same associations that they do.

All told, our findings on the political views of young Americans, and especially the effect of the war in Iraq on those views, tells us a great deal about tomorrow's political landscape. We can expect that the Democratic and Republican Parties of tomorrow will have a similar balance to the parties of today, though current issues make it likely that Democrats will have an extended advantage in Congress. We can also expect that both parties will become more united on issues of war and peace, and anything else related to the current conflict, and that an increasingly unified Democratic Party will have a marked advantage on these issues. In some ways, then, the politics of twenty to thirty years from now—when today's young people are the dominant force in their parties—will be similar to those of today. There is no telling, though, how important the small changes will turn out to be.

7
Conclusion

Researchers, as well as citizens, have long been curious about the voting behavior of young Americans. It is cliché, but they are the future, and we understandably want to know what's going to happen. When suffrage was extended to eighteen-year-olds in 1971, the expectation was that young people would turn out to vote in droves, but it never happened. Rather, the elections gave us an opportunity to measure the apathy of our young people, and we've been doing it ever since. There have been many explanations given for this: young people have too many things to deal with (Jowell and Park 1998), they're living at home longer (Kimberlee 1998), they don't trust the politicians (Bentley et al. 1999). The shared assumption, though, is that young people's apathy is monolithic: that they're all disengaging for the same reasons.

Our interviews have shown clearly that this simply isn't the case. In all cases, the apathy comes from the inability of young people to relate to aspects of the political world, but there are enormous differences in the aspects that they find lacking. While the root cause of this apathy may be the same across political groups—the commoditization of politics—any solutions to it must take account of the differences among young people. Republican-leaning youth are rendered apathetic by the lack of relatable leaders. Like conservatives of past generations, they're looking for a consistent, forceful leader—but the way in which politicians seem to be bought and sold to appeal to as many disparate interests as possible renders today's leaders unpalatable to them. Among the youth who identify with the Democratic Party, there is a substantial disconnect between the issues at play in the political system and the issues that they consider to be important. They don't care about Social Security reform because they don't think that they will ever receive Social Security. They don't care

213

about a potential draft because they don't think they'll be called upon to fight. Abortion has been a decided issue for as long as they've been alive, so even that has no particular resonance. While Republican youth like the issues, but not the leaders, Democratic young people have no particular problem with the politicians, but simply don't think any of the issues are relevant to them. The focus-group-tested issues that are supposed to excite them are falling flat. Our final category—independent young people—simply believes that the structure of the political system prevents anything meaningful from happening. This may be the hardest of the groups to mobilize, because the independents can't be excited merely by presenting more relevant issues or more relatable leaders. Rather, these youth will seemingly only be mobilized by evidence that the system really can be changed.

It's also important to note that the inability of these youth to relate to political issues is not a great source of angst to them. For a generation that has grown up entirely in the world where parties, politicians, and policies have been sold like soap, opting out from politics is no more consequential a decision than one to avoid pop music or shop at The Gap. Despite the fact that we've divided up young people by their self-professed partisan affiliation, their partisanship is shockingly ideological. Attachment to a party is superficial, saying no more about an individual than the clothes they wear. Certain brands are more desirable than others of course, but it's a matter of taste more than anything. This is obvious in their descriptions of members of partisan groups, which rely far more on a listing of the brands that partisans are associated with than any insight into what might lead someone to affiliate with that party or ideology. To them, it's as if stockbrokers are Republicans for the same reason that stockbrokers buy European cars: it just comes with the territory.

Our research has shown that one of these brands, though, can have a positive impact. Unlike other political media outlets, *The Daily Show* is seen as youthful and cool—as opposed to boring and old, like NPR and Fox News. The appeal of this program may be as superficial as the appeal of political parties, but the process of being associated means that they're exposed to a great deal of political information, as well as discussing that information with their peers. Our experiment shows that viewers with low levels of political knowledge learn more about politics from *The Daily Show* than from traditional news broadcasts, and more importantly, the significantly strengthen their political knowledge structures. This means that they have a much better idea what Republicans and Democrats, what the president, and members of Congress are likely to do. This is the sort of understanding that leads people to be more able to understand novel political concepts and allows viewers to pull themselves up by their boostraps into greater political sophistication.

Finally, we looked at the defining political issue of the last few years: the war in Iraq. It seems possible that the reason young people are less engaged in politics than previous generations is that they don't see politics as being consequential, and if this were the problem, war would be a solution. Debates over campaign finance, Social Security reform, and prescription drug benefits may be arcane, but a debate over war and peace, over big issues of constitutional prerogatives—that should excite the imagination of anyone interested in politics. Moreover, an increasingly overstretched military has raised the specter, to many commentators, of a draft: a step that would make the issue of the war very relevant to young men.

To some extent, the war has made it more likely that young people will take one side or the other in the partisan debate. Young people are more likely than their older counterparts to adopt a partisan stance because of their view of the war, but it seems unlikely that the war in Iraq will have the sort of long-term impact on American politics that Vietnam did. In what will certainly be a disappointment to liberal activists, the eventual balance of the two parties as a result of the war will be almost identical to the balance today.

PLACING THE BLAME

In some sense, asking "what's wrong with today's young people" is blaming the victim. There is nothing intrinsic to this generation that prevents them from engaging in politics in the same way that their parents and grandparents did. It could be argued that they are simply adapting their behaviors and attitudes rationally in response to the tenor of politics around them. For at least forty years, politics, partisanship, and leadership have become commoditized. Difficult political decisions are guaranteed to alienate some segments of the population; by replacing the substance of politics with branding, it's possible to please everyone. We've spent decades selling politicians and policies like soap, and so it should be little surprise that the differences between consumption items and partisan politics have fallen away. Of course young people react with cynicism and apathy: no one's ever showed them why they should care. The culprit, then, is a political system that's adapted the tools of direct marketing to political ends, and news sources that value the sound bite over the debate.

But we may be placing the blame wrongly here, too. After all, news broadcasts and political consultants are reacting to the public as well: if they wanted substance, they'd get it. Flawed as they are, Nielsen ratings don't lie. *Charlie Rose* doesn't get high marks, and the highest rated news programs on cable television are those that are the most crass and confrontational: *The O'Reilly Factor, Hannity and Colmes*. People don't have time, the argument goes, to worry about nuance: they need the quick version, and they need it now. Governance is, for the most part, not about what policies to adopt, but how to put those policies into action. Perhaps we can all agree that we should reduce emissions of greenhouse gasses: the debate comes when we ask what to do about it. Do we put a cap and trade program into place? Increase subsidies to Iowa corn farmers to make ethanol? Build wind farms? Tax SUVs? Use taxes to push up the price of gasoline? There's no consensus on these, rendering any consensus on the general point meaningless. In sum, the quick version doesn't tell us anything about the real issues at stake.

There is reason to believe, though, that the problem isn't with the content of the policy-centered programming, but rather on its format. Only a few years ago, *The West Wing* had remarkable critical and commercial success while routinely spending episodes discussing the minutiae of the policy-making process. One episode, for instance, focused almost entirely on the question of whether the census should be conducted as a head count or through statistical sampling.[1] Another featured an extended discussion of whether the United States should switch textbooks from the Mercator map projection to the more accurate Peters projection.[2] Today, *The Daily Show* has become a popular cultural phenomenon because it combines an enormous amount of political information with a humorous, ironic bent that makes the presentation of that information interesting. As we can see from the success of these shows, it isn't that people don't want content, it's that they don't want the content as it's generally given out.

In general, broadcast television features a constant flow of audio and visual information, and there are any number of successful programs—*Lost, 24, Desperate Housewives*—that require the viewer to piece together clues laid out of literally dozens of hours of viewing (Johnson 2005). Even local news broadcasts have adopted the "action news" format, in which every story is accompanied by flashy visuals and breathless descriptions of crime and disaster. Political programs, with almost the sole exception of *The Daily Show*, operate entirely on the opposite end of the spectrum. Turn on an afternoon show on CNN or MSNBC, or a Sunday morning talk show on any of the broadcast networks, and you're likely to see several old, often unattractive, people talking, with no graphics but an occasional quote from a newspaper article that the host reads to the audience. To repeat, for emphasis, a staple of political shows in the United States is the host reading on-screen text to the viewers. It is difficult to imagine a poorer use of the dynamic medium of television. While the rest of the medium has evolved, serious political news broadcasts remain largely as they have been for fifty years. Every week, NBC's *Meet the Press* ends by showing a historic appearance on the program from twenty or more years past, and if we ignore the clothing and the poor signal quality, the clips are scarcely different from what's on the program now. In this light, it's easy to see why the confrontational programs do better: at least there the people are *shouting* at each other.

The challenge, then, of the politically oriented media is to present the talking heads in a more interesting way, and the programs that have done this have proven immensely successful. *The Daily Show* blends serious political information with almost constant visual gags, from the title of the story to the fake backgrounds behind the correspondents, and the political content is filled with jokes and innuendo. *The West Wing* featured characters talking about serious political issues, but became famous for having them do so while almost running through crowded hallways and speaking almost impossibly complex sentences at a breakneck pace. British writer Warren Ellis has noted his jealousy that the show's creator, Aaron Sorkin, was able to get almost 50 percent more dialogue in a minute of television than anyone else has managed. On *The Daily Show*'s recent offspring, *The Colbert Report*, the surest laughs come from the host's monologue, "The Word." In this segment, Colbert launches into a straight-faced diatribe designed to visually and tonally reference Bill O'Reilly, while the updating graphics on the screen next to him provide ironic commentary, undercutting his every sentiment. The common thread of these successful, content-heavy political programs is the adaptation of modern television techniques to political content, which doesn't have to dilute that content. As our experimental results show, viewers can actually learn more about the day's political issues from *The Daily Show* than from a standard news broadcast, and the learning seems to build up ideological structures, making future learning easier.

There's no question that this sort of program is much more difficult to make than a traditional political talk show. In addition to researchers, you need writers, graphic designers, multiple cameras—but the benefits of this investment are enormous on both sides. Viewers learn more about politics and gain the foothold in the political debate necessary to learn even more in the future, and creators get the ratings and advertisers that they need for the program to survive. So why hasn't this happened more? Certainly programmers and network executives know more about ratings and revenues than we do. Inertia is one explanation; a desire for gravitas is another. The hosts and guests of the programs no doubt feel more comfortable with them as they are now, and it isn't hard to imagine an argument that politics is too important to denigrate with the trappings of modern television. So long as this continues, though, the choice that's given to young people in terms of political media is between dull and meaningless, and so it's no surprise that they choose neither and drop out of the partisan debate entirely.

In a very real way, political content itself has been branded as "dull," and this represents a very real threat to representative democracy. As we've seen, the virtues of the independent voter are largely a myth: those individuals who opt out of partisanship know less about the issues, are less likely to vote, and have a harder time learning about politics. The dealignment from partisanship in recent years, then, is more than just an expansion of the number of voters who could go either way in a close election. It's also a sign that our party system is broken, and it isn't going to get better by itself. Rather than just curse the youth for not being engaged, we have to follow Stewart's lead, and do all that we can to rebrand politics, to make it both interesting and important: our democracy depends on it.

Appendix 1: Survey Questions

A detailed description of this questionnaire can be found in the introduction. Responses given to the questions can be found in chapters 1 through 4.

Section A. For the first few questions, we want you to think about typical members of a group. There are no right or wrong answers to these questions; just tell us about a typical member of the group, in as much detail as you can.

1. Describe a typical Republican.
2. Describe a typical Democrat.
3. Describe a typical Starbucks employee.
4. Describe a typical McDonald's employee.
5. Describe a typical Fox News viewer.
6. Describe a typical *Daily Show* viewer.
7. Describe a typical NPR listener.
8. Describe a typical person who's really interested in politics.

Section B. In the next few questions, we want you tell us whether you agree with certain statements that people make about politics or not. For each, just say if you agree with the statement or not, and explain why you feel that way. Add as much detail as you would like.

1. A lot of government policies affect me directly.
2. There are a few bad apples, but most people in government are trying to do a good job.
3. There are big differences between the two major parties on a lot of issues.
4. There isn't much any one person can do to change the political system.
5. We'd all be better off if the government would just leave us alone.
6. Most people don't have time to worry about political issues.
7. Today's political leaders are as good as those in years past.

8. I don't feel like there are many political issues I can relate to.
9. The political system makes sure that no change ever really happens.

Section C. Here we just want to know a few things about how you feel about the political situation today.

1. Do you approve or disapprove of how President Bush is doing his job as president?
2. All in all, do you think that invading Iraq was a good idea or a bad idea?
3. Do you think there's much of a chance that the government will reinstate the draft if the war continues or another one starts?
4. How politically involved would you say that you are?
5. Where, specifically, do you get your political information?
6. How, if at all, would you say that your political views have changed over the last few years?

Section D. In this section, we just need some basic information about you. None of this information will be used to personally identify you.

1. How would you describe yourself politically? Republican, Democrat, or Independent?
2. Aside from this one, what political science classes have you taken?
3. Aside from being a student, do you work? Full time or part time?
4. In what year were you born?
5. How many of your grandparents were born in the United States?
6. Are you male or female?
7. Do you attend religious services? If so, how often?
8. How many houses did you live in when you were growing up?

Appendix 2: Experimental Questions

Descriptions of the experimental procedures used to administer these questions can be found in chapter 5.

[Article one was a news analysis of President Bush's surprise trip to Iraq in early September 2007.]

Take a couple of sentences to summarize the article you just read. What was President Bush doing in Anbar province? What's going on with the benchmarks?

Some of the following statements were included in the article that you just read, and others were not. Of the following 15 statements, circle the **eight** that you think *were* included. [Included statements in normal text; not included, noncongruent statements in italics; not included, congruent statements in bold]

1. **According to President Bush, progress in Anbar province shows that we are winning the war on terror.**
2. *According to several new reports, Iraqi leaders have met nearly all of the benchmarks set by Congress.*
3. *Congressional leaders called for additional time to allow the Al-Maliki government to meet the benchmarks.*
4. **Democrats in Congress compared Bush's to his "Mission Accomplished" visit to an aircraft carrier in 2004.**
5. *During the trip, President Bush called for a partition of Iraq into three states as a way to stabilize the country.*
6. It's not clear how strong the links between Al-Qaeda in Mesopotamia and Osama Bin Laden's Al-Qaeda network are.
7. **President Bush took the opportunity to call for an end to Iranian involvement in the conflict.**
8. Rather than the benchmarks he set last year, President Bush is pushing for new ways to measure success in Iraq.
9. Sunnis in Anbar province are fighting alongside the Americans against Al-Qaeda forces.

10. The National Intelligence Estimate and the Government Account-ability Office report on Iraq both painted a bleak picture of Iraq's future.
11. **The president declined comment on whether progress had been made by the government in Iraq.**
12. *The president praised the progress made by Prime Minister Nuri Al-Maliki's government in Baghdad.*
13. Today, it seems likely that Iraq will be divided up into three areas.
14. *Tribal leaders in both northern and central Iraq are uniting in the fight against Al-Qaeda in Mesopotamia.*
15. **While forces in Anbar province are working with American forces, Iraqi forces in other provinces are increasingly turning against coalition forces.**

[Article two was detailed a Senate Armed Services Committee hearing about a report they commissioned regarding progress in Iraq. The head of the commission issuing the report was Marine General James L. Jones.]

In a few sentences, summarize the article you just read. What did the independent commission find about the Iraqi army? What did senators on the panel have to say about it?

Some of the following statements were included in the article that you just read, and others were not. Of the following 15 statements, circle the **eight** that you think *were* included. [Included statements in normal text; not included, noncongruent statements in italics; not included, congruent statements in bold]

1. *According to the report, Iraqi forces are now operating without American help in much of the country.*
2. **Critics of the president's policy said that no political gains will be made unless we threaten withdrawals.**
3. Currently, only seven of Iraq's eighteen provinces are controlled by the central government in Baghdad.
4. **Democrats like Ted Kennedy argued that we should make it clear that we will eventually leave Iraq.**
5. *Democrats were pleased with the pace of talks between the different factions going on in Baghdad.*
6. General Jones said that we may be able to reduce American forces as early as next year.
7. *It seems likely that President Bush will take the findings seriously when deciding what should be done next.*
8. **Like Democrats, Republican Senators are increasingly frustrated with the slow pace of political progress.**

9. *Most Democratic committee members said that the findings justified giving the Iraqi government more time before withdrawing troops.*

10. **Republican Senators are hoping for good news from Iraq in advance of next year's elections.**

11. *Republicans were hoping that General Jones would speak in favor of a firm deadline for troop withdrawal.*

12. Senate Democrats used the report to challenge White House claims made that the current strategy is working.

13. Senator John McCain argued that a deadline for the withdrawal of American troops would be against U.S. interests.

14. **Support among Republicans is building for a small troop withdrawal that would silence critics of the war.**

15. The commission recommended disbanding the Iraqi police force because it is corrupt and contributes to sectarian violence.

Appendix 3: Political Knowledge Scale

Match each of the following individuals with the position that he or she
currently holds. Each answer may be used once, twice, or not at all.
[Correct answers in brackets]

1. Condoleezza Rice [G]
2. Gordon Brown [A]
3. Hillary Clinton [I]
4. John Edwards [B]
5. John McCain [I]
6. Mahmoud Abbas [E]
7. Mahmoud Ahmadinejad [C]
8. Nancy Pelosi [J]
9. Robert Gates [F]
10. Tony Blair [B]

A. British Prime Minister
B. No Current Position
C. President of Iran
D. President of Iraq
E. President of the Palestinian Authority
F. Secretary of Defense
G. Secretary of State
H. Secretary of the Interior
I. Senator
J. Speaker of the House

Appendix 4: Post-Experiment Knowledge Scale

[Correct answer in bold]

1. How many troops does the U.S. currently have in Iraq?
   a. Less than 25,000
   b. Between 25,000 and 75,000
   c. Between 75,000 and 125,000
   d. Between 125,000 and 175,000
   e. More than 175,000

2. Approximately how many casualties have U.S. forces sustained in Iraq to date?
   a. About 3,700 dead, about 27,000 wounded
   b. About 4,400 dead, about 20,000 wounded
   c. About 2,300 dead, about 32,000 wounded
   d. About 3,300 dead, about 18,000 wounded
   e. About 3,900 dead, about 25,000 wounded

3. What is the name of the general who recently gave the report to Congress?
   _____ **(Petraeus)**

4. Who is currently the U.S. ambassador to Iraq?
   _____ **(Crocker)**

5. How do U.S. forces refer to the fortified zone in Baghdad where most of the governing takes place?
   a. The Blue Zone
   b. The Green Zone
   c. The End Zone
   d. The Demilitarized Zone
   e. The Emerald City

225

6. How likely is it that President Bush will follow the recommendations made by the general who testified?
   a. Not at all likely
   b. Somewhat unlikely
   c. Somewhat likely
   d. Almost certain
   e. Don't know

7. Why did some groups attack that general in advance of his testimony? They said that he . . .
   a. Lied in previous reports to Congress
   b. Was politically motivated
   c. Wanted the troops to leave too soon
   d. Didn't understand the realities of war

8. Which party currently controls the two houses of Congress?
   a. Democrats
   b. Republicans
   c. Democrats control the Senate, Republicans control the House
   d. Republicans control the Senate, Democrats control the House

9. How did the general begin his testimony? He said that . . .
   a. His testimony hadn't been edited by anyone
   b. He was optimistic about the progress that has been made
   c. We cannot afford to pull troops out now
   d. Agreed with the president's general strategy
   e. Didn't want the debate to be political

10. According to the general, what will happen if we begin removing troops?
    a. There will be increased pressure on the Iraqi government to make political progress
    b. Iran will become more powerful
    c. Iraq will fall into a civil war
    d. No one knows
    e. A, B, and C
    f. B and C

Appendix 5: Summaries of Programs Used in the Experiment

As with every episode, this broadcast of *The Daily Show* begins with the announcement that it comes from Comedy Central's world news headquarters in New York. In some ways, this is an unusual episode: the show had just returned from a two-week hiatus the previous day and had a great deal of catching up to do. In others ways, it's a typical episode: as expected, the majority of the program's content is centered on national politics and on many of the same issues covered by other nightly news broadcasts. The one thing this episode lacks is a produced segment from a correspondent in the field—a surprising omission, since these have been some of the most reliable sources of humor on the show, deflating ideologues who aren't quite in on the joke—but an understandable one, given how much news there is to catch up on. For our purposes, this is actually a good thing, as it means that all of the news segments leading up to the interview portion of the broadcast (about fourteen minutes of the twenty-two minute program) are national news, making the comparison with network news broadcasts easier. We're going to do just that: compare how much young people learn about political issues, specifically the war in Iraq from a network news broadcast and from *The Daily Show,* to see how well our model of the program's impact holds up. As such, it's important to describe the relevant contents of the episode that we're using for comparison, as well as to give a general idea of what the show is like for readers who may not have seen it.

After the intro and the announcement of that night's guest, actress Jodie Foster, Stewart immediately begins his discussion of the highly anticipated report of General David Petraeus on the progress of the war in Iraq, and whether any troop withdrawals should be made. The jokes begin with a montage of clips from (mostly) Republican politicians saying that they'll withhold judgment about the situation on Iraq until the general's report in September, interspersed with clips from the movie

Braveheart, in which Mel Gibson's character tells his army to "hold" before charging into battle, the army charging only when an ABC news anchor announces that "the time has finally arrived." Before getting to his report, though, and the reactions to it in the press, Stewart brings up a graphic of a *Washington Post* op-ed piece Petraeus wrote just a few weeks before the 2004 presidential election, in which he said that there was "momentum," "optimism" and "tangible progress" in Iraq. The claims proved inaccurate, to put it mildly, and Stewart hopes aloud that one "incredibly relevant" mistake won't cause the media to be too critical of the general. This leads into another montage of pundits, mostly on cable news channels, calling Petraeus everything from "the most talented man I've ever met," to "a miracle worker" with "the heart of a lion." This is contrasted almost immediately with Petraeus not being able to get the microphone to work at the start of the hearings, being handed another microphone, and having no success with that one either. The clip ends with the general looking sheepish and confused, and Stewart mouthing the words "Are you [expletive] kidding me?" The same ironic structure is used throughout: politicians and the media saying one thing, while the actions clearly show something else: in this case, on Petraeus's competence.

While they're "waiting" for the general's microphone to begin working, Stewart launches into some facts about the war: it costs $2 billion per week; 4 million Iraqis have been displaced, 2 million of whom are now refugees; there have been 30,000 American casualties. This segment is closely mirrored in the *World News* broadcast, which shows graphics about the toll of the war, and uses the same clip afterward as Stewart's show, in which Petraeus begins by saying that his report has not been cleared with the White House or anyone else and is entirely his own work. Stewart then interrupts the clip to say what the White House line has been—the surge has been working, and we need more time to assess progress—and shows Petraeus saying the exact same thing. "My God," Stewart says to reinforce the point, "the President has been right the whole time," before showing Petraeus and Bush issuing the same talking points about success in Iraq. Similarly, after showing the general saying that it's impossible to predict what will happen in Iraq, a series of clips show him predicting doom if there is troop withdrawal. The clips end with Stewart noting that all of the consequences that the general is discussing happened when we entered in the first place. With an appeal to M.C. Escher to help the nation out of this apparent Möbius strip, the first segment ends after just shy of nine minutes.

The second segment of the show begins with Stewart introducing the show's resident expert John Hodgman (better known as PC in the "I'm a PC, I'm a Mac" commercials) to discuss the situation. Hodgman tells Stewart that he knows that the surge is successful, even without looking at any of the indicators, because the president is following what boils down to the power of positive thinking. He's put up a "Mission Accomplished" banner, talked about how Iraq will be a beacon of democracy in the Middle East, downplayed expectations, ignored "small" things like bombings. So long as you redefine failure as success, he says, you can be sure that you'll always be successful.

With the end of the segment, a bit more than fifteen minutes into the program, the discussion of national politics is over. The next few minutes are spent in an interview with Jodie Foster about her movie, *The Brave One.* The interview doesn't touch on national politics, and a description wouldn't be relevant to our needs here. A final segment, the "Moment of Zen," shows the committee taking Petraeus's testimony waiting for the microphones to be fixed.

September 10, 2007, 6:30 pm, NBC

Because the format of the network evening news broadcasts is so familiar, there's no need to discuss it in as much depth as we did *The Daily Show* broadcast with which we are contrasting it. There are some points we need to address to ensure that it's a fair comparison, and one of them is the date of the broadcast: *The World News Tonight* episode we're using is from the day before *The Daily Show* episode. The main reason for this is that both programs, on these nights, spent about fifteen minutes discussing the Petraeus report and progress in Iraq. The second is that, as mentioned previously, Stewart's program had just returned from a two-week hiatus on September 10, and thus didn't cover that day's news, but rather what they had missed in previous weeks.

The first five minutes of *The World News* broadcast are taken up by clips from Petraeus's testimony and congressional leader's questions, along with analysis from Pentagon correspondent Jim Miklaszewski. In many cases, these are the same clips as were used in Stewart's broadcast, though the context is rather different. As Baym (2005) notes, *The Daily Show* uses clips almost as a dialectical technique, constantly questioning them and putting them up against other, contradictory, clips. The traditional broadcast uses the clips straight, piecing them together into sound bites in the hopes of giving a general overview of what went on in as short a time as possible. The attempts to get the microphone to work are, unsurprisingly, not included.

This is not to say, though, that the Petraeus's comments pass entirely without criticism. Miklaszewski points out that the possible troop reductions the general spoke about aren't a reduction at all, but a return to the numbers of troops before the president's surge strategy took effect. He doesn't point out, as other media sources at the time did, that such a reduction was necessitated by troop rotations, but it is clear that the comments aren't simply repeated without being evaluated.

Coverage of Petraeus's testimony continues after the first segment, with a three-minute segment discussing the political ramifications of Petraeus's testimony. Republican members of Congress, for instance, blasted liberal groups for advertisements taken out in *The New York Times* and other newspapers questioning whether Petraeus could be trusted. What isn't noted here, though, are the charges behind the advertisement: the ones that Stewart laid out in his broadcast without making reference to the ads. A series of political figures opine on the potential impact of Petraeus's report, generally agreeing that it is Bush's best chance to buy more time in Iraq.

A final segment on the war, "Assessing the Surge," shows footage taken from digital cameras and interviews with Iraqis on the streets. All told, just less than fourteen minutes of the broadcast are spent discussing various elements of the war in Iraq. Afterward, there are a series of shorter articles. There is a one minute segment about an increase in the number of complications due to prescriptions, two minutes about a U.S. scholar ("and grandmother," the report notes) that had been held in Iran, obituaries, and a stock market report. The program ends with a segment called "The Secret to Her Success," described as "how women meet all kinds of challenges, like finances, friends, and work." While this segment isn't exactly paralleled in *The Daily Show* broadcast, the final minutes of both deal with issues completely removed from the political issues that dominate the first two-thirds of both shows.

Notes

CHAPTER 1. WORK, POLITICS

1. Though there has been some debate over the exact nature of these leaners: see Niemi, Reed and Weisberg 1991 and Kieth et al. 1986.

2. As widely used as this scale has become, it hasn't been immune from criticism. The 1980 American National Election Study included an alternate scale that asked people to place themselves on a seven-point scale measuring their closeness to the two parties. This was a response to the fact that many of the people who claim to be independents leaning toward a party are, in fact, more partisan than people who claim to identify with a party weakly: they are, it seems, responding to social pressures to be independent, rather than admitting their partisan views. As valid as the criticisms of the traditional party identification scale have been (see Dennis 1988 for a round-up), the traditional measure has stayed. Whether this is because of its superiority or because of scholarly inertia is anyone's guess, but even those who have conceptual problems with the scale continue to use it, as do we.

3. We'll talk more about this process of political socialization in chapter 6, which deals with the long-term effects of political events on young people's partisanship.

4. As we'll discuss in chapter 6, party identification is different from these other facets of identity in that it is learned as much as experienced. Until individuals have answered the question many times, their response to the question of partisanship may vary, and may vary even afterward, depending on the circumstances and what is on the top of the respondent's head at the time. Political scientists have, however, been treating as an essential aspect of identity for long enough that it would be remiss not to do so here.

5. These figures are always difficult. For instance, calculating the percentage turnout by looking at the number of individuals age eighteen and over means that we're including felons, green card holders, and other people over eighteen who aren't eligible to vote. However, the figures given here are good enough for the purposes of comparison.

6. There are some problems with applying the education variable to young people—namely that many haven't finished their educations yet. However, it isn't really the years of education that matter here, so much as the social and economic background that leads someone to get those years of education. As such, we can model the results of the partisanship model for a college-

educated young person even at an age when not all of them have necessarily finished college.

7. Other lifestyle brands in Forbes's (2007) top 100 best companies to work for include Nordstroms, Yahoo, Microsoft, Four Seasons, Nike, Timberland, IKEA, and, of course, Starbucks.

8. This leaves us with just a bit more than a thousand of the young people we're interested in for this analysis: a relatively small figure. However, we don't necessarily need a large number of young people in the data in order to make judgments about their preferences and predispositions. Instead of splitting up the dataset to look only at young people, we're going to assume linear effects of age and leverage the variance in the age effects of older individuals to tell us about what's going on with young people. This approach has the added advantage of allowing us to compare the views of young and old people to ensure that age has a significant effect.

9. The interactions here include work status by age, work status by education, and a three-way interaction of work status by education by age. A separate model including dummy variables for part-time work and nonworking students was also run; neither of these dummies, nor their interactions, had significant effects on strength of partisanship. For the sake of clarity in the estimated effects, these variables were excluded from the final model.

10. Essentially, the ordered logit model assumes that people are operating on a spectrum between independent and strong partisan and uses the specified variables to guess where someone should be on that scale. Because we're trying to predict a discrete outcome—independent or leaner, for example—the best metric to see how good a job the variables do is the PCP, or percent correctly predicted, which tells us how often the model guessed correctly.

11. Monte Carlo analyses were carried out using Clarify 2.1, as discussed in King, Gary, Michael Tomz and James Wittenberg 2000. "Making the most of Statistical Analyses: Improving Interpretation and Presentation." *American Journal of Political Science* 44(2): 341–55.

12. Robert Putnam, in his widely read 2000 book *Bowling Alone,* as well as other work, refers to this as "social capital," borrowing a phrase from Bourdieu (1977, 1983).

13. While we don't have a direct measure of the difference between expected and actual tax revenue—and, to be fair, the Congress doesn't seem to have a reliable indicator of this either—the unemployment indicator used here is certainly an acceptable leading indicator of government revenues.

14. The use of objective economic indicators is important here. Initial studies of macropartisanship used subjective economic indicators: how well people thought that the economy was doing, how they expected it to be doing in six months. It has been argued (as in Lebo and Cassino 2007), however, that these subjective economic measures are at least partially endogenous to partisanship. People who like the president say that the economy is going well and will continue to do so; people who don't like him are more pessimistic.

15. It could be argued that the size of this effect is due to the health of the economy in the mid 1990s; the effects look bigger because the unemployment rate simply didn't change very much. However, the contrast in effects among

young people, who see the *smallest* effects of unemployment during the Clinton years, would argue otherwise.

16. In reality, the unemployment rate during the George W. Bush administration has fluctuated a bit more than two points, from 4.2 percent (February 2001) to 6.3 percent (June 2003).

CHAPTER 2. REPUBLICANS

1. Briefly, the Downs-Hotelling (Downs 1997 [1957]) model argues that people will vote for whichever candidate is ideologically closest to themselves. Assuming that voters are normally distributed across ideologies, the candidate closest to the middle of the distribution will get the greatest number of votes. As such, it is in the best interest of both candidates to be as close to the middle as they can possibly manage. This is, of course, more difficult than it sounds, as locating the middle of the distribution isn't a trivial task, but it provides some explanation as to why the parties in American politics often seem to offer so little choice on many issues.

2. The amendment regarding flag burning was passed by the House of Representatives in June 2005, and failed by one vote to receive the necessary two-thirds margin in the Senate in June 2006. The Federal Marriage Amendment failed even to get sufficient votes to invoke cloture, also in June 2006.

3. In their individual-level models, trust in government had a significant effect on support for government spending in all eight issues that they considered, but only among conservatives. Among liberals, trust in government was a significant predictor of support for only one of the questions they modeled, aid to mothers. Trust had a significant effect on moderate's support of distributive, but not redistributive, policies.

4. The issue positions predicted by ideology may be more stable for domestic than for foreign policy issues (Cronin and Fordham 1999). Since the 1960s, the parties seem to have completely flipped on foreign policy, with Republicans becoming internationalist, and Democrats nationalist (and they may well have flipped again since then). In America government, politics is said to "stop at the water's edge": and so it isn't surprising that the links between ideology and policy are weaker in the international arena than they are in the domestic. Thankfully, little of our analysis relies on foreign policy stances, minimizing the effects of this problem going forward.

5. According to Census Bureau statistics, real median household income in the Northeast, Midwest and West were almost identical, at about $46,000 per year. The South not only had a significantly lower median household income ($39,823), but one that was declining, while the others remained stable.

6. This link between specific political and ideological views and the Holocaust has been roundly criticized as the result of a left-wing bias in academia (as in Durrheim 1997). However, any linkage between psychological predispositions and ideological views is, as Jost et al. (2003) argue, an empirical question, and should be approached as such.

7. As widely cited and influential as *The Authoritarian Personality* is, the argument is rather dated, with authoritarianism resulting from child-rearing practices. However much we may scoff at the Freudian overtones of the work, the basic idea—political and social views as the result of deep psychological traits, rather than day-to-day calculation—is even more influential today than when the book was first published.

8. The interpretation of these results vary. Milgram (1963) himself posited the existence of an "agentic state," in which people consciously gave over responsibility for their actions to a higher power. Therefore, rather than applying their own morality or desires to a subject, they simply sought to confirm that the higher authority really wanted them to do something. Others find an explanation in Solomon Asch's (1951, 1956) conformity experiments, and argue that the participants in Milgram's experiments were simply trying to conform to the social script put before them.

9. Sadly, little is known of Frenkel-Brunswik's life. Just as her research was first being recognized, her husband, also a professor of psychology, killed himself: she followed a few years later, overdosing on barbiturates in 1958.

10. Others, most notably Sidanius, see this racism and sexism arising from a different psychological predisposition: the desire to dominate outgroups like racial minorities (Sidanius 1993; Sidanius and Pratto 1993, 1996). This social dominance orientation has been widely cited, but in our studies, it is difficult to distinguish it from the intolerance of ambiguity explanation given in the text. Empirically, though, the results are the same. Just as our respondents would be unlikely to answer questions in an overtly racist way, they would be unlikely to do so in a way that overtly revealed a desire to dominate other racial or ethnic groups. Rather, the indicators would most likely be references to principled political views that *happen* to have negative consequences for the groups in question, by cutting governmental aid programs or downplaying the need for equal opportunity programs such as affirmative action.

11. The best evidence for this comes from the work of researchers on the modern racism scale, which makes the case that modern taboos against overt racism have simply driven that racism underground. Rather than telling pollsters that they think blacks are less intelligent or hardworking than whites, racist individuals have learned to hide their views behind opinions that can be supported without racist appeals. According to these theories, much of the opposition to forced bussing, affirmative action, welfare, and other issues tainted with race is due to racism, rather than conservative principles.

12. While it is certainly the case that superhero comic books—and their attendant themes of power and mastery—had peaks in the 1930s and 1960s (the decades identified as having high ambient social threat), the relationship is weak at best. In the 1930s, for instance, superheroes such as Superman and Captain America were immensely popular, but not until 1939, and were much more a phenomenon of the 1940s than 1930s. The superhero renaissance of the 1960s, on the other hand, was less the result of a fretful public looking for super authority figures to save them than a reaction to Stan Lee's embrace of social discord in making comics "relevant." His characters were more likely to be seen as counterculture figures than defenders of the status quo. Finally, the third boom

in comic book sales took place in the early to mid 1990s, one of the least threatening periods of recent history, and the substantial increase in ambient threat post–9/11 has done little to boost the sales of superheroes.

Chapter 3. Democrats

1. According to a July 2007, Zogby poll, 58 percent of Americans think that the political bias of college professors is a serious problem, with about two-thirds of those rating it as a "very serious" problem.

2. These figures were taken from a 2005 poll carried out by researchers at George Mason University (Rothman, Lichter and Nevitte 2005).

3. There is some debate as to whether egalitarianism or humanitarianism is most important in determining American's positions on issues (see Feldman and Steenbergen 2001). What seems most likely is that egalitarianism—the belief that everyone should be treated equally—is most often implicated in legal matters, and humanitarianism—the belief that people should be helped when possible—is most prevalent in economic matters.

4. There's also a substantial racial element to American's opposition to welfare policy. Many Americans believe—mistakenly—that blacks are the primary beneficiaries of welfare benefits and use opposition to them as a form of covert racism (Gilens 1995, 1996).

5. The results change little when independent leaners are included in the calculation. With leaners included, 46 percent of Democrats are on the egalitarian side of the scale, compared with 17 percent of Republicans. 28 percent of Democrats come out on the individualistic side, compared with 67 percent of Republicans.

6. By recent, we mean since the ideological polarization of the parties, as discussed in chapter 4. Before then, the parties were highly mixed on such issues, especially in the South.

7. This was a volunteered response, only given by 22 respondents in the poll. Six of those 22 were strong Republicans. No one polled said that rich people don't pay any taxes (though that may well be more accurate).

8. This characteristic of liberals has been used to explain the liberalism of American Jews (Levey 1995; Walzer 1995), the argument being that the argumentative, complex nature of Democratic rhetoric is similar to that of traditional Jewish scholars, and therefore intrinsically appealing to Jews. Despite the discomfort associated with making judgments about why a group of people do something based on expectations about their traditions, this has been seen as an explanation for why American Jews, for whom a combination of religiosity and income would lead us to expect Republicanism, would support the Democratic Party. See Cohen and Liebman (1997) for a full discussion.

9. The blame placed by some Democratic groups—such as Daily Kos and MoveOn.org—on Gonzales, Cheney, and Rove can be seen, in this way, as a complex way of dealing with anger toward Bush. He isn't necessarily bad, but he's surrounded by bad people who are using him.

Chapter 4. Independents

1. Even these analyses give little hope to those hoping for the truly independent to exhibit sophisticated political behavior, as they focus mostly on individuals who initially claim to be independent, but lean toward one party or the other.

2. This vote, on the Byrd-Hagel resolution, actually came before the terms of the treaty had been finalized. It rejected the basis of the Kyoto Protocols—binding targets for industrialized nations, lower standards for developing nations—and, as a result, the treaty itself was never presented to the Senate for approval.

3. Actually, it increased by thirteen points because of a decrease in the number of blacks identifying themselves as apolitical, presumably out of fear of reprisals or laws preventing them from registering to vote.

4. The decrease in the number of independents in 2002 is largely due to a sudden increase in the percentage of individuals identifying themselves as Republicans in the immediate aftermath of the September 11 attacks. As can be seen in Figures 4.1 and 4.2, this trend reversed itself rather quickly. A discussion of why this may have happened is in chapter 6.

5. The exact question used for most of Chanley, Rudolph, and Rahn's analysis was "How much of the time do you think you can trust the government in Washington to do what is right—just about always, most of the time, or only some of the time?" Different questions were used to fill the gaps in the series created by this question, using Stimson's (1999) matching techniques to iron out any differences in the question wording.

6. While it's a matter of some contention whether there's actually been an increase in the number or severity of political scandals, there's no doubt that media attention to these scandals has increased substantially.

7. One of the fourth-graders in Hershey and Hill's (1974) study put it this way: "He's just going off about the gas shortage and the high prices, like, 'The people can worry about that. I'm worried about *me*.' He is trying to prove he is so innocent, you know, and he is the best, you know, and he didn't do nothing wrong or anything."

8. We discuss this process in greater detail in the chapter dealing with Republicans. It also seems likely that this is an emergent process, in which top-down and bottom-up pressures come together to create otherwise unexpected outcomes.

9. Part of this difference may also be due to the increased use of the "conservative" label by Republican candidates. Especially since Reagan's two terms in office, Republican candidates have fought to be called conservative, while Democrats continue to shy away from being labeled as "liberal." However, it's unlikely that this results in the entire difference in Figure 4.3, which deals with the proportion calling the parties "moderate, middle of the road" and "extremely" conservative or liberal.

10. Briefly, Duverger's law (1954) holds that the maximum number of competitive parties in any given district is equal to the number of seats that district is electing, plus one. Any other parties that try and run will be subject to strategic defection, as their supporters turn to a less preferred party that has a better

chance of winning (Riker 1982). Note that this rule applies only to a single district: theoretically, each district could have two different parties competing, though this is limited by the single grand prize of a presidential system. Regardless, it seems unlikely that many of the respondents to the survey are aware of this structural barrier, though they may have some experience with legal barriers to third-party competition, such as ballot access and debate entry.

CHAPTER 5. *THE DAILY SHOW*

1. The program has won two George Foster Peabody Awards for excellence in radio and television broadcasting: one each for coverage of the 2000 and 2004 presidential election campaigns.

2. An alternative explanation might come from Kressel's (1987) work on perceptions of media bias in the Israeli-Palestinian conflict. Essentially, individuals on the extreme political right see even right-wing media sources as being biased toward the left, and moderate news sources as being extremely left. However, there is no indication in this particular respondent's other responses that he is so far right as to make this plausible.

3. As before, part of this is almost certainly due to confusion over what *liberal* and *conservative* even mean. As one of our respondents said about *The Daily Show*, "They are pro-war and support the fight against terrorist. They are the exact opposite of CNN, because they are more liberal."

4. As Baum (2002) notes, there isn't a commonly accepted definition of "soft" news: it's whatever hard news *isn't*.

5. The top ten cable Nielsen shows that week:

1. *High School Musical 2* (Disney)
2. *Hannah Montana* (Disney)
3. *High School Musical 2* (Disney)
4. *Hannah Montana* (Disney)
5. *The Suite Life of Zack and Cody* (Disney)
6. *High School Musical 2* (Disney)
7. *The Closer* (TNT)
8. *High School Musical* (Disney)
9. *The Suite Life of Zack and Cody* (Disney)
10. *Hannah Montana* (Disney)

That week wasn't necessarily representative—it's obviously slanted by the large numbers for *High School Musical 2* and its lead-ins, including Billy Ray Cyrus comedy *Hannah Montana*, but it does reflect how skewed the cable Nielsen results can be.

6. According to a June 2007 Harris poll, about 11 percent of Americans use only cellular phones. However, more than half of these (55 percent) were under the age of thirty.

7. The fight between O'Reilly and *The Daily Show* for the top cable news show has occasionally become heated, with O'Reilly expressing outrage at what he calls the "stoned slackers" and "dopey kids" watching Stewart's show, and claiming that nearly 90 percent of them are intoxicated while they watch

(a comment he was widely criticized for, coming, as it did, just before an Annenberg Study showing that *Daily Show* viewers were actually more educated and informed than his own audience).

8. Median ages for *The Daily Show* (11 PM showing) and *The O'Reilly Factor* (8 PM showing) from Nielsen's Npower Market Breaks of the two programs.

9. The coders that analyzed the media appearances in Baum's study found several criticisms per minute in traditional hard news interviews of Kerry, but no comments harsh enough to qualify as criticisms in Kerry's interview on the Letterman program. This is despite the length of time given to Kerry's interview there: Farnswoth and Lichter (2003) find that Kerry had more speaking time in that single interview than he did on the three evening news broadcasts, for that entire month, combined.

10. The exact quotes, from CNN's transcript of Stewart's October 15, 2004, interview.

> STEWART: You're on CNN. The show that leads into me is puppets making crank phone calls.
> (*Laughter*)
> STEWART: What is wrong with you?
> CARLSON: Well, I'm just saying, there's no reason for you—when you have this marvelous opportunity not to be the guy's butt boy, to go ahead and be his butt boy. Come on. It's embarrassing.
> STEWART: I was absolutely his butt boy. I was so far—you would not believe what he ate two weeks ago.

11. Olbermann's ratings swing up or down rather dramatically depending on whether they include the viewers who watch the program (via TiVo or other means) outside of its broadcast time of 8 PM. Without these viewers, he averages about 650,000 viewers per night, subject to the same provisos governing ratings calculations for *The Daily Show* (which, presumably because of its late hour, and next-day reruns doesn't have nearly as many people recording it to watch later). Regardless of which number is used, the interpretation remains substantively the same.

12. National Public Radio, often referred to as liberal by those claiming that radio is not biased toward the right, doesn't seem to offer much to our young respondents. Few of them had heard of NPR before the survey, and those that had heard of it didn't know much about it.

13. Results taken from the National Annenberg Election Study, carried out between July 15 and September 19, 2004.

14. If we include the "Moment of Zen" and the footage shown along with the credits at the very end of the show, both of which are offered without comment, the total for *The Daily Show* increases by just shy of a minute, meaning that Stewart's program, arguably, spent about two minutes more on national politics. However, this is countered by oblique references to national issues in several stories on the NBC broadcast, including an obituary for President Ronald Reagan's first wife and an interview with a former prisoner in Iran.

15. In many cases, a Poisson-related model is used for the sort of count variables used in this analysis. However, the distribution of the data across the categories is fairly uniform, and there aren't so many zero values as to require a

zero-inflated Poisson or related model. As such, the added complexity of a Poisson-related model, especially given the small n of the experiment, buys us very little.

Furthermore, in this set of analyses, the difference between the Poisson results and the ordered logit results are minimal. All of the significant effects remain in the same direction, and the magnitude of the main effects relative to the interaction effects is the same. The only notable difference is the increase in the relative standard errors of the Poisson regression due to the relative inefficiency of the MLE technique used, and, even so, the significant effects remain significant (with the p-values approximately doubled) in the Poisson results.

16. Using the tenth and ninetieth percentiles, or the minimum or maximum, rather than the twenty-fifth and seventy-fifth percentiles, would lead to even larger effects, but at the risk of overstating the results.

17. As before, a Poisson or Poisson-related model would also be appropriate for the analyses, though such models are less desirable in this case because of their relative inefficiency. In two of the analyses (those for the number of items answered correctly of those that were and were not contained in the broadcast), there is no notable difference between the ordered logit and Poisson models: not surprising, given the lack of results in the ordered logit. In the third model, for the number of implied items answered correctly, there is some difference. Though the coefficients are in the same direction, and the main and interaction effects are of the same relative magnitude, the z-scores of the Poisson model are much lower. For instance, the z-score for the main effect of experimental condition in the ordered logit model is –1.69, with a corresponding p-value of .045 (one-tailed). In the Poisson regression, the z-score is reduced to –.90, with a one-tailed p-value of .184. The question, then, is not of the direction or magnitude of the effects, but rather of the likelihood that the effects were the result of random chance, an issue that can only be resolved—in any case—by examining the theoretical base for the hypotheses being tested and their correspondence to previous findings.

CHAPTER 6. WHAT DOES TOMORROW HOLD?

1. Helmut Norpoth (i.e., Norpoth 1995, 2001, 2004) has been among the most successful. In past election years, an issue of *Political Science and Politics* has been devoted to predictions about the outcome of presidential elections, with mixed results.

2. The model of answering questions described later in this chapter owes a great deal to the online processing model described by Lodge and his colleagues. The simplest version of the online processing model holds that when people process political information, they figure out if the information is good or bad and adjust their overall evaluation of the person the information is about accordingly. So, you hear that a senator is involved in a sex scandal and decide that you don't like him as much as you used to. Lodge's key insight is that, at that point, there's really no need to hold on to the information that led you to change the evaluation, and you can safely forget why, exactly, it is that

you don't like him quite as much anymore. All that you need to know is the "affect" associated with the candidate—the summation of all the likes and dislikes. This model has proved compelling to many political scientists because it allows a public that is demonstrably ignorant of many of the basic facts of politics to make good decisions about them, in what's often called "high information rationality." The people may not know much, but their opinions are valid, and based on all of the information that you would hope they would have.

3. Former New York City mayor and 2008 candidate for the Republican presidential nomination Rudolph Giuliani, for instance, has said that he became a Republican after watching the Humphrey-Nixon debates in 1968. These debates however, didn't actually happen, making the claim either an example of political theater, confusion, or faulty flashbulb memory.

4. We owe this formulation to John Zaller and Stanley Feldman's "Simple Model of the Survey Response," which puts forward a model for the construction of summary evaluations of political candidates and objects from the considerations that come to mind when the candidate or object is mentioned. This notion of constructed evaluations has often been put at odds with the stored evaluations proposed by the online processing model, the so-called "Stony Brook school," names after the State University of New York at Stony Brook, where Lodge has enjoyed a long tenure. Of course, the conflict is vastly overstated: Feldman is at Stony Brook with Lodge, and the model described in this chapter, among others, liberally combines the two approaches.

5. This sort of analogy is common in cognitive psychology, perhaps because the vast increase in the understanding of the mind (the "cognitive revolution" that began in the 1950s) was spurred on by an increase in the ability of computers to model these concepts of memory and accessibility. For instance, it isn't at all uncommon to hear the brain referred to as a "Turing machine."

6. There's some debate over the extent to which a "node" is a node, with some cognitive and social psychologists arguing that many concepts are represented by a group of nodes tied together so closely as to be inseparable, sometimes referred to as a "schema." To the extent that a schema represents one chunk of information in working memory, just as one node does, this is, for our purposes, a distinction without much of a difference.

7. Other theories—notably those proposed by Taber and Lodge—propose that the affect is stored with the node, rather than distributed as a connection with other nodes. Certainly, the stored affect has points to recommend it, especially the seemingly automatic activation of affect upon the activation of a node. However, there is no reason that a model where affect is stored via connections doesn't require the added complexity of stored affect. In this model, the affective component of a node can be created in the same way as the semantic associations, through the process often referred to as "wire by fire." According to this model, connections are formed between nodes when those nodes are activated simultaneously. The more often those nodes are activated simultaneously, the stronger the connection between the two becomes. For instance, the nodes representing "bird" and "wing" are often activated at the same time, so the mention of one is likely to lead to the activation of the other. In addition to wings, birds also have livers, but the fact that "liver" and "bird" are less likely to be simultaneously activated means that the connection between the two of them is much weaker.

In practice, the difference between the affect by association model and the affective tags are fleeting at best, and the overall model is not at all impacted by the replacement of affective associations with tags.

8. To anyone familiar with the workings of neurons within the brain, this is all going to sound very familiar. It's tempting to map nodes onto neurons, and connections between nodes onto synapses, and so on. However, the analogy breaks down fairly quickly. As far as we can tell, nodes don't have refractory periods, or required levels of activation before firing, the way that neurons do. The mind—what we're talking about here—arises from the brain, the meat and wires where the neurons are, but it isn't the same thing.

9. Of course, political sophisticates are very good are refusing to alter their evaluations regardless of the salience of dissonant considerations: bring up the Lewinsky scandal all you want, but James Carville isn't going to speak ill of Bill Clinton. Two main reasons for this inability (or refusal) to deal with discordant information have been offered. The first rests on the ability of political sophisticates to counterargue or otherwise dismiss such information: consciously finding reasons why the information isn't at odds with their existing beliefs. This sort of behavior is detectable because of the cognitive effort involved in it: you have to put effort into ignoring or explaining away information. Alternately, this can be seen as the partner of the Bayesian anchoring and adjustment effects discussed earlier. Political sophisticates have enough information—a strong enough anchor—that no amount of new information is sufficient to make their opinions change.

10. We can see this in a classic University of Chicago study, in which students were asked, by phone, to evaluate their relationships and their lives in general. Those students who were asked on rainy days evaluated their lives and relationships more negatively than those who were asked on sunny days. That, in and of itself, isn't surprising: rainy days lead to negative moods, which can be thought of as an increased activation of the negative affective network, so positive things about their lives and relationships are less likely to come to mind, and negative things are more likely to. What's interesting here is that the effects disappeared completely when respondents were first asked what the weather was like. Even without apparent cognitive effort—after all, no one really thinks "My girlfriend is probably going to leave me, but I only think that because it's raining"—the respondents were able to correct for the temporarily increased negative affect.

11. It would be the minimum effect because some proportion of the sample that was not reminded of the scandal would be thinking about it anyway. As this proportion of people who were thinking about it regardless approaches the proportion in the group that was reminded that are thinking about it, the difference disappears. Outside of the laboratory, we can't measure these proportions, and it's a dicey proposition even in the laboratory, so the most we can say is that the difference in evaluations due to the scandal is at least as large as the difference between the reminded and not-reminded groups.

12. Eisenhower, as a former commander of NATO forces, was largely immune from this criticism, one of the reasons he was such a strong candidate in 1952. Still, he faced harsh criticism for his internationalist stances from members of his own party like Robert Taft, who came very close to denying him the nomination.

13. Vietnam, it may seem, gets short shrift in our discussion of the long-term effects of recent political events. The main reason for this is empirical. To sort out the effects of the Vietnam War, we have to control for all of the other events going on at the same time. This wouldn't be a problem, but many of those events were unique, and coincided with events in the war that could be expected to shift partisanship. Without some separation between these events there's no way to determine their individual contributions to any shift in partisanship, and no way to compare the shift to any other shift in recent history. In the absence of such empirical evidence, it is better, we think, to say little, than to overstate what can be proven.

14. Wright (1977) finds that those members of Nixon's own party who voted against impeachment were significantly more likely to lose their seats in the 1974 midterms than Republicans who had voted in favor of impeachment.

15. This can, of course, be beneficial to some politicians. Bill Clinton, for instance, was able to get the 1992 Democratic presidential nomination largely because none of the big names—most notably Mario Cuomo—wanted to run against a then-popular George H. W. Bush, preferring to wait for 1996.

16. In contrast, other analyses, including one by one of the authors, have shown a relatively modest effect on Nixon's approval. Mackuen, Erikson, and Stimson show a twelve-point decline in presidential approval as a result or Watergate; Lebo and Cassino (2007) show a decline of only about five points in his approval (the difference is almost certainly due to the increased specification of Lebo and Cassino's model). However, it isn't at all odd that more people would switch parties than would change their evaluation of Nixon, given Nixon's already low levels of support at the revelation of his role in the scandal.

17. The surveys were taken beginning in the July before the election, with polls coming in July, August, October, and the week before the election. The average number of respondents for the polls was 572. More details on these polls can be found in two articles written for *The Polling Report* (Cassino and Woolley 2006a, 2006b) and *Survey Practice* (Cassino, Jenkins and Woolley 2007).

18. There was always the possibility that respondents might be differently affected by mentions of President Bush and mentions of the war in Iraq. The common wisdom about Bush is, after all, that he was personally liked even as his policies were disliked. To ensure that this didn't confound the results of the priming, the first survey (carried out in July) had three, rather than two, priming conditions. In the first, respondents were asked about President Bush and Iraq at the beginning of the poll (unprimed), in the second, they were asked about President Bush at the beginning of the poll, and Iraq at the end (primed only with Iraq), and in the third they were asked about both Bush and Iraq immediately before the party identification questions (primed with both). No differences between the first and second conditions were detectable, implying that President Bush is so linked with the war and Iraq that mentioning one necessarily brings the other to mind. This is supported by the strong relationship between the answers to these questions. For instance, the correlation between views of progress in Iraq ("How well is the military effort in Iraq going?") and Bush's job performance is .65. The correlation between the rightness of going into Iraq ("Was invading Iraq the right thing to do, or the wrong thing?") and Bush's job performance is .69. In the analyses discussed in the text, the second

condition from the first study was excluded to ensure that it didn't contaminate the results of the priming condition in the subsequent surveys.

19. The primary purpose of these polls was to estimate the effects of the war in Iraq on vote choice. Thus, the questions on Iraq were designed to come immediately before questions about which candidate the respondent preferred in the Senate race or well after that. The only challenge faced by adapting these questions to measure the effect of Bush and Iraq on partisanship is that all of the respondents receive questions about Bush and Iraq before answering questions about partisanship. However, the length of time between the initial questions about national issues and the partisanship questions is great enough—about ten minutes, as noted in the text—and filled with the mention of so many other political issues and ideas, that the increased activation of Bush and Iraq due to the initial questions about them should have long since faded. Also, it should be noted that any residual activation of these issues should work *against* our hypotheses, reducing the difference between the control and experimental groups.

20. For instance, the inclusion of the "national view X priming condition X age" variable affects the interpretation of the "national view X priming condition" variable such that the latter only represents individuals for whom the age variable is zero. Since age in the model is represented by year of birth, this is a highly hypothetical case, extending only, perhaps, to Mel Brooks, as interviewed by Carl Reiner.

21. Predictors in the model not previously discussed include education (measured on a five-point scale, with categories for no high school diploma, high school education, some college education, a college degree, and graduate degrees), gender (males at one, females at two) and race (one for white, two for all others).

22. As before, these effects are estimated with Tomz, King, and Wittenberg's (2003) CLARIFY routine for Stata 9.

23. For the purposes of equivalence across conditions, all of these figures assume a white male respondent with some college education. This means, of course, that there are rather more Republicans than there would be if the model were based on women or non-whites. However, these demographic factors are modeled only as main effects, not interactions, so their inclusion would only shift the results up or down for either of the partisanship categories. The comparisons between the groups would remain the same. For instance, a non-white respondent, in all cases, would be about twelve points less likely to be a Republican and about nine points more likely to be a Democrat, but the differences between the priming conditions within these categories would be unaffected.

24. These figures are taken from the responses of primed twenty-five-year-olds in the model. It is assumed that if Bush and Iraq were always associated with partisan politics, or the Republican Party, respondents would have approximately the same views of these issues as they do now. For instance, in the New Jersey surveys, about two-thirds of respondents with a view have a negative view of the direction that the country is going. Therefore, the overall percentage share of the Democratic Party would be $2/3$ * (proportion of primed twenty-five-year-old Democrats who say that the country is on the wrong track) + $1/3$ * (proportion of primed twenty-five-year-old Democrats who say that the country is on the wrong track). In the New Jersey surveys, this amounts to 17.2

percent of respondents expected to be Democrats with negative views of Bush and Iraq, and 4.5 percent expected to be Democrats with positive views of Bush and Iraq. Democrats with positive views of Bush and Iraq would therefore represent about 20 percent of all Democrats, a figure that can be compared with the percent of Democrats in the unprimed category who currently have a positive view of Bush and Iraq, a bit less than half of those who have an opinion. Currently, 20 percent of unprimed twenty-five-year-old respondents who say that the country is on the right track are Democrats, and 23 percent of those who say that the country is on the wrong track are Democrats. Therefore, 20/43, or about 46 percent of unprimed twenty-five-year-old Democrats currently say that the country is on the right track, and a drop to 4.5/22, or about 20 percent, represents a huge loss in the diversity of opinion within the Democratic Party.

25. One interesting exception to this pattern comes in the effect of priming on fifty-five-year-olds who feel that the country is on the wrong track. They should be more likely to identify with the Democratic Party—but in fact become more likely to identify with the Republican Party by 2.4 percent. This is especially surprising as most of the other effects in the category are in the expected direction: priming led the individuals to be slightly less likely to be Democrats or to lean toward the Democrats. Among twenty-five-year-olds, the effect was in the expected direction. Because of the strength of the results otherwise, we don't feel that this calls the other results into question. While we can't identify the exact cause of this discrepancy without further studies, it seems possible that it's the result of the one question included in the national study not in the New Jersey study: 2008 candidate choice. Individuals who feel that the country is going in the wrong direction could easily choose a Republican candidate who they see as representing an alternative to the current administration, and, in doing so, reinforce their allegiance to the Republican Party.

26. This can be most easily seen in the changes in Poole and Rosenthal's D-Nominate scores (Poole and Rosenthal 1991, 2001, among others), which use roll-call votes to estimate the ideological views of members of Congress. While this approach certainly present some problems (and see Segal and Cover 1989 for a solution applied to the Supreme Court), it is the most widely accepted measure in political science research. Alternatives, such as the scores given out by Americans for Democratic Action, have generally the same result.

27. Perhaps the clearest example of party change through attrition is the shift in the stance of the Democratic Party on civil rights from the 1950 through the 1980s. Over time, pro–civil rights liberals like Hubert Humphrey (mostly from the north) replaced the old-line conservative Democrats. The children of these conservative "boll weevil" Democrats became Republicans.

28. Such a situation is by no means new to American politics. Richard Nixon campaigned on a promise to bring "peace with honor" to our conflict in Vietnam. Exactly what this meant, or how he was going to do it wasn't really discussed, and it isn't clear that he even knew.

29. Again, these figures represent the views of young white males: the overall composition of either party on these issues would be rather different, reflecting the diverse coalitions making up the parties.

30. The polarization is expected to occur because a large proportion of the Democratic Party will have similar affective associations for Bush and the war,

and a similar semantic relationship between those issues and the Republican Party. As such, nodes with a semantic relationship with Bush or Iraq can be expected to share that negative affect, and engender a similar response from a large proportion (92 percent of those with a view of the issue) of the party.

CHAPTER 7. CONCLUSION

1. Episode entitled "Mr. Willis of Ohio," original airdate November 3, 1999. Its airing led then White House press secretary, Joe Lockhart, to say, "Make the Census interesting; who'd have thought?"

2. Episode entitled "Someone's Going to Emergency, Someone's Going to Jail," original airdate February 28, 2001. According to a report from the *Hartford (Conn.) Courant* (July 5, 2001) about the impact of the episode, the company making the Peters projection maps typically sold about six per week before the episode was first broadcast, and sold three hundred the following week. Almost six months later, the company reported that about 80 percent of its sales were of the controversial projection.

Bibliography

Abramowitz, Alan, L. 1995. It's abortion, stupid: Policy voting in the 1992 presidential election. *The Journal of Politics* 57(1):176–86.

Abramson, Paul R. and Charles W. Ostrom, Jr. 1991. Macropartisanship: An empirical reassessment. *American Political Science Review* 85(1):181–92.

Adams, Greg D. 1997. Abortion: Evidence of an issue evolution. *American Journal of Political Science* 41(3):718–37.

Adorno, Theodor W., Else Frenkel-Brunswik, Daniel J. Levinson, and R. Nevitt Sanford. 1950. *The authoritarian personality.* New York: Harper.

Altemeyer, Robert A. 1996. *The authoritarian spectre.* Cambridge: Harvard University Press.

———. 1998. The other 'authoritarian personality.' In M. P. Zanna, ed., *Advances in experimental social psychology* (Vol. 30, pp. 47–91). New York: Academic Press.

Arendt, Hannah. 1958. *The human condition.* Chicago: University of Chicago Press.

Asch, Solomon E. 1951. Effects of group pressure upon the modification and distortion of judgment." In H. Guetzkow (ed.) *Groups, leadership and men.* Pittsburgh: Carnegie Press.

———. 1956. Studies of independence and conformity: A minority of one against a unanimous majority. *Psychological Monographs* 70 (Whole no. 416).

Asher, Herbert. 1980. *Presidential elections in American politics.* Homewood: Dorsey.

Avery, R. K. 1979. Adolescents' use of the mass media. *American Behavioural Scientist.* 23:53–70.

Baker-Brown, G., E. J. Ballard, S. Bluck, B. de Vries, P. Suedfeld, and P. E. Tetlock. 1992. The conceptual integrative complexity scoring manual. In *Motivation and Personality: Handbook of thematic content analysis,* edited by C. P. Smith, 400–18. Cambridge: Cambridge University Press.

Ballard, E. J. 1983. Canadian prime ministers: Complexity and political issues. *Canadian Psychology* 24:125–30.

Bastedo, Ralph W., and Milton Lodge. 1980. The meaning of party labels. *Political Behavior* 2 (3):287–308.

Baum, Matthew A. 2002. Sex, lies, and war: How soft news brings foreign policy to the inattentive public. *The American Political Science Review* 96(1):91–109.

———. 2005. Talking the vote: Why presidential candidates hit the talk show circuit. *American Journal of Political Science* 49(2):213–34.

Baym, Geoffrey. 2005. The daily show: Discursive integration and the reinvention of political journalism. *Political Communication* 22:259–76.

Belk, Russell W. 1988. Possessions and the extended self. *Journal of Consumer Research*, 15 (September):139–68.

Bennett, Stephen Earle. 1996. "Know-Nothings" revisited again. *Political Behavior* 18(3):219–33.

Benoit, W. L., J. P. McHale, G. J. Hansen, P. M. Pier and J. P. McGuire. 2003. *Campaign 2000: A Functional Analysis of Presidential Campaign Discourse.* Lanham, MD: Rowman and Littlefield.

Bentley, T., K. Oakley, S. Gibson, and K. Kilgour. 1999. *The real deal: What young people really think about government, politics and social exclusion.* London: Demos.

Berelson, Bernard R., Paul F. Lazarsfeld, and William N. McPhee. 1954. *Voting: A study of opinion formation in a presidential campaign.* Chicago: University of Chicago Press.

Besen, Yasemin. 2004. It's not like a job: A study of part-time youth labor in suburban America. *Contexts* 3(4):60–61.

———. 2005. Consumption of production: A study of part-time youth labor in suburban America. *Berkeley Journal of Sociology* 49(1):58–75.

———. 2006[a]. Pay or play? Labor market entry decisions of youth in the United States. *Regional Labor Review* 9(3):30–40.

———. 2006[b]. Fun or exploitation: The lived experience of work in suburban America. *Journal of Contemporary Ethnography* 35 (3):319–41.

Blanchette, Isabelle. 2006. Snakes, spiders, guns and syringes: How specific are evolutionary constraints on the detection of threatening stimuli? *Quarterly Journal of Experimental Psychology* 59(8):1484–1504.

Bourdieu, Pierre. 1977. *Outline of a theory of practice.* New York: Cambridge University Press.

———. 1983. Ökonomisches kapital, kulturelles kapital, soziales kapital in soziale ungleichheiten (Soziale Welt, Sonderheft 2), edited by Reinhard Kreckel. Goettingen: Otto Schartz & Co. pp. 183–98.

Buckley, William S. 1955. Publisher's statement. *National Review* 1(1):1.

Budner, S. 1962. Intolerance of ambiguity as a personality variable. *Journal of Personality* 30:29–59.

Burden, Barry C., and Joseph Neal Rice Sanberg. 2003. Budget rhetoric in presidential campaigns from 1952 to 2000. *Political Behavior* 25(2):97–118.

Campbell, Angus, Phillip E. Converse, W. E. Miller, and Donald E. Stokes. 1960. *The American voter.* New York: Wiley.

Carlson, L., and S. Groosbart. 1988. Parental style and consumer socialization. *Journal of Consumer Research* 15:77–94.

Carmines, Edward G., and Geoffrey C. Layman. 1997. Issue evolution in postwar American politics: Old certainties and fresh tensions. In Byron E. Shafer, ed., *Present Discontents.* Chatham, NJ: Chatham House.

Carmines, Edward G., and James A. Stimson. 1980. The two faces of issue voting. *American Political Science Review* 74(1):78–91.

———. 1989. *Issue evolution: Race and the transformation of American politics.* Princeton: Princeton University Press.

Cassino, Dan, Krista Jenkins, and Peter J. Woolley. 2007. Measuring "What if?" standard versus priming methods for polling counterfactuals. *Survey Practice* forthcoming.

———. 2007. Just talking? The effects of open-ended answers on candidate evaluations. Paper Presented at the 65th Annual Meeting of the Midwest Political Science Association, Chicago, April 12–15, 2007.

Chaffee, S. H., and Diana C. Mutz. 1988. Comparing mediated and interpersonal communication data. In R. P. Hawkins, J. M. Wiemann, and S. Pingree, eds., *Advancing communication science: Merging mass and interpersonal processes.* Newbury Park, CA: Sage. Pp. 19–43.

Chambers, S. 1996. *Reasonable democracy.* Ithaca: Cornell University Press.

Chanley, Virginia A., Thomas J. Rudolph, and Wendy M. Rahn. 2000. The origins and consequences of public trust in government: A time series analysis. *Public Opinion Quarterly* 64(3):239–56.

Chaplin, Lan Nguyen, and Deborah Roedder John. 2005. The development of self-brand connections in children and adolescents. *Journal of Consumer Research* 32:119–29.

Cohen, Steven M., and Charles S. Liebman. 1997. American Jewish liberalism: Unraveling the strands. *Public Opinion Quarterly* 61(3):405–30.

Coleman, J. S. 1961. *The adolescent society.* New York: Free Press of Glenco.

Converse, Philip E. 1966. Information flow and the stability of partisan attitudes, in Angus Campbell, Philip E. Converse, Warren E. Miller, and Donald E. Stokes, eds., *Elections and the political order.* New York: Wiley. Pp. 136–57.

———. 1970. Attitudes and non-attitudes: Continuation of a dialogue. In E. Tufte, Ed. *The Quantitative Analysis of Social Problems.* Reading, MA: Addison-Wesley.

———. 1974. Nonattitudes and American public opinion: Comment, the status of nonattitudes. *American Political Science Review* 68(2):650–60.

———. 1969. Of time and partisan stability. *Comparative Political Studies* 2: 139–71.

Cronin, Patrick, and Benjamin O. Fordham. 1999. Timeless principles or today's fashion? Testing the stability of the linkage between ideology and foreign policy in the senate. *Journal of Politics* 61(4):967–98.

D'Amico, Ronald 1984 "Does Employment During High School Impair Academic Progress?" in *Sociology of Education* 57(3):152–64

Davis, J. 1990. Youth and the condition of Britain: Images of adolescent conflict. London: Athlone Press.

Delli Carpini, Michael X., and Scott Keeter. 1991. Stability and change in the U.S. public's knowledge of politics. *Public Opinion Quarterly* 55(3):583–612.

———. 1993. Measuring political knowledge: Putting first things first. *American Journal of Political Science* 37(4):1179–1206.

Dennis, Jack. 1975. "Trends in Pubic Support for the American Party System." *British Journal of Political Science* 5(1):187–230.

———. 1988. Political independence in America, part I: On being an independent partisan supporter. *British Journal of Political Science* 18(1):77–109.

Dillon, Michele. 1993. Argumentative complexity of abortion discourse. *Public Opinion Quarterly* 57(3):305–14.

Doty, R. M., B. E. Peterson, and D. G. Winter. 1991. Threat and authoritarianism in the United States, 1978–1987. *Journal of Personality and Social Psychology* 61:629–40.

Downs, Anthony. 1997 (1957). *An economic theory of democracy.* New York: Addison-Wesley.

Dunlop, R., and J. Eckstein, eds. 1995. *Cultural trends 1994, 23 film, cinema and video: The benefits of public art.* London: Policy Studies Institute.

Durrheim, K. 1997. Theoretical conundrum: The politics and science of theorizing authoritarian cognition. *Political Psychology* 18:625–56.

Duverger, Maurice. 1954. *Political parties.* London: Methuen.

Eliasoph, Nina. 1998. *Avoiding politics: How Americans produce apathy in everyday life.* Cambridge: Cambridge University Press.

Entwisle, Doris R., Karl L. Alexander, and Linda Steffel Olson. 2000. Early work histories of urban youth. *American Sociological Review* 65(2): 279–97.

Erikson, Robert S., Michael B. MacKuen, and James A. Stimson. 1998. What moves macropartisanship? A response to Green, Palmquist, and Schickler. *American Political Science Review* 92(4):901–12.

Farnsworth, S. J., and S. R. Lichter. 2003. *The nightly News nightmare: Network television's coverage of U.S. presidential elections, 1988–2000.* Lanham, MD: Rowman and Littlefield.

Feldman, Stanley, and John Zaller. 1992. The political culture of ambivalence: Ideological responses to the welfare state. *American Journal of Political Science* 36(1):268–307.

———, and Karen Stenner. 1997. Perceived threat and authoritarianism. *Political Psychology* 18(4):741–70.

———, and Marco Steenbergen. 2001. The humanitarian foundation of public support for social welfare. *American Journal of Political Science* 45(3):658–77.

Fournier, Susan. 1998. Consumers and their brands: Developing relationship theory in consumer research. *Journal of Consumer Research* 24:343–73.

Fox, Julia R., Gloria Koloen, and Volkhan Sahin. 2007. No joke: A comparison of substance in *The Daily Show* with Jon Stewart and broadcast network television coverage of the 2004 Presidential Election Campaign. *Journal of Broadcasting and Electronic Media* 51(2):213–27.

———, J. R. Angelini, and C. Goble. 2005. Hype versus substance in network television coverage of presidential election campaigns. *Journalism and Mass Communication Quarterly* 82(1):97–109.

Frenkel-Brunswik, E. 1948. Tolerance toward ambiguity as a personality variable. *American Psychologist* 3:268.

————. 1949. Intolerance of ambiguity as an emotional perceptual personality variable. *Journal of Personality* 18:108–43.

————. 1951. Personality theory and perception. In R. Blake and G. Ramsey, eds. *Perception: An approach to personality.* New York: Oxford University Press. Pp. 356–419.

Furnham, A. 1987. The determinants and structure of adolescents' beliefs about the economy. *Journal if Adolescence* 10(35):3–71.

Gardner, Burleigh B., and Sidney J. Levy. 1955. The product and the brand. *Harvard Business Review* 33:33–39.

Giddens, A. 1998. *The third way: The renewal of social democracy.* Cambridge: Polity Press.

Gilens, Martin. 1995. Racial attitudes and opposition to welfare. *Journal of Politics* 57(4):994–1014.

————. 1996. Race coding and white opposition to welfare. *American Political Science Review* 90(3):593–604.

Gilkison, P. 1973. Teenagers' perceptions of buying frame of reference: A decade of retrospect. *Journal of Applied Psychology* 28:16–27.

Gladwell, Malcolm. 2005. *Blink: The power of thinking without thinking.* New York: Little Brown and Company.

Glaser, Barney G. 1992. *Basics of grounded theory analysis.* Mill Valley, CA: Sociology Press.

Glaser, Barney G. and Anselm L. Strauss. 1967. *The discovery of grounded theory: Strategies for grounded research.* Piscataway, NJ: Aldine Transaction.

Gopoian, J. David. 1993. Images and issues in the 1988 presidential election. *Journal of Politics* 55(1):151–66.

Graber, Doris A. 1976. Press and TV as opinion resources in presidential campaigns. *Public Opinion Quarterly* 40:285–303.

————. 1980. *Mass media and American politics.* Washington, DC: Congressional Quarterly Press.

Green, D., B. Palmquist, and Eric Schickler. 1998. Macropartisanship: A replication and critique. *American Political Science Review* 92(4):883–900.

Gunter, Barrie, and Adrian Furnham.1998. *Children as consumers: a psychological analysis of the young people's market.* London: Routledge.

Gutmann, A., and D. Thompson. 1996. *Democracy and disagreement.* Cambridge: Harvard University Press.

Hallin, D. 1992. Sound bite news: Television coverage of elections, 1968–1988. *Journal of Communication* 42(2):5–24.

Halperin, Mark, and John F. Harris. 2006. *The way to win: Taking the White House in 2008.* New York: Random House.

Hansen, John Mark. 1998. Individuals, institutions and public preferences over public finance. *American Political Science Review* 92:513–31.

Hartz, Louis. 1955. *The liberal tradition in America.* New York: Harcourt Brace Jovanovich.

Hershey, Marjorie Randon, and David B. Hill. 1975. Watergate and preadults' attitudes toward the president. *American Journal of Political Science* 19(4): 703–26.

Hess, Robert D., and Judith V. Torney. 1967. *The development of political attitudes in children.* Chicago: Aldine.

Hetherington, Marc J. 2004. *Why trust matters: Declining political trust and the demise of American liberalism.* Princeton: Princeton University Press.

Hutcheson, J. D. Domke, A. Billeaudeaux, and P. Garland. 2004. U.S. national identity, political elites and a patriotic press following September 11. *Political Communication* 21:27–51.

Hyman, Herbert H., and Paul B. Sheatsley. 1947. Some reasons why information campaigns fail. *Public Opinion Quarterly* 11(3):412–23.

Jacobs, A. J. 2004. *The know-it-all: One man's humble quest to become the smartest person in the world.* New York: Simon and Schuster.

Jacobson, Gary C., and Samuel Kernell. 1981. *Strategy and choice in congressional elections.* New Haven: Yale University Press.

Jamieson, Kathleen Hall, and Christopher Adasiewicz. 2000. What voters can learn from election debates. In S. Coleman, ed., *Televised election debates: International perspectives.* New York: St. Martin's Press. Pp. 25–42.

John, D. R. 1984. The development of knowledge structures in children. In E. C. Hirschman and M. B. Holbrook, eds., *Advances in consumer research.* 6:413–19.

Johnson, Steven. 2005. *Everything bad is good for you: How today's pop culture is actually making us smarter.* New York: Riverhead.

Jost, John T., Jack Glaser, Arie W. Kruglanski, and Frank J. Sulloway. 2003a. Political conservatism as motivated social cognition. *Psychological Bulletin* 129(3):339–75.

———, B. W. Pelham, O. Sheldon, and B. Sullivan, 2003b. Social inequality and the reduction of ideological dissonance on behalf of the system: Evidence of enhanced system justification among the disadvantaged. *European Journal of Social Psychology* 33:13–36.

Jowell, R., and A. Park. 1998. *Young people, politics and citizenship: A disengaged generation?* London: Citizenship Foundation.

Kamptner, N. 1991. Personal possessions and their meaning: A lifespan perspective. *Journal of Social Behavior and Personality* 6:209–28.

Keeter, Scott. 2006. Election '06: Big changes in some key groups. http://pew research.org/pubs/93/election-06-big-changes-in-some-key-groups. Accessed on August 19, 2007.

Keith, Bruce E., David B. Magleby, Candice L. Nelson, Elizabeth Orr, Mark C. Westlye, and Raymond E. Wolfinger. 1986. The partisan affinities of independent "leaners." *British Journal of Political Science* 16:155–85.

Kernell, Samuel. 1978. Explaining presidential popularity. *American Political Science Review* 72: 506–22.

Key, V. O., Jr. 1955. A theory of critical elections. *The Journal of Politics* 17(1): 3–18.

———. 1966. *The responsible electorate.* New York: Vintage Books.

Kiewiet, Roderick D., and Douglas Rivers. 1985. The economic basis of Reagan's appeal. In *The new direction in American politics,* John E. Chubb and Paul E. Peterson, eds. Washington: Brookings Institute.

Kim, J., R. O. Wyatt, and E. Katz. 1999. News, talk, opinion, participation: The part played by conversation in deliberative democracy. *Political Communication* 16:361–85.

Kimberlee, R. 1998. Politically apathetic youth: A new generation? *Renewal* 6(2): 87–90.

King, Gary. 1989. *Unifying political methodology.* Cambridge: Cambridge University Press.

Kleine, Susan Schultz, Robert E. Kleine III, and Chris T. Allen. 1995. How is a possession "me" or "not me"? Characterizing types and an antecedent of material possession attachment. *Journal of Consumer Research.* 22: 327–43.

Kline, S. 1993. *Out of the garden: Toys, TV, and children's culture in the age of marketing.* New York: Verso.

Knorr, K., and P. Morgan. 1983. *Strategic military surprise: Incentives and opportunities.* London: Transaction Books.

Kovach, Bill, and Tom Rosenstiel. 1999. *Warp speed: America in the age of mixed media.* New York: Century Foundation Press.

Kressel, Neil J. 1987. Biased judgments of media bias: A case study of the Arab-Israeli dispute. *Political Psychology* 8(2):211–27.

Kuiper, Giselinde. 2005. "Where was King Kong when we needed him?" Public discourse, digital disaster jokes, and the functions of laughter after 9/11. *Journal of American Culture* 28(1):70–84.

Lakoff, George. 1996. *Moral politics.* Chicago: University of Chicago Press.

Lavine, Howard, Diana Burgess, Mark Snyder, John Transue, John L. Sullivan, Beth Haney, and Stephen H. Wagner. 1999. Threat, authoritarianism, and voting: An investigation of personality and persuasion. *Personality and Social Psychology Bulletin* 25(3):337–47.

Lebo, Matthew, and Dan Cassino. 2007. The aggregated consequences of motivated reasoning. *Political Psychology* 28(6):719–46.

Levey, Geoffrey Brahm. 1995. Toward a theory of disproportionate American Jewish liberalism. In *Values, interests, and identity: Jews and politics in a changing world: Studies in contemporary Jewry,* vol. 11, ed. Peter Y. Medding. New York and Oxford: Oxford University Press. Pp. 64–85.

Libet, Benjamin. 2004. *Mind time: The Temporal factor In consciousness.* Cambridge: Harvard University Press.

Lindaman, Kara, and Donald P. Haider-Markel. 2002. Issue evolution, political parties and the culture wars. *Political Research Quarterly* 55(1):91–110.

Lyle, J., and H. R. Hoffman. 1971. "Children's Use of Television and Other Media." In E. A. Rubinstein, G. A. Camstock, and J. P. Murray, eds., *Television and Social Behaviour.* Washington, DC: US Government Printing Office. Pp. 129–256.

MacKuen, Michael B., Robert S. Erikson and James A. Stimson. 1989. Macropartisanship. *American Political Science Review* 83(4):1125–42

Manning, Wendy D. 1990. Parenting employed teenagers. *Youth and Society* 22: 184–200.

Martinez, Michael D., and Michael M. Gant. 1990. Partisan issue preferences and partisan change. *Political Behavior* 12(3):243–64.

McGinniss, Joe. 1969. *The selling of the president 1968*. New York: Simon and Schuster.

McNeal, J. U. 1992. *Kids as customers: A handbook of marketing to children*. New York: Lexington Books.

Mendelberg, Tali. 2001. *The race card: Campaign strategy, implicit messages, and the norm of equality*. Princeton: Princeton University Press.

———. 2002. The deliberative citizen: Theory and evidence. *Political Decision Making, Deliberation and Participation*. 6:151–93.

Merriam, Charles E., and Harold F. Gosnell. 1949. *The American party system*. New York: Macmillan.

Milgram, Stanley. 1963. Behavioral study of obedience. *Journal of Abnormal and Social Psychology* 67:371–78.

———. 1974. *Obedience to authority*. New York: Harper.

Mills, C. Wright. 1959. *The sociological imagination*. New York: Grove Press.

Mintel, 1990. *Youth lifestyles*. London: Mintel Publications LTD.

Modigliani, André, and Franco Modigliani. 1987. The growth of the federal deficit and the role of public attitudes. *Public Opinion Quarterly* 51:459–80.

Monroe, Kristen R. 1978. Economic influences on presidential popularity. *Public Opinion Quarterly* 42: 360–69.

Moschis, G. P., and G. A. Moschis. 1978. Consumer socialization: A theoretical and empirical analysis. *Journal of Marketing* 43:40–48.

———, R. P. Moore. 1979. Decision making among the young: A socialization perspective. *Journal of Consumer Research* 6:101–12.

———, and R. L. Moore. 1981. The effects of family communication and mass media use on adolescent consumer learning. *Journal of Communication*, 31.

———, J. T. Lawton, and R. W. Stampfl. 1980. Preschool children and consumer learning. *Home Economics Journal* 9:64–71.

Mowen, J. C., and M. Minor. 1998. *Consumer behavior*, 5th ed. London: Prentice-Hall.

Moy, Patricia, Michael A. Xenos, and Verena K. Hess. 2005. Communication and citizenship: Mapping the political effects of infotainment. *Mass Communication and Society* 8(2):111–31.

Muniz, Albert M., Jr., and Thomas C. O'Guinn. 2001. Brand community. *Journal of Consumer Research* 27:412–32.

Nappi, Andrew. 1973. Children as consumers. *The Elementary School Journal* 73(5):239–43.

NcNeal, J. U. 1969. The child as consumer: A new market. *Journal of Retailing* 15 (Summer): 22, 84.

Niemi, Richard G., David R. Reed, and Herbert F. Weisberg. 1991. Partisan commitment: A research note. *Political Behavior* 13(3):213–21.

Norpoth, Helmut. 1985. Economics, politics, and the cycle of presidential popularity. In *Economic conditions and electoral outcomes*, ed. Heinz Eulau and Michael S. Lewis-Beck. New York: Agathon.

———. 1995. Is Clinton doomed? An early forecast for 1996. *PS: Political Science and Politics* 28(2):201–7.

———. 2001. Primary colors: A mixed blessing for Al Gore. *PS: Political Science and Politics* 34(1):45–48.

———. 2004. From primary to general election: A forecast of the presidential vote. *PS: Political Science and Politics* 37(3):737–40.

———, and Jerrold G. Rusk. 1982. Partisan dealignment in the American electorate: Itemizing the deductions since 1964. *The American Political Science Review* 76(3):522–37.

———, and Milton Lodge. 1985. The difference between attitudes and nonattitudes in the mass public: Just measurements. *American Journal of Political Science* 29(2):291–307.

———, and Thom Yantek. 1983. Macroeconomic conditions and fluctuations of presidential popularity: The question of lagged effects. *American Journal of Political Science* 27: 785–807.

Nye, Joseph S., Jr. 1997. Introduction: The decline of confidence in government. In *Why people don't trust government*, ed. Joseph S. Nye, Jr., Philip D. Zelikow, and David C. King. Cambridge: Harvard University Press.

———, and Philip D. Zelikow. 1997. Conclusion: Reflections, conjectures, and puzzles. In *Why people don't trust government*, ed. Joseph S. Nye, Jr., Philip D. Zelikow, and David C. King. Cambridge: Harvard University Press.

O'Brien, M., and S. Ingels. 1985. The effects of economics instruction in early years. *Theory and Research in Social Education* 4:279–94.

Orren, Gary. 1997. Fall from grace: The public's loss of faith in government. In *Why people don't trust government*, ed. Joseph S. Nye, Jr., Philip D. Zelikow, and David C. King. Cambridge: Harvard University Press.

Ostrom, Charles W., and Dennis M. Simon. 1989. The man in the Teflon suit? The environmental connection, political drama and popular support in the Reagan administration. *Public Opinion Quarterly* 53: 353–87.

Patterson, Thomas E. 1977. The 1976 horserace. *The Wilson Quarterly* 1:73–79.

———. 2000. Doing well and doing good. Faculty Research Working Paper Series, RWP01–001 (December). Cambridge: John F. Kennedy School of Government, Harvard University.

———, and Robert D. McClure. 1976. *The unseeing eye: The myth of television power in national politics.* New York: Paragon Books.

Perachhio, L. A. 1992. How young children learn to be consumers? A crypt processing approach. *Journal of Consumer Research* 18:425–39.

Pierce, John C., and Douglas D. Rose. 1974. Nonattitudes and American public opinion: The examination of a thesis. *American Political Science Review* 68(2):626–49.

Pomper, Gerald. 1975. *Voters' choice: Varieties of American electoral behavior.* New York: Dodd, Mead.

Poole, Keith T., and Howard Rosenthal. 1991. Patterns of congressional voting. *American Journal of Political Science* 35(1):228–278.

———, and Howard Rosenthal. 2001. D-Nominate after 10 Years: A comparative update to congress: A political-economic history of roll-call voting. *Legislative Studies Quarterly* 26(1):5–30.

Postman, Neil. 1986. *Amusing ourselves to death: Public discourse in the age of show business.* New York: Penguin.

Pringle, Hamish, and Marjorie Thompson. 1999. *Brand spirit: How cause related marketing builds brands.* New York: Wiley.

Putnam, Robert D. 2000. *Bowling alone: The collapse and revival of American community.* New York: Simon and Schuster.

Rawls, John. 1999. *A theory of justice: Revised Edition.* Oxford: Oxford University Press.

RePass, David. 1971. Issue salience and party choice. *American Political Science Review* 65:389–400.

Reynolds, F. D., and W. D. Wells. 1977. *Consumer behaviour.* New York: McGraw-Hill Book Company.

Riker, William H. 1982. The two-party system and Duverger's law: An essay on the History of Political Science. *American Political Science Review* 76(4): 753–66.

Rokeach, Milton. 1973. *The nature of human values.* New York: Free Press.

Rosenthal, Jack. 1973. Youth vote held of little impact: Study finds less than half of young cast ballots. *New York Times,* January 4, sec A.

Rothman, Stanley S., Robert Lichter, and Neil Nevitte. 2005. Politics and professional advancement among college faculty. *The Forum* (3):1: Article 2.

Rudolph, Thomas J., and Jillian Evans. 2005. Political trust, ideology, and public support for government spending. *American Journal of Political Science* 49(3):660–71.

Sales, S. M. 1972. Economic threat as a determinant of conversion rates in authoritarian and non-authoritarian churches. *Journal of Personality and Social Psychology* 23:420–28.

———. 1973. Threat as a factor in authoritarianism. *Journal of Personality and Social Psychology* 28:44–57.

Schouten, John W., and James H. McAlexander.1995. Subcultures of consumption: An ethnography of the new bikers. *Journal of Consumer Research* 22: 43–61.

Schuman, H., and S. Presser. 1980. Public opinion and public ignorance: The fine line between attitudes and nonattitudes. *American Journal of Sociology* 85(5):1214–25.

Sears, David O., Donald R.Kinder, Tom R. Tyler, and Karen S. Rook. 1974. Symbolic heroes and villains in children's views of oil and the mideast. Paper prepared for delivery at the Seventieth Annual Meeting of the American Political Science Association, Chicago, IL: August 29–September 2, 1974.

Segal, Jeffrey A., and Albert Cover. 1989. Ideological values and the votes of U.S. supreme court justices. *The American Political Science Review* 83(2): 557–65.

Sidanius, Jim. 1993. The psychology of group conflict and the dynamics of oppression: A social dominance perspective. In S. Iyengar and W. J. McGuire, eds., *Explorations in political psychology*. Durham, NC: Duke University Press. Pp. 183–219.

———, and F. Pratto. 1993. The inevitability of oppression and the dynamics of social dominance. In P. Sniderman, P. E. Tetlock, and E. G. Carmines, eds., *Prejudice, politics, and the American dilemma*. Stanford, CA: Stanford University Press. Pp. 173–211.

———. 1999. *Social dominance: An intergroup theory of social hierarchy and oppression*. New York: Cambridge University Press.

———, and B. Ekehammer. 1979. Political socialization: A multivariate analysis of Swedish political attitude and preference data. *European Journal of Social Psychology* 9:265–79.

Sigel, Roberta S. 1965. An exploration into some aspects of political socialization: School children's reactions to the death of a president. In Martha Wolfenstein and Gilbert Kliman, eds., *Children and the Death of a President*. Garden City, New York: Doubleday. Pp. 30–61.

Sirgy, M. Joseph. 1982. Self-concept in consumer behavior: A critical review. *Journal of Consumer Research* 9:287–300.

Smolkin, Rachel. 2007. What the mainstream media can learn from Jon Stewart. *American Journalism Review* (June/July).

Solomon, Michael. 1983. The role of products as social stimuli: A symbolic interactionism perspective. *Journal of ConsumerResearch* 10:319–29.

Staney, Harold. 1988. Southern partisan changes: Dealignment, realignment or both? *The Journal of Politics* 50(1):64–88.

Stewart, F. 1992. The adolescent as consumer. In J. C. Coleman and C. Warren Adamson, eds., *Youth policy on the 1990s: The way forward*. London: Routledge.

Stimson, James A. 1999. *Public opinion in America: Moods, cycles, and swings*. 2d ed. Boulder, CO: Westview.

Strauss, Anselm L. 1987. *Qualitative analysis for social scientists*. Cambridge: Cambridge University Press.

Streufert, S., and S. C. Streufert. 1978. *Behavior in complex environments*. Washington, DC: Winston.

Tetlock, Philip E. 1984. Cognitive style and political belief systems in the British House of Commons. *Journal of Personality and Social Psychology* 46:365–75.

———. 1986. A value pluralism model of ideological reasoning. *Journal of Personality and Social Psychology* 50:819–27.

———, and Jane Bernzweig, and Jack L. Gallant. 1985. Supreme Court decision making: Cognitive style as a predictor of ideological consistency of voting. *Journal of Personality and Social Psychology* 48:1227–39.

Tomz, Wittenberg, and Gary King. 2003. *CLARIFY: Software for interpreting and presenting statistical results Version 2.1*. Cambridge, MA.

Tootelean, D. H., and R. M. Gaedecke 1992. The teen market: An exploratory analysis of income, spending and shopping patterns. *Journal of Consumer Marketing* 9:35–45.

Torrance, K. 1998. *Contemporary childhood: Parent-child relationships and child culture*. Leiden: DSWO Press.

Uslaner, Eric M., and M. Margaret Conway.1985. The responsible congressional electorate: Watergate, the economy, and vote choice in 1974. *American Political Science Review* 79(3):788–803.

Valkenburg, Patti M., and Joanne Cantor. 2001. The development of a child into a consumer. *Applied Developmental Psychology* 22: 61–72.

Wallace, Michael D., Peter Suedfeld, and Kimberley Thachuk. 1993. Political rhetoric of leaders under stress in the Gulf Crisis. *Journal of Conflict Resolution* 37(1):94–107.

Wallendorf, Melanie, and Eric Arnould (1988). My favorite things: A cross-cultural inquiry into object attachment, possessiveness, and social linkage. *Journal of Consumer Research* 14:531–47.

Walzer, Michael. 1995. Liberalism and the Jews: Historical affinities, contemporary necessities. In *Values, interests, and identity: Jews and politics in a changing world: Studies in contemporary Jewry*, vol. 11, ed. Peter Y. Medding. New York and Oxford: Oxford University Press. Pp. 3–10.

Ward, S., E. Popper, and D. Wackman. 1977. *Parent under pressure: Influences on mothers' response to children's purchase requests*. Report No. 77–104. Cambridge: Marketing Research Institute.

Wartella, E., D. Wackman, S. Ward, J. Shamir, and A. Alexander. 1979. The young child as a consumer. In E. Wartella, ed., *Children communicating: Media and development of thought, speech, understanding*. Beverly Hills, CA: Sage.

Weber, Max. 1958 (1930). *The Protestant ethic and the spirit of capitalism*. New York: Scribners.

Weisberg, Herbert F. and Charles E. Smith, Jr. 1991. The influence of the economy on party identification in the Reagan years. *Journal of Politics* 53(4): 1077–92.

Weiss, Michael J. 2000. The Clustered World: How We Live, What We Buy, and What It All Means About Who We Are. New York: Little, Brown.

Wilson, G. 1973. *The psychology of conservatism*. New York: Academic Press.

Woolley, Peter J., and Dan Cassino. 2006a. Bush withers republican in Garden State senate race. *The Polling Report* 22(16):1, 7–8.

———. 2006b. Why Menendez won. *The Polling Report* 22(22):1, 5–6.

Wright, G. C. 1977. Constituency response to congressional behavior: The impact of the House Judiciary Committee impeachment votes. *Western Political Quarterly* 30:401–10.

Wuthnow, Robert. 1991. *Acts of compassion: Caring for others and helping ourselves*. Princeton: Princeton University Press.

Zajonc, Robert B. 1968. Attitudinal effects of mere exposure. *Journal of Personality and Social Psychology* 9(2):1–27.

Zukin, Cliff, Scott Keeter, Molly Andolina, Krista Jenkins, and Michael X. Delli Carpini. 2006. *A new engagement? Political participation, civic life, and the changing American citizen.* Oxford: Oxford University Press.

Index